THE OFFICIAL
PEAKY BLINDERS
QUIZ BOOK

THE OFFICIAL
PEAKY
BLINDERS

— ♘ —

QUIZ BOOK

HODDER &
STOUGHTON

First published in Great Britain in 2020 by Hodder & Stoughton
An Hachette UK company

1

WITH THANKS TO MATT WHYMAN AND JAMIE GLAZEBROOK

A CIP catalogue record for this title is available from the British Library

Hardback ISBN 978 1 529 34749 4
eBook ISBN 978 1 529 34750 0

Designed by Nicky Barneby, Barneby Ltd
Typeset in 10/12pt Appareo by Barneby Ltd

Printed and bound in Great Britain by Clays Ltd, Elcograf S.p.A.

Hodder & Stoughton policy is to use papers that are natural, renewable
and recyclable products and made from wood grown in sustainable forests.
The logging and manufacturing processes are expected to conform to
the environmental regulations of the country of origin.

Hodder & Stoughton Ltd
Carmelite House
50 Victoria Embankment
London EC4Y 0DZ

www.hodder.co.uk

INTRODUCTION

It was during the editing stage of Series 2 that it first truly hit me just how immersive the world of *Peaky Blinders* is.

We lucky executive producers got to watch, for the first time, two episodes one after another, Episodes 4 and 5. That's Arthur's invasion of the Eden Club, Tommy's seduction of May, Michael's bar brawl, Alfie's betrayal, the return of Grace ... And after a while it didn't feel like we were merely watching it: it felt like we were in it.

How does this happen? In large part, I think it's because across the five series so far we have kept the emphasis on feelings, especially Tommy's feelings. So you can't help but empathise, and be part of the story.

But it's also to do with the details.

Creator and writer Steve Knight has this uncanny ability to inhabit the minds of everyone in his tale − from gangsters to cops, penniless to posh − and to deftly show us their fears and dreams. Characters such as Michael's foster mother, Devlin the factory guy, Levitt the journalist ... they're not on screen for long, but we feel as if we know them.

And so often it's the details that tell us their stories.

Remember the Digbeth Kid in Series 2? He was only in one episode, but we know that he goes to see Tom Mix cowboy films, that he has a sister who makes things for him, that the woman he calls his mother isn't his real mother, that he can't read. And that he's an innocent, because he doesn't know what Tommy means when he says he can 'stand him up'.

The whole world of *Peaky Blinders* is full of these beautiful details. They're part of the show's poetry. Tommy's specific negotiating tactics. Polly's belief that 'bucks taste better'. Alfie's feelings regarding rum versus whiskey. And all those names – names of streets, of people, of racehorses, pubs, suburbs, songs, brands of beer ...

And when we make the show, our incredible cast and crew add another layer still. (Remember that swan image that production designer Nicole Northridge threaded through Series 5?)

All this was going through my head when I sat down with Matt Whyman's ingenious set of trivia questions. They take one through the entire *Peaky Blinders* saga thus far, episode by episode. I've not tried to commit the show to memory, but I found endless details or lines popping back into my head. (Though Matt did have me stumped on a good few occasions.)

It's a brilliant way to relive the story, a whole other way to appreciate our world, and I hope you love it as much as I do.

Jamie Glazebrook
Executive Producer

SEASON
ONE

1. The Peaky Blinders wear a distinct, oversized cap that was popular at the time among working men. What is concealed in the brim?

- ○ A NEEDLE
- ○ A RAZOR BLADE
- ○ A HAND-ROLLED CIGARETTE
- ○ A BULLET

2. In the opening scene, Tommy Shelby rides through the Birmingham slums on horseback. What is the name of his horse?

- ○ BY ORDER
- ○ MONAGHAN BOY
- ○ PAPER MONEY
- ○ IN THE CUT

3. Tommy summons a girl from the Chinese quarter who is said to cast magic spells. What is the colour of the powder she blows at his horse so that onlookers believe it'll win its next race?

- ○ YELLOW
- ○ RED
- ○ BLUE
- ○ GOLD

4. Where is the race due to take place?

- ○ AINTREE
- ○ KEMPTON PARK
- ○ CARLISLE
- ○ CHELTENHAM

5. In what year does Season 1 begin?

- ○ 1909
- ○ 1919
- ○ 1929
- ○ 1915

SEASON ONE ▮ EPISODE ONE

6. Name the song by Nick Cave & The Bad Seeds that accompanies the opening credits.

   ○ STRAIGHT TO YOU
   ○ RED RIGHT HAND
   ○ THE MERCY SEAT
   ○ UP JUMPED THE DEVIL

7. What is the name of the Birmingham quarter the Peaky Blinders call home?

   ○ SMALL HEATH
   ○ HAY MILLS
   ○ HEATH SIDE
   ○ LITTLE BROMWICH

8. Where is the Garrison Tavern located?

   ○ GARRISON NARROWS
   ○ GARRISON LANE
   ○ GARRISON STREET
   ○ GARRISON WAY

9. What does Tommy assure his brother when it comes to building the gambling business? 'I _____, Arthur. That's what I do. I _____ so that you don't have to.'

   ○ TALK
   ○ KILL
   ○ THINK
   ○ STEAL

10. Where is the Shelby house located?

   ○ 4 WASHER LANE
   ○ 6 VICTORY WAY
   ○ 4 WILLOW ROAD
   ○ 6 WATERY LANE

11. What military unit did Tommy Shelby serve in during World War I?

   ○ XVI BRIGADE
   ○ 179TH TUNNELLING COMPANY
   ○ 74TH YEOMANRY DIVISION
   ○ MACHINE GUN CORPS

12. Who is Billy Kimber?

   ○ A FOUNDRY FOREMAN
   ○ A RACECOURSE BOSS
   ○ A POLICE INSPECTOR
   ○ THE GARRISON LANDLORD

13. Union representative Freddie Thorne rallies the workers at the British Small Arms Company to take strike action. What is his political allegiance?

   ○ LIBERAL
   ○ COMMUNIST
   ○ FASCIST
   ○ CONSERVATIVE

14. Drinking at the Garrison, Freddie tells Tommy that the Peaky Blinders have been implicated in an arms robbery. He warns that police are travelling up from London to investigate. According to Freddie, how serious do the authorities consider the crime to be?

   ○ OF LOCAL INTEREST
   ○ A REGIONAL SECURITY ISSUE
   ○ OF NATIONAL SIGNIFICANCE
   ○ AN INTERNATIONAL INCIDENT

15. Danny Whizz-Bang crashes into the Garrison in the grip of a panic attack. Why?

   ○ HE'S FLEEING FROM DEBT COLLECTORS
   ○ HE'S JUST BEEN MUGGED
   ○ HE'S SHELL-SHOCKED FROM HIS WAR EXPERIENCE
   ○ HE'S SCARED OF HORSES

SEASON ONE ▮ EPISODE ONE

16. Why does Polly draw a pistol on her nephew, John?

- ○ JOHN HAS STOLEN MONEY FROM POLLY
- ○ POLLY IS TESTING JOHN'S CALM UNDER PRESSURE
- ○ THE PISTOL BELONGS TO JOHN, AND HIS YOUNGER BROTHER, FINN, HAD BEEN FOUND PLAYING WITH IT
- ○ JOHN WAS SUPPOSED TO BE LOOKING OUT FOR FINN THAT DAY

17. At a family meeting, Arthur reveals that a police chief inspector has been recruiting men to come to Birmingham to 'clean up the city'. Who are these men?

- ○ ITALIAN MAFIA
- ○ PROTESTANT IRISHMEN
- ○ JEWISH LONDONERS
- ○ GLASWEGIAN DOCKWORKERS

18. Where does Tommy confess to Polly that the Peaky Blinders were behind the factory theft?

- ○ THE GARRISON
- ○ CHARLIE STRONG'S YARD
- ○ THE CHURCH
- ○ A NARROWBOAT GALLEY

19. Tommy claims the theft of machine guns, semi-automatic rifles and pistols was down to a mix-up over crates. What had his men been instructed to steal?

- ○ TWO LATHES
- ○ THREE BICYCLES
- ○ FOUR MOTORBIKES
- ○ FIVE GEARBOXES

20. Tommy tells Polly he thinks his men were drunk, having found a gin still inside the factory. What variety of gin does he believe they were drinking?

- ○ BATHTUB
- ○ TRAMLINE
- ○ SINKHOLE
- ○ TRAIN TRACK

21. In a secret tryst under the canal bridge at night, who tells Freddie Thorne, 'You love me more than you fear them'?

- ○ POLLY GRAY
- ○ ADA SHELBY
- ○ LIZZY STARK
- ○ ZILPHA LEE

22. When undercover agent Grace Burgess first visits the Garrison Tavern, what does she claim to be seeking?

- ○ A MEETING WITH TOMMY SHELBY
- ○ EMPLOYMENT AS A BARMAID
- ○ A SHOWDOWN WITH ARTHUR SHELBY
- ○ DIRECTIONS TO THE RAILWAY STATION

23. When Chief Inspector Campbell arrives in Birmingham and addresses the police, he vows to decapitate the 'three-headed beast' menacing the city. As well as the Peaky Blinders and the communists, who else are in the inspector's sights?

- ○ THE ANARCHISTS
- ○ THE IRA
- ○ THE FASCISTS
- ○ THE TRADE UNIONISTS

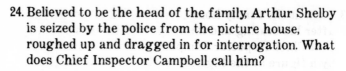

24. Believed to be the head of the family, Arthur Shelby
    is seized by the police from the picture house,
    roughed up and dragged in for interrogation. What
    does Chief Inspector Campbell call him?

    ○ TOP DOG
    ○ KINGPIN
    ○ LEAD PACK DOG
    ○ GANG BOSS

25. 'After _____ of dealing with animals like you,'
    Chief Inspector Campbell tells Arthur Shelby when
    questioning him about the munitions robbery, 'I can
    tell just by sniffing the air whether or not you're
    lying.' How long has he been in the police force?

    ○ 5 YEARS
    ○ 10 YEARS
    ○ 25 YEARS
    ○ 35 YEARS

26. On Grace's first day as a barmaid, the Garrison is
    packed with football supporters. Landlord Harry
    Fenton tells her they've gathered to drink before
    heading off to St Andrew's, home of Birmingham FC,
    to watch the match. By what nickname does he refer
    to the team?

    ○ THE SEAGULLS
    ○ THE GREENS
    ○ THE CANARIES
    ○ THE BLUES

27. When Grace first serves Tommy, she's advised to give
    him whatever drink he wants on the house. What
    bottle does Tommy request?

    ○ GIN
    ○ WHISKEY
    ○ RUM
    ○ STOUT

28. Back at the family house, Arthur is in a bad way after his beating and interrogation. He tells Tommy that Chief Inspector Campbell has been dispatched by a figure at the highest level to investigate the missing munitions box. Who is it?

- ○ DAVID LLOYD GEORGE
- ○ WINSTON CHURCHILL
- ○ NANCY ASTOR
- ○ KING GEORGE V

29. 'You went to one first-aid class in the church hall and got thrown out for giggling.' Who is John Shelby addressing when he casts doubt on their ability to tend to Arthur's injuries?

- ○ HIS AUNT, POLLY
- ○ HIS SISTER, ADA
- ○ HIS YOUNGEST BROTHER, FINN
- ○ A NEIGHBOUR WITH A FIRST-AID KIT

30. What popular song of the time does Grace sing in the pub, encouraging the men to join in?

- ○ IT'S A LONG WAY TO TIPPERARY
- ○ KEEP THE HOME FIRES BURNING
- ○ THE BOY I LOVE IS UP IN THE GALLERY
- ○ SEND ME AWAY WITH A SMILE

31. Plagued and tormented by his war experience, Danny Whizz-Bang is triggered by a waiter outside a café and knifes him. In which quarter of the city does this take place?

- ○ THE JEWISH QUARTER
- ○ LITTLE ITALY
- ○ THE IRISH QUARTER
- ○ CHINATOWN

SEASON ONE ▮ EPISODE ONE

32. On board a train at the station, Chief Inspector Campbell meets the Secretary of State, Winston Churchill, who compliments him on his top hat. What does Campbell tell him the hat is made from?

   ○ BEAVER
   ○ BLACK SILK
   ○ BADGER
   ○ MINK

33. Bargeman, scrapyard owner and Peaky Blinder associate Charlie Strong agrees to Tommy's request to smuggle stolen goods out of the city. What condition does Charlie put on this?

   ○ HE ONLY HAS ROOM FOR HALF THE CONSIGNMENT
   ○ HE WILL ONLY MAKE THE JOURNEY WHEN THERE'S NO MOON IN THE NIGHT SKY
   ○ HE REQUIRES PROTECTION
   ○ HE NEEDS PAYMENT UP FRONT

34. 'Fortune drops something valuable into your lap, you don't just dump it on the back of the cut.' Tommy decides to hold onto the goods. Where does he tell Charlie to hide them?

   ○ GAS STREET BASIN
   ○ THE OLD TOBACCO WHARF
   ○ EDGBASTON RESERVOIR
   ○ THE PORT LOOP

35. Where does Chief Inspector Campbell meet Grace, who reports to him in her role as an agent of the Crown?

   ○ THE RACECOURSE
   ○ THE MUSEUM
   ○ THE RAILWAY STATION
   ○ PENNY CRUSH CINEMA

36. Grace tells the chief inspector that she suspects neither the Peaky Blinders nor the communists were behind the theft, but the IRA. Why does Campbell believe her judgement may be clouded?

   ○ SHE'S IN LOVE WITH TOMMY SHELBY
   ○ SHE FEARS THE PEAKY BLINDERS WILL KILL HER IF THEY FIND OUT HER TRUE ROLE
   ○ HER FATHER WAS MURDERED BY THE IRA
   ○ SHE'S A COMMUNIST SYMPATHISER

37. To head off a gang feud following the death of the waiter, Tommy agrees to execute Danny Whizz-Bang in the presence of two Italian mobsters. What is Danny's last request at the canal side before he is shot and falls into Charlie Strong's barge?

   ○ A CIGARETTE
   ○ A NIP FROM TOMMY'S HIP FLASK
   ○ TO BE BURIED ON A HILL, BUT NOT IN MUD
   ○ TO TELL THE FAMILY OF THE MURDERED WAITER THAT HE IS SORRY

38. When Danny regains consciousness, Charlie explains that Tommy faked the execution using a shell containing sheep's blood. To show gratitude for saving his life, Danny must now undertake a job for the Peaky Blinders in which city?

   ○ GLASGOW
   ○ LIVERPOOL
   ○ LEEDS
   ○ LONDON

39. Arthur is furious when Tommy's horse wins its next race. As a bookmaker, he's made a loss because so many people witnessed the 'blessing' scam and backed it. What is Tommy's plan to make money?

- ○ TO PERFORM THE SAME SCAM BUT WITH A SLOWER HORSE
- ○ TO GET OUT OF BOOKMAKING AND INTO PROTECTION
- ○ TO BUILD THE HORSE'S WINNING REPUTATION THEN FIX A RACE SO THAT IT LOSES
- ○ TO BACK THE HORSE HIMSELF AT THE NEXT RACE

KILLER QUESTIONS

40. The rusting hull of a barge sits on the wharf beside the canal opposite Charlie Strong's yard. What is the yard's name?

- ○ HAYES HILL COAL MERCHANTS LTD
- ○ HARTS HILL IRON CO LTD
- ○ IRON HILL CO LTD
- ○ HARTS MILL IRON CO LTD

41. According to street preacher Jeremiah Jesus, as Tommy rides his horse back from the 'blessing', 'God does not care if you live in a slum or in a _____.' Fill in the blank.

- ○ ... PALACE
- ○ ... CASTLE
- ○ ... MANSION
- ○ ... HALL

42. Which of these characters does not travel by narrowboat in Episode 1?

- ○ DANNY WHIZZ-BANG
- ○ CHARLIE STRONG
- ○ CURLY
- ○ ARTHUR SHELBY

SEASON ONE ▮ EPISODE ONE

1. The episode opens with the Shelby brothers travelling along a country lane. Where does Arthur believe they are heading before Tommy stops off at the Lee family gypsy camp to see Johnny Dogs about a horse?

   ○ THE COAST
   ○ A CONVALESCENT HOME FOR SOLDIERS
   ○ THE FAIR
   ○ A STATELY HOME

2. What is the game that Tommy Shelby and Johnny Dogs play, where the winner keeps both horse and car?

   ○ PENNY IN THE HOLE
   ○ FIVE FINGER FILLET
   ○ TWO UP
   ○ ROCK, PAPER, SCISSORS

3. Johnny Dogs attempts to diffuse tension between Tommy and the Lee boys by reminding them that the Shelby brothers' grandfather was a man of standing in the Romany community. What was he?

   ○ A WARLORD
   ○ A KING
   ○ A FORTUNE TELLER
   ○ A HEALER

4. Tommy and his brothers attack the Lees when one of them insults their mother's name. What does he call her?

   ○ A BEARCAT
   ○ A DIDICOI WHORE
   ○ A LOOSE WITCH
   ○ AN UGLY KNACKER

5. How does Chief Inspector Campbell arrive in Small Heath ahead of the dawn police raid?

- ○ BY CAR
- ○ ON FOOT
- ○ ON HORSEBACK
- ○ BY BICYCLE

6. 'We will take them before last night's beer turns to piss and wakes the devils up,' Campbell instructs his officers. What does he demand is brought to him for inspection?

- ○ EVERY WEAPON
- ○ EVERY GUN AND BULLET
- ○ EVERY MAN AND WOMAN
- ○ EVERY VALUABLE ITEM THAT HAS NO PLACE HERE

7. Freddie Thorne and Ada Shelby escape from his bedroom before the police crash in. What do they find in his room as evidence that she has been there?

- ○ A LOVE NOTE SIGNED BY HER
- ○ A PRESCRIPTION IN HER NAME
- ○ A CARDIGAN WITH HER NAME TAG
- ○ A BOOK WITH A HANDWRITTEN DEDICATION TO HER FROM FREDDIE

8. Name one of the pubs searched by the police because it pays protection to the Peaky Blinders.

- ○ THE LOCK
- ○ THE KEY
- ○ THE CHAIN
- ○ THE BOLT

SEASON ONE ▮ EPISODE TWO

9. Chief Inspector Campbell encounters Polly Gray in the church. She tells Campbell something that leads him to believe the Shelbys have looked into his past. What is it?

   ○ HE DIDN'T FIGHT IN FRANCE
   ○ HIS MOTHER WAS CATHOLIC
   ○ HE IS FEARED BY THE BELFAST UNDERWORLD
   ○ HE IS SECRETLY IN LOVE WITH GRACE

10. As his officers search the church, Campbell instructs Polly to have Tommy meet him on Friday at 10a.m. Where?

   ○ THE GARRISON
   ○ THE TEA ROOM
   ○ THE BOATYARD
   ○ THE POLICE STATION

11. When the Shelby brothers return home, they find that Chief Inspector Campbell has suggested the raid was staged with their blessing. How has he done this?

   ○ HANDED OUT FLYERS NAMING THE PEAKY BLINDERS AS 'MOST WANTED'
   ○ ALLOWED ADA SHELBY TO SUCCESSFULLY HIDE DURING THE HOUSE-TO-HOUSE SEARCH
   ○ MADE SURE THE BROTHERS WERE OUT OF TOWN BEFORE THE RAID TOOK PLACE
   ○ LEFT THE BETTING SHOP UNTOUCHED

12. How does Tommy propose that they regain their reputation on the streets?

   ○ KILLING A COPPER
   ○ HANDING OUT CASH TO THE RAIDED PUBS
   ○ RECOMPENSING THOSE WHOSE HOMES HAVE BEEN DAMAGED IN THE RAID
   ○ STANDING ON A SOAPBOX AND ADDRESSING THE PEOPLE

13. Polly believes the stolen guns in Tommy's possession are a liability because a revolution is coming. What odds does she give for this happening?

   ○ 3:1
   ○ 5:2
   ○ EVENS
   ○ 10:1

14. 'You don't parley when you're on the back foot.' What is Tommy referring to here?

   ○ A FORTHCOMING BOXING MATCH
   ○ THE PROPOSED MEETING WITH CHIEF INSPECTOR CAMPBELL
   ○ NEGOTIATING WITH COMMUNIST STRIKERS AT THE BRITISH SMALL ARMS COMPANY
   ○ THE FEUD WITH THE LEE FAMILY

15. In a bid to send out a message to the authorities, the Shelbys stage a bonfire in the street at Watery Lane. They burn portraits of a national figurehead. Who is it?

   ○ THE PRIME MINISTER, DAVID LLOYD GEORGE
   ○ THE LIBERAL LEADER, HENRY ASQUITH
   ○ KING GEORGE V
   ○ THE AMERICAN PRESIDENT, WOODROW WILSON

16. To help spread the word, Tommy gives a tip-off about the bonfire to a journalist from which newspaper?

   ○ BIRMINGHAM DAILY GAZETTE
   ○ BIRMINGHAM MAIL
   ○ BIRMINGHAM EVENING DISPATCH
   ○ BIRMINGHAM POST

SEASON ONE ▩ EPISODE TWO

17. 'These new coppers over from Belfast, breaking into our homes and interfering with our women,' says Tommy to the reporter, 'we don't think the King would _____.' Complete the sentence.

   ○ ... STAND BY AND LET HIS SUBJECTS BE MISTREATED IN THIS WAY
   ○ ... WANT TO SEE THAT HAPPENING
   ○ ... SANCTION OR APPROVE SUCH BEHAVIOUR
   ○ ... GIVE HIS BLESSING FOR SUCH MISTREATMENT OF HIS PEOPLE

18. To cover for her time with Freddie Thorne, Ada tells Polly she had a bad night. What is in the dream she describes?

   ○ A BEAR AND A BOAT
   ○ A BADGER AND A BATHTUB
   ○ A HARE IN A SNARE
   ○ A FOX IN A HENHOUSE

19. Charlie Strong shows Tommy a bullet with his name on it. Who sent it?

   ○ CHIEF INSPECTOR CAMPBELL
   ○ FREDDIE THORNE
   ○ THE IRA
   ○ THE LEE FAMILY

20. Who is Scudboat?

   ○ A FOUNDRY WORKER
   ○ A BOOKMAKER
   ○ A BUTCHER
   ○ A BARMAN

21. Having learned that **Ada** is pregnant, **Tommy** finds her at the Penny Crush Picture House. Who is the star of the movie she is watching?

    ○ HAROLD LLOYD
    ○ DOUGLAS FAIRBANKS
    ○ RUDOLPH VALENTINO
    ○ CHARLIE CHAPLIN

22. **Tommy** finally fixes it so that **Monaghan Boy** loses a race and the **Shelbys'** betting enterprise cleans up. How many races has the horse won before?

    ○ TWO
    ○ THREE
    ○ FOUR
    ○ SIX

23. What does **Polly** advise **Tommy** to do with some of the takings?

    ○ THROW A PARTY FOR THE PEOPLE
    ○ DISTRIBUTE IT TO THE LOCALS
    ○ OPEN A BANK ACCOUNT
    ○ BURY THE MONEY OUT IN THE COUNTRYSIDE

24. **Ada** writes a letter to **Freddie**, telling him she is pregnant. She gives the letter to **Polly**, who hands it to **Tommy** to pass on to his former friend. What does **Tommy** do with the letter?

    ○ READS IT
    ○ LOSES IT
    ○ BURNS IT
    ○ DELIVERS IT TO FREDDIE

SEASON ONE ▮ EPISODE TWO

SEASON ONE ▬ **EPISODE TWO**

25. Polly arranges for Ada to visit a backstreet abortionist. Where?

- ○ WARWICK
- ○ LEEDS
- ○ CONWY
- ○ CARDIFF

26. What does Polly suggest they do afterwards as a treat?

- ○ SPEND THE AFTERNOON IN THE PARK
- ○ VISIT THE CASTLE
- ○ TRAVEL TO THE SEASIDE
- ○ GO TO THE PICTURES

27. Tommy meets Chief Inspector Campbell to strike a deal. He wants the police to turn a blind eye to his business affairs. What does he offer in return?

- ○ A GUARANTEE THAT CAMPBELL WILL NOT BE KILLED BY THE PEAKY BLINDERS WHILE HE REMAINS IN BIRMINGHAM
- ○ DETAILS OF FREDDIE THORNE'S WHEREABOUTS
- ○ THE RETURN OF THE STOLEN CRATE FROM THE BRITISH SMALL ARMS COMPANY
- ○ LIFELONG PROTECTION

28. At the opera house, Grace is briefed by Chief Inspector Campbell about her mission to get close to Tommy in order to gather intelligence. What does he hand her before she leaves?

- ○ MONEY
- ○ A PISTOL
- ○ A LUCKY CHARM
- ○ A LOVE LETTER

29. What performance are they watching?

- ○ THE MARRIAGE OF FIGARO
- ○ MADAME BUTTERFLY
- ○ TOSCA
- ○ CARMEN

30. Curly rushes through the rainswept night to tell Tommy that his white horse is showing symptoms of a fatal curse by the Lee family. What form does this curse take?

- ○ BLINDNESS
- ○ A BUCKLED HORSESHOE
- ○ BRITTLE BONES
- ○ A BAD SEED IN THE HOOF

31. Tommy learns that Grace's background as a barmaid from a rough pub in Dublin is a cover story. What does he believe she's hiding?

- ○ SHE'S A GIRL FROM A GOOD FAMILY WHO FELL PREGNANT
- ○ SHE MURDERED A PATRON AND FLED
- ○ SHE ROBBED THE PUB OF A NIGHT'S TAKINGS
- ○ SHE HAD AN AFFAIR WITH THE MARRIED LANDLORD

32. Alone in the Garrison, Tommy asks Grace to get up on a chair and sing for him. What does he request?

- ○ A WARTIME SONG
- ○ A HAPPY SONG
- ○ A SAD SONG
- ○ A FOLK SONG

SEASON ONE ▮ EPISODE TWO

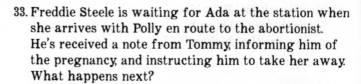

33. Freddie Steele is waiting for Ada at the station when she arrives with Polly en route to the abortionist. He's received a note from Tommy, informing him of the pregnancy, and instructing him to take her away. What happens next?

   ○ HE URGES HER TO GET ON THE NEXT TRAIN WHEREVER IT'S HEADING
   ○ HE BREAKS UP WITH HER, UNABLE TO HANDLE THE PRESSURE
   ○ HE PROPOSES TO HER, BUT INSISTS THEY REMAIN IN BIRMINGHAM
   ○ HE PRODUCES TWO BOARDING TICKETS FOR A PASSAGE TO NEW YORK

34. As it dawns on Arthur and John that their brother is drawn to Grace, they remind Tommy of an old saying by their father. Fill in the blank: 'Fast women and slow _____ will ruin your life.'

   ○ ... MOTOR CARS
   ○ ... HORSES
   ○ ... GREYHOUNDS
   ○ ... WITS

35. Billy Kimber pays the Shelby brothers a visit at the Garrison. How does he draw them from the back room?

   ○ BY SHOOTING A GUN AT THE CEILING
   ○ BY SHOOTING A BOTTLE FROM THE BAR
   ○ BY SHOOTING OUT THE GLASS FROM THE BACK ROOM DOOR
   ○ BY THREATENING TO KILL EVERYONE PRESENT

36. Billy is unhappy that Tommy fixed a race without his permission, but agrees to join forces in order to prevent the Lees taking control of the racecourses. They agree to work together at which race?

   ○ LINGFIELD
   ○ NEWMARKET
   ○ CHELTENHAM
   ○ ASCOT

37. 'He's the oldest,' Billy Kimber says, pointing at Arthur Shelby, before jabbing his finger at another Shelby, 'and you're the thickest.' Who is he referring to?

- ◌ FINN
- ◌ TOMMY
- ◌ JOHN
- ◌ ARTHUR SNR

38. Who is Billy Kimber's associate, Roberts?

- ◌ HIS ACCOUNTANT
- ◌ HIS HENCHMAN
- ◌ HIS APPRENTICE
- ◌ HIS LAWYER

39. Roberts outlines their suspicions that the Peaky Blinders fixed the race at Kempton Park. How much money does he say was riding on Monaghan Boy to win, a firm favourite who uncharacteristically came last?

- ◌ £3,000
- ◌ £3,200
- ◌ £3,500
- ◌ £3,700

SEASON ONE ▮▮▮ EPISODE TWO

KILLER QUESTIONS

40. Tommy asks Curly to fetch him a saddle so he can ride the horse won from Johnny Dogs. What kind of saddle is it?

   ○ A LEATHER SADDLE
   ○ A SPANISH SADDLE
   ○ A VELVET SADDLE
   ○ A TURKISH SADDLE

41. When Tommy agrees to Grace's request to allow singing in the Garrison, John jokes that it sounds like they're 'strangling cats out there'. What song is bringing everyone together in the saloon bar?

   ○ THE GARDEN OF YOUR HEART
   ○ WHEN MY SHIPS COME SAILING HOME
   ○ THE SUNSHINE OF YOUR SMILE
   ○ HOMEWARD BOUND

42. According to the scrawl on the betting shop blackboard, name one other horse racing alongside Monaghan Boy on Tuesday 8th at Kempton Park?

   ○ MERCY ME
   ○ PERCY PIPER
   ○ PIPER BAND
   ○ PRAY FOR MERCY

1. Grace tells Tommy that she's decided not to accompany him to the races unless he gives her more money for a dress. How much more does she ask for?

   - ○ THREE SHILLINGS
   - ○ TWO POUNDS, TEN SHILLINGS
   - ○ WHATEVER HE FEELS SHE'S WORTH
   - ○ TWENTY POUNDS

2. 'Oh, I don't pay for suits,' Tommy tells Grace when she asks how much his clothing costs. 'My suits are on the house, or _____.' Complete the sentence.

   - ○ ... I SEIZE THE HOUSE
   - ○ ... THE HOUSE BURNS DOWN
   - ○ ... THE TAILOR LEAVES TOWN
   - ○ ... I STITCH THEM UP

3. Two men join Tommy in the back room of the Garrison. They're interested in acquiring the crate stolen from the British Small Arms Factory. Who do these men represent?

   - ○ THE BILLY BOYS
   - ○ THE ITALIAN MAFIA
   - ○ THE IRA
   - ○ THE COMMUNISTS

4. Which quarter of Birmingham are they from?

   - ○ SPRING FIELD
   - ○ SPARKHILL
   - ○ HALL GREEN
   - ○ SPARKBROOK

SEASON ONE ▮ EPISODE THREE

27

5. How do the pair claim to have raised enough money to acquire the stolen items?

   ○ BLACKMAIL
   ○ PUB COLLECTIONS
   ○ A BANK ROBBERY
   ○ A LOAN

6. When Tommy won't be drawn on whether the crate is in his possession, how does one of the men respond?

   ○ INVITES HIM OUTSIDE FOR A FIGHT
   ○ SINGS A PROVOCATIVE SONG
   ○ THREATENS THE SAFETY OF THE SHELBY FAMILY
   ○ THREATENS TO INFORM THE POLICE

7. 'Whiskey is good _____,' Tommy tells Grace as the two men leave. 'It tells you who's real and who isn't.' Fill in the blank.

   ○ ... TRUTH MEDICINE
   ○ ... PROOFING WATER
   ○ ... FIRE WATER
   ○ ... TRUTH TONIC

8. Freddie Thorne waits anxiously for Ada so they can get married in secret. What's set to surprise him?

   ○ ADA BRINGS A BRIDESMAID
   ○ TOMMY SHOWS UP, AND HE'S UNHAPPY
   ○ ADA ARRIVES, HAVING RUN THROUGH THE STREETS IN A WEDDING DRESS
   ○ POLLY INFORMS HIM THE WEDDING IS OFF

9. Grace updates Chief Inspector Campbell on the meeting. When he summons Sergeant Moss to discuss the situation, what is the name of the pub he has noted on a strip of a paper where the two men who met Tommy are said to drink?

   ○ THE BLUE IDOL
   ○ THE BLACK SWAN
   ○ THE RED LION
   ○ THE GREEN MAN

10. For such a formidable character, Chief Inspector Campbell is easily needled by what fact about his past?

    ○ HE WAS INJURED EARLY IN THE WAR AND RETURNED HOME
    ○ HE DIDN'T FIGHT IN THE WAR AT ALL
    ○ HE NEVER MARRIED
    ○ HE HAS NO CHILDREN

11. Grace follows one of the suspect men into a back alley, where he turns on her. The scene ends with a gunshot. Who fires the round?

    ○ THE MAN SHE FOLLOWED
    ○ A POLICE OFFICER
    ○ GRACE
    ○ TOMMY

12. Before Polly breaks the news to Tommy about Freddie and Ada's marriage, what does she ask him?

    ○ TO TAKE A SEAT
    ○ TO POUR A DRINK
    ○ WHETHER OR NOT HE'S ARMED
    ○ IF HE'S IN A GOOD MOOD

SEASON ONE EPISODE THREE

13. Sergeant Moss refers to Chief Inspector Campbell's unnamed female 'spy'. Campbell corrects him. What does he insist she is called?

- ○ AN INSIDER
- ○ AN OPERATIVE
- ○ A DOUBLE AGENT
- ○ AN INFORMER

14. Polly visits Freddie to persuade him to leave town with his new bride. What does she offer him?

- ○ A NEW JOB IN LONDON
- ○ LODGINGS IN LIVERPOOL
- ○ THE KEYS TO THE FAMILY CAR
- ○ MONEY

15. 'A communist in the family is _____,' Polly tells Freddie as her reason for wanting him gone. Fill in the blank.

- ○ ... UNTHINKABLE AND INTOLERABLE
- ○ ... A DEAD MAN
- ○ ... BAD FOR BUSINESS
- ○ ... LIKE A CUCKOO IN THE NEST

16. When Freddie refuses, what does Polly produce from her purse?

- ○ A GUN
- ○ TICKETS FOR THE NEXT PASSAGE TO AMERICA
- ○ ANOTHER £200
- ○ A KNIFE

17. Chief Inspector Campbell meets Grace at the museum. He reminds her of her remit. What is it?

- ○ OBSERVE AND REPORT
- ○ WATCH AND LEARN
- ○ CATCH AND KILL
- ○ SHOOT FIRST, ASK QUESTIONS LATER

18. What is on display in the room where they meet?

   ○ TAPESTRIES
   ○ WHITE STATUES
   ○ PORTRAIT PAINTINGS
   ○ LANDSCAPE PAINTINGS

19. 'Killing a man affects the _____.' Finish Chief
    Inspector Campbell's sentence.

   ○ SOUL
   ○ TEMPERAMENT
   ○ MIND
   ○ HEART

20. Tommy visits the Chinese quarter. There, he admires
    a suit on the rack in the dry cleaning den. What does
    Mr Zhang, the owner, tell him?

   ○ IT NEEDS CLEANING
   ○ IT BELONGS TO BILLY KIMBER
   ○ THERE'S A BULLET HOLE IN THE BACK THAT NEEDS STITCHING
   ○ IT'S ON THE HOUSE

21. Freddie Thorne addresses the workers at the
    factory in a bid to muster strike action. He cautions
    that Chief Inspector Campbell has forbidden them
    from what?

   ○ SPREADING COMMUNIST PROPAGANDA
   ○ GATHERING IN GROUPS OF MORE THAN THREE
   ○ LISTENING TO FREDDIE THORNE
   ○ CIVIL DISOBEDIENCE OF ANY KIND

SEASON ONE ▮ EPISODE THREE

31

22. John warns Tommy that their brother, Arthur, is suffering from the _____ Blues again. Fill in the blank.

- ◌ ... WHISKEY
- ◌ ... SOLDIER
- ◌ ... VERDUN
- ◌ ... FLANDERS

23. Where does Tommy find Arthur?

- ◌ IN A CHURCH PEW, NURSING A BOTTLE OF SPIRITS
- ◌ IN THE BACK ROOM AT THE GARRISON, DRINKING SHOTS
- ◌ AT HOME, IN A TIN BATH
- ◌ IN THE BOXING RING, SPARRING WITH AN OPPONENT

24. In a bid to cheer him up, what does Tommy gift his older brother?

- ◌ A RACEHORSE
- ◌ THE GARRISON PUB
- ◌ A PROSTITUTE
- ◌ A MOTOR CAR

25. When Tommy leaves his brother for the car outside, what does he discover?

- ◌ IT'S BEEN STOLEN
- ◌ A FLAT TYRE
- ◌ IT'S BEEN SCRATCHED
- ◌ POLLY IS WAITING FOR HIM IN THE PASSENGER SEAT

26. Sergeant Moss is waiting for Tommy. He knows Freddie is still in town, and responsible for the strike action at the factory. Unless Tommy deals with it, Moss threatens to have Freddie's new bride charged. What prison term is Ada looking at?

○ TWO YEARS FOR AIDING AND ABETTING A MEMBER OF THE COMMUNIST PARTY
○ THREE YEARS FOR SEDITION
○ ONE YEAR FOR SHELTERING A KNOWN CRIMINAL
○ FIVE YEARS FOR TREASON

27. Tommy distracts Freddie for long enough to draw his own gun. What does he say to seize the advantage?

○ HE POINTS OUT FREDDIE'S SAFETY CATCH IS ON
○ HE ASKS IF THEY COULD STILL SWIM ACROSS THE WATER LIKE THEY DID WHEN THEY WERE YOUNG
○ HE REMINDS FREDDIE OF THE HARDSHIP THEY BOTH FACED DURING THE WAR
○ HE PRETENDS THAT ADA IS APPROACHING THEM

28. What are Tommy's parting words once they put their guns down?

○ 'LEAVE THIS CITY BY DAWN TOMORROW.'
○ 'YOU'LL NEVER SEE ADA AGAIN.'
○ 'THIS MARRIAGE WILL NOT STAND.'
○ 'YOUR CHILD IS DESTINED TO BE FATHERLESS.'

29. Tommy takes Freddie's money and returns it to Polly. What is she doing when Tommy informs her that he'll be dealing with his new brother-in-law in his own way from now on?

○ SMOKING A CIGARETTE AT THE WINDOW
○ DRINKING AT THE WINDOW
○ COUNTING THE TAKINGS FOR THE DAY AT THE TABLE
○ CRADLING THE HEAD OF YOUNG FINN, WHO IS ASLEEP BESIDE HER ON THE SOFA

SEASON ONE ▪ EPISODE THREE

30. That night, Tommy dreams about his time in the tunnels during the war. Who is down there with him?

   ○ FREDDIE AND DANNY WHIZZ-BANG
   ○ ARTHUR AND FREDDIE
   ○ ARTHUR AND JOHN
   ○ DANNY WHIZZ-BANG AND ARTHUR

31. Back from London, Danny Whizz-Bang visits Tommy. Where has he overheard news about the killing of the IRA man and the belief that the Peaky Blinders were responsible?

   ○ A MARKET
   ○ A PUB
   ○ HIS LODGINGS
   ○ A FOOTBALL MATCH

32. 'Lies _____ faster than the truth.' Complete Tommy's response to Danny about the accusation. Complete the sentence.

   ○ ... SPREAD
   ○ ... VANISH
   ○ ... TRAVEL
   ○ ... CORRUPT

33. Danny leaves a note for Tommy, which he finds at first light. What does it read?

   ○ I WILL DO MY DUTY, SIR
   ○ I WON'T LET YOU DOWN
   ○ GONE TO SEE MY SWEETHEART
   ○ UNITED WE STAND, TOMMY

34. Arthur briefs the Peaky Blinders on the operation to take down the Lee family at Cheltenham, as well as Kimber's men who have gone 'rotten'. What are his parting words?

- ○ 'TAKE NO PRISONERS.'
- ○ 'KILL OR BE KILLED.'
- ○ 'WE ARE FAMILY.'
- ○ 'TRUST ONLY KIN.'

35. At the racecourse, Tommy asks Grace to pretend she's from high society in order to gain access to the VIP rooms. What is the name he asks her to use?

- ○ LADY SUSAN DUNNANT OF BENGOWER
- ○ LADY SARAH DUGGAN OF CONNEMARA
- ○ LADY SALLY WALSH OF DERRYCLARE
- ○ LADY CARA QUINN OF BENBRACK

36. In sneaking in, Tommy tells Grace to say that he's from overseas and speaks no English. What nationality does he suggest?

- ○ ITALIAN
- ○ AUSTRIAN
- ○ PRUSSIAN
- ○ POLISH

37. In a lavatory at the races, Arthur, John and the gang stop a member of the Lee family from shaking down one of Kimber's bookies. With razor cap in hand, how does Arthur scar him?

- ○ BLINDS HIM
- ○ SLICES HIS EAR
- ○ SLICES HIS CHEEK
- ○ SLICES HIS THROAT

SEASON ONE EPISODE THREE

38. Tommy takes the recovered money from all the shakedowns and dumps it in front of Kimber and Roberts, the accountant. He proposes that the Peaky Blinders take over protection in return for what?

- ○ CONTROL OF ONE HIS RACECOURSES
- ○ CONTROL OF THE ODDS ON ALL RACES
- ○ A RACING STABLE AND £500 A YEAR
- ○ A PERCENTAGE OF THE TAKE AND BETTING PITCHES AT HIS RACECOURSES

39. On finalising a deal that involves the promise of sex as much as money, who says: 'Everyone's a whore, Grace, we just sell different parts of ourselves.'

- ○ BILLY KIMBER
- ○ ARTHUR
- ○ TOMMY
- ○ ROBERTS THE ACCOUNTANT

40. Back at his grand house, Billy is set to have his way with Grace when Tommy crashes in. What does he make up about her that persuades Billy to back off?

- ○ SHE'S A MAFIA MOLL
- ○ SHE HAS SYPHILIS
- ○ SHE'S A JEWEL THIEF
- ○ SHE'S A BLACKMAILER

KILLER QUESTIONS

41. Which one of these Irish whiskies from the early 1900s is visible on the shelf when Tommy first walks into the Garrison?

○ JAMESON
○ REDBREAST
○ MOONEYS
○ POWERS

42. When Freddie holds a gun to Tommy's head at the docks, and drops money at his feet intended to pay for him to leave the city with Ada, what is the name of the Cunard liner on the ticket that he also rejects?

○ SAMATRA
○ SAXONIA
○ CARONIA
○ ORDUNA

43. What is the registration number of the car in which Tommy collects Grace before driving to the races?

○ DL 6947
○ LD 3631
○ DS 9746
○ DS 1744

SEASON ONE ▮ EPISODE THREE

1. Freddie has returned from London, where he accepted money from a Russian towards instigating revolution. Where did the pair meet?

   ○ A TURKISH BATH
   ○ A CHINESE RESTAURANT
   ○ A RUSSIAN TEA ROOM
   ○ AN ITALIAN CAFÉ

2. 'Our revolution is international, and _____,' says Freddie's contact, delighted by the commission. Complete the sentence.

   ○ ... THE WORLD AWAITS OUR NEXT MOVE
   ○ ... IT GROWS BY THE DAY
   ○ ... IT HAS BECOME AN UNSTOPPABLE FORCE
   ○ ... SOON OUR BROTHERS AND SISTERS WILL BE FREE FROM ALL OPPRESSION

3. Jeremiah Jesus reports to Tommy that Freddie is back in town, but keeps giving him the slip. What does Jeremiah compare him to?

   ○ A SNAKE
   ○ A FISH
   ○ AN EEL
   ○ A SERPENT

4. Tommy makes his way to the Shelby betting office. Inside, a customer has just had his bet refused. Why?

   ○ HE'S IN DEBT TO THE SHELBYS
   ○ THE RACE HAS STARTED
   ○ THE HORSE BELONGS TO THE LEE FAMILY
   ○ HE DISRESPECTED ARTHUR

5. Polly and Tommy leave for a family meeting at the Garrison. Scudboat locks the door behind them. Who is left hiding in the office?

   ○ GRACE BURGESS
   ○ A SMALL BOY
   ○ ADA SHELBY
   ○ SERGEANT MOSS

6. The Lee family stage a robbery as payback for Cheltenham. Where have they been hiding, waiting to be let in?

   ○ IN A HOUSE ACROSS THE STREET
   ○ IN A CAR AROUND THE CORNER
   ○ UNDER CANVAS IN A HORSE-DRAWN CART
   ○ IN THE GARRISON

7. At the family meeting, John announces that he's proposed to Lizzie Stark. The family react with incredulity. Why?

   ○ LIZZIE IS MUCH OLDER THAN JOHN
   ○ SHE'S A PROSTITUTE
   ○ SHE'S AN ALCOHOLIC
   ○ SHE'S AN OPIUM ADDICT

8. When Tommy learns of the robbery, how many cash boxes does he discover have been stolen?

   ○ ONE
   ○ TWO
   ○ THREE
   ○ FOUR

9. The robbers leave behind a pair of wire-cutters. Why?

   ○ THE SAFE WAS PADLOCKED
   ○ THEY WANTED TO SEVER THE TELEPHONE LINES
   ○ THERE'S A BOOBY TRAP
   ○ THEY WERE PREPARED TO TORTURE TO GET WHAT THEY WANTED

SEASON ONE EPISODE FOUR

10. Tommy figures out the trap has been set for him, but it isn't in the betting office. Where is it?

   ○ THE GARRISON
   ○ THE SHELBY PARLOUR ROOM
   ○ THE CAR
   ○ THE STABLES

11. Tommy and Johnny Dogs visit the Lee family for a parlay. What is Johnny holding as they approach?

   ○ A WHITE HANDKERCHIEF
   ○ A RIFLE
   ○ THE WIRE-CUTTERS
   ○ A WHITE SCARF ON A STICK

12. Johnny Dogs has arranged for Tommy to parlay with Zilpha Lee, the head of the family. 'You could at least say thank you,' Johnny complains. 'It's easier to see the _____ nowadays.' Fill in the blank.

   ○ ... KING
   ○ ... ARCHANGEL
   ○ ... PRIME MINISTER
   ○ ... POPE

13. Before attempting to settle the dispute between the two families, why does Tommy say he won't swear on the Bible?

   ○ HE HAS NO TIME FOR SUPERSTITION
   ○ HE DOESN'T BELIEVE
   ○ HE WANTS ZILPHA TO KNOW SHE CAN'T TRUST HIM COMPLETELY
   ○ HE CONSIDERS IT TO BE BAD LUCK

14. What does he present to her to symbolise his proposal and bring the Lees and the Shelbys together again?

○ AN INVITATION TO THE GARRISON TO BURY THE HATCHET
○ HALF OWNERSHIP OF THE BETTING SHOP
○ A BULLET WITH BILLY KIMBER'S NAME ON IT
○ A PLAN TO HOLD HIS WIFE HOSTAGE FOR RANSOM

15. Wise to the reason for his London trip, Ada questions whether Freddie's more committed to the communist cause or their future together. Where is he when this exchange takes place?

○ A TIN BATH
○ THE FACTORY FLOOR
○ THE TOWPATH
○ THE GARRISON

16. Tommy arranges to meet Chief Inspector Campbell. He has an address for the Communist Party contact holding the money Freddie picked up from the Russian agent. What is the contact's name?

○ CYRIL CHAPMAN
○ STANLEY CHAPMAN
○ SAMUEL CHAPMAN
○ STIRLING CHAPMAN

17. What does Chief Inspector Campbell agree to give him in return?

○ A TIP-OFF AHEAD OF FREDDIE'S ARREST, SO ADA CAN GET AWAY
○ A CHANCE FOR FREDDIE TO LEAVE THE CITY WITH ADA
○ AN EXTRA WEEK TO RETURN THE STOLEN CRATE
○ IMMUNITY FROM PROSECUTION FOR ADA

SEASON ONE ▮ EPISODE FOUR

18. Polly tells Freddie about the arrest of his communist associate, urging him to leave Birmingham with Ada before the police come for him. Where does this take place?

    O THE CHURCH
    O THE PENNY CRUSH PICTURE HOUSE
    O THE RAILWAY STATION
    O THE CEMETERY

19. 'If you want me out of Birmingham,' Freddie tells Polly, 'it'll have to be _____.' Complete the sentence.

    O ... WHEN I ALONE DECIDE
    O ... IN A WOODEN BOX
    O ... AFTER THE BABY'S BORN
    O ... WHEN THE REVOLUTION COMES

20. Billy Kimber grants Tommy the licence for a racecourse betting pitch for his good work. Tommy introduces him to his team for the pitch: John will take care of the book, with Scudboat serving as bagman. What is Lovelock's role?

    O LOOKOUT
    O PROTECTION
    O RUNNER
    O DRIVER

21. The pitch will be at Warwick Racecourse. What condition does Billy place on this?

    O IT HAS TO BE AT LEAST FIFTY YARDS FROM THE BEER TENT
    O THE TRIO MUST NOT SWEAR AT THE CUSTOMERS
    O THE THREE CANNOT DRINK UNTIL THE RACING IS OVER
    O THEY ARE FORBIDDEN FROM ENTERING THE VIP AREA

22. As Arthur counts the takings at the Garrison, Grace fetches a consignment of cigarettes from the cellar to stock at the bar. She knows they're contraband but why does she suggest they're not fit to sell?

   ○ THEY'RE STALE AND THE TOBACCO FALLS OUT
   ○ THEY SMELL OF ROTTING WATER AND THE RATS HAVE GOT TO THEM
   ○ THEY'RE COUNTERFEIT
   ○ THEY'RE A GERMAN BRAND

23. What information does Grace pass onto Chief Inspector Campbell about the Peaky Blinders' contraband that leads to a secret raid?

   ○ IT'S KEPT ON DREDGERS
   ○ IT'S KEPT AT CANAL JUNCTIONS
   ○ IT'S KEPT ON BARGES
   ○ IT'S KEPT IN WATERTIGHT BOXES AT THE BOTTOM OF THE CANAL

24. After the raid, Tommy takes Grace to the church so they can talk. What tells him she has secrets?

   ○ HE REGISTERS THE GUN IN HER PURSE
   ○ SUPPOSEDLY A CATHOLIC, SHE DOESN'T MAKE A SIGN OF THE CROSS AT THE DOOR
   ○ SHE HASN'T BEEN SEEN AT A SERVICE SINCE HER ARRIVAL IN SMALL HEATH
   ○ SHE'S BEEN SEEN AT THE PROTESTANT CHURCH

25. The scene ends with Tommy inviting Grace to work for him, which he seals with a kiss. What does Grace say in response to this?

   ○ 'AM I IN YOUR EMPLOYMENT NOW?'
   ○ 'MY APPETITE FOR THE WORK HAS ONLY INCREASED.'
   ○ 'THERE ARE RISKS IN MIXING BUSINESS WITH PLEASURE.'
   ○ 'I AM APPREHENSIVE ABOUT THE WORK YOU HAVE IN MIND FOR ME.'

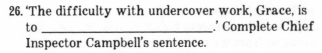

26. 'The difficulty with undercover work, Grace, is to _____.' Complete Chief Inspector Campbell's sentence.

   ○ ... REMEMBER WHAT YOU ARE
   ○ ... STAY IN CHARACTER AT ALL TIMES
   ○ ... RECOGNISE WHO REALLY HAS YOUR BEST INTERESTS AT HEART
   ○ ... NEVER FORGET YOUR LIFE IS IN DANGER

27. When Tommy invites Lizzie into the car to discuss her engagement to his brother John, what does he place on the back seat for her before she climbs in?

   ○ A BASKET OF APPLES
   ○ A BASKET OF GROCERIES
   ○ A BASKET OF WASHING
   ○ A BOTTLE OF WHISKEY

28. How does Tommy test if Lizzie is genuine about his brother?

   ○ BY OFFERING HER MONEY TO DISAPPEAR
   ○ BY OFFERING HER MONEY TO BREAK OFF THE ENGAGEMENT
   ○ BY OFFERING HER MONEY TO SLEEP WITH HIM FOR OLD TIMES' SAKE
   ○ BY OFFERING TO SET HER UP WITH ANOTHER MAN

29. John is polishing the car, preparing for a day out with Lizzie, when Tommy tells him about her response to his test. What does John do with the car key?

   ○ HURLS IT AT TOMMY
   ○ TOSSES IT IN THE CANAL
   ○ THROWS IT ON THE FLOOR
   ○ POCKETS IT AND LEAVES

30. When Tommy brings Grace a contract of employment, she presents him with a bottle of champagne from what department store?

- ○ HENRYS
- ○ RACKHAMS
- ○ BARROWS
- ○ GREYS

31. What is Tommy's first job for Grace?

- ○ WATCH OVER FINN
- ○ AUDIT THE BOOK AT THE BETTING SHOP
- ○ DELIVER AN INVITATION TO ADA
- ○ TAKE OVER THE GARRISON ACCOUNTS FROM ARTHUR

32. Climbing the stairs, Tommy hears activity in his room. With gun cocked, he rushes in. Who has been attempting to smoke his opium pipe?

- ○ FINN
- ○ JOHN
- ○ ADA
- ○ POLLY

33. John is distraught about Lizzie. How did he confirm the truth about her?

- ○ ASKING LIZZIE DIRECTLY
- ○ BUYING DRINKS FOR HER SISTER AND HER COUSIN
- ○ ASKING AROUND IN THE PUB
- ○ SPYING ON HER

34. Tommy orders the Peaky Blinders to assemble the next morning to 'finish the war with the Lees once and for all'. What time do they meet?

- ○ 6.00AM
- ○ 8.00AM
- ○ 9.15AM
- ○ 10.00AM

SEASON ONE ▮ EPISODE FOUR

35. Yards before the Lee camp, Tommy halts the gang and turns to John. What does he produce from his pocket for his brother?

   U A GUN
   U A BLADE
   U A BUTTONHOLE FLOWER FOR A WEDDING
   U A WHISKEY FLASK

36. 'There's a girl from the Lee family who's going a bit wild. They need to marry her off.' Reacting in horror at Tommy's plan to strike peace between the families, what derogatory name does John use to describe his as-yet unseen bride?

   U A FRUIT PICKER
   U A MUSHROOM PICKER
   U A STRAWBERRY PICKER
   U A PICKPOCKET

37. Arthur attempts to sweeten the deal by telling John his prospective new father-in-law has bought them what?

   U A CARAVAN
   U A HOUSE
   U A CAR
   U A FRUIT FARM

38. What is the full name of John's bride?

   U ESME MARTHA LEE
   U ESME MARIA LEE
   U ESME MERCY LEE
   U ESME MASILDA LEE

39. What is the symbolic act that joins the two families?

   U THE FIRST KISS
   U THE MINGLING OF BLOOD
   U A RIFLE ROUND SHOT INTO THE AIR
   U A TOAST

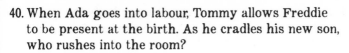

40. When Ada goes into labour, Tommy allows Freddie to be present at the birth. As he cradles his new son, who rushes into the room?

○ ARTHUR SHELBY
○ THE POLICE
○ FREDDIE'S UNION COLLEAGUES
○ GRACE BURGESS

SEASON ONE ▣ EPISODE FOUR

KILLER QUESTIONS

41. What is the name of the barge carrying Freddie and Ada in the opening scene?

- ○ CORMORANT
- ○ KENNET
- ○ KESTREL
- ○ CONNAUGHT

42. What is the name of the coroner Chief Inspector Campbell recommends to record the death of the communist during interrogation as an accident?

- ○ GREGSON
- ○ GRAYSON
- ○ DICKINSON
- ○ GREEN

1. Tommy pays his respects at the grave of Daniel Owen, also known as Danny Whizz-Bang. What is the year of death on the gravestone?

   ○ 1901
   ○ 1910
   ○ 1915
   ○ 1919

2. Polly visits Ada and the new baby. She brings provisions in a basket. What two items does she say it contains?

   ○ EGGS AND BREAD
   ○ APPLES AND BUTTER
   ○ PEARS AND SUGAR
   ○ SAUSAGES AND LEEKS

3. With another basket of her provisions outside the door, untouched given Tommy's apparent act of treachery following the birth, Polly begs Ada to rethink her refusal to accept family help. 'Babies don't _____,' she says. Complete the sentence.

   ○ ... UNDERSTAND STUBBORNNESS
   ○ ... HAVE PRINCIPLES
   ○ ... THRIVE ON AIR
   ○ ... DESERVE TO SUFFER

4. Tommy visits Grace as she works on the Garrison accounts. What drink does she offer him?

   ○ WHISKEY
   ○ RUM
   ○ TEA
   ○ CHAMPAGNE

SEASON ONE ▮ EPISODE FIVE

5. Tommy marks a date in the diary when he plans to take out Billy Kimber and his men. What symbol does he use?

   ○ RED CIRCLE
   ○ BLACK CIRCLE
   ○ RED STAR
   ○ BLACK STAR

6. John and Arthur discuss who shopped Freddie Thorne as they visit an underground bare-knuckle fight. John sides with Polly in thinking it was Tommy. Who does Arthur suggest might be responsible?

   ○ THE LEE FAMILY
   ○ NEIGHBOURS
   ○ STREET KIDS
   ○ THE IRA

7. Arthur notes the popularity of the fight and asks, 'Who's running this _____?'

   ○ SCAM
   ○ BRAWL
   ○ CARNY
   ○ SIDESHOW

8. Seeking to profit from the event, the pair seek out the ringmaster and demand he obtains what?

   ○ PROTECTION
   ○ A LICENCE
   ○ INSURANCE
   ○ AN EXIT FEE

9. As one of the fighters floors his opponent and raises his fists in victory, John and Arthur are struck dumb in surprise. Why?

   ○ THEIR FATHER IS RINGSIDE
   ○ THEIR FATHER IS THE REFEREE
   ○ THEIR FATHER IS THE VICTOR
   ○ THEIR FATHER IS THE FIGHTER ON THE FLOOR

10. Invited back to the house, after years of absence, it's clear that there's bad blood between Arthur Shelby Snr and his family. When Polly tells him to sling his hook, how does he address her?

    ○ POLLY
    ○ POL
    ○ ELIZABETH
    ○ POLLYANNA

11. Discovering their father at the table, Tommy insists that he leaves. Afterwards, how does he describe him to Arthur?

    ○ 'A THIEF AND A LIAR.'
    ○ 'A DESERTER OF THE WORST KIND.'
    ○ 'A SELFISH BASTARD.'
    ○ 'NOT FIT TO CALL HIMSELF A FATHER.'

12. In dispute with Tommy about whether their father can stay, Arthur heads to the Garrison. There, with Grace behind the bar, what does he help himself to?

    ○ A SHOT OF RUM
    ○ MONEY FROM THE TILL
    ○ A BOTTLE OF WHISKEY
    ○ A PACKET OF CIGARETTES

SEASON ONE EPISODE FIVE

13. Grace is working on the accounts. She questions why a dead man, Daniel Owen, is on the payroll. What is Arthur's explanation?

   ○ IT'S PART OF A MONEY-LAUNDERING OPERATION
   ○ IT'S A MEANS OF HIDING MONEY FROM THE TAX INSPECTOR
   ○ DANIEL OWEN IS STILL ALIVE
   ○ IT'S A MISTAKE

14. Arthur meets his father at the underground boxing ring. Where does Arthur Snr say he's been all these years?

   ○ SOUTH AMERICA
   ○ AMERICA
   ○ SCOTLAND
   ○ SPAIN

15. What is responsible for his claim that he's a changed man?

   ○ REGRET
   ○ RELIGION
   ○ BUSINESS SUCCESS
   ○ LOVE

16. Arthur Shelby Snr has returned with a business proposition. What Stateside project does he invite his eldest son to invest in?

   ○ GOLD MINES
   ○ CASINOS
   ○ OIL
   ○ CONSTRUCTION

17. With Arthur expressing an interest, how does his father finish the conversation?

   ○ HE GIVES HIM TWENTY-FOUR HOURS TO COMMIT
   ○ BY INVITING HIM TO STEP INTO THE RING FOR A FATHER-TO-SON FIGHT
   ○ BY INVITING HIM TO PLACE A BET ON THE NEXT FIGHT
   ○ BY ENCOURAGING YOUNG FINN INTO THE RING

18. An IRA man, Byrne, visits Tommy in the Garrison, pressing to purchase the contents of the stolen crate. What does Tommy offer him to drink?

   ○ WHISKEY
   ○ RUM
   ○ WATER AND CORDIAL
   ○ ALE

19. Byrne tells him that Danny Whizz-Bang has divulged in a moment of drunkenness that Tommy has the goods. Before Tommy confirms this, he points out that his former brother in arms is shell-shocked and sees German infantrymen on the back of milk carts. According to Tommy, what does Danny use to shoot them?

   ○ A PISTOL
   ○ A BROOMSTICK
   ○ A RIFLE
   ○ A MACHINE GUN

20. What is Byrne's rank in the IRA?

   ○ QUARTERMASTER
   ○ INTELLIGENCE OFFICER
   ○ COMMANDING OFFICER
   ○ VOLUNTEER

SEASON ONE ▮ EPISODE FIVE

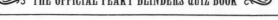

21. Arthur hands his father the money he needs for the casino venture. What day does Arthur Shelby Snr say they'll set sail for America?

   ○ SATURDAY
   ○ MONDAY
   ○ WEDNESDAY
   ○ FRIDAY

22. Towards midnight, Tommy rushes into the Garrison. He tells Grace two IRA men are coming for the stolen crate, but they also plan to kill him. What does he ask Grace to do?

   ○ LEAVE IMMEDIATELY
   ○ WAIT FOR HIS SIGNAL BEFORE BRANDISHING A GUN
   ○ LOCK THE DOORS AND EXTINGUISH THE LAMPS
   ○ WAIT FOR HIS NOD BEFORE RAISING THE ALARM

23. Who is lying in wait outside?

   ○ ARTHUR AND JOHN
   ○ SERGEANT MOSS AND HIS MEN
   ○ THE LEE FAMILY
   ○ BILLY KIMBER AND HIS MEN

24. What does Tommy give Byrne and his associate in return for the money?

   ○ THE CRATE
   ○ A MAP WITH DIRECTIONS
   ○ AN EMPTY CRATE
   ○ A NOTE WITH WRITTEN INSTRUCTIONS

25. When Sergeant Moss and his men enter the Garrison, the two IRA men lie dead. Tommy reacts with fury because, according to a prearranged plan, they were supposed to come when?

○ ON THE STROKE OF MIDNIGHT
○ ON THE SIXTH CHIME
○ WHEN THE IRA MEN WALKED INTO THE PUB
○ WHEN TOMMY RAISED HIS GLASS AND PROPOSED A TOAST

26. When Grace reports to Chief Inspector Campbell, what does he say he's done with Sergeant Moss's report of the pub killing?

○ FILED IT
○ MISLAID IT
○ BURNED IT
○ SENT IT TO LONDON

27. What reason does Grace give for shooting one of the IRA men?

○ SHE PANICKED
○ SHE WANTED TO PROTECT TOMMY
○ VENGEANCE FOR THE KILLING OF HER FATHER
○ SHE THOUGHT SHE WAS ABOUT TO BE SHOT

28. Grace believes she knows where the contents of the stolen crate are hidden. In return for the information, she asks Chief Inspector Campbell to promise not to harm Tommy as she has 'a residue of _____.' Complete the sentence.

○ ... SYMPATHY
○ ... AFFECTION
○ ... CHARITY
○ ... EMPATHY

29. Acting on Grace's intelligence, where do Chief Inspector Campbell and his men unearth the stolen guns?

- ○ DOCKSIDE WAREHOUSE
- ○ DANIEL OWEN'S GRAVE
- ○ IRENE THORNE'S GRAVE
- ○ AT A CANAL JUNCTION

30. Arthur sits anxiously at a ringside table in an empty club with two drinks on the table. Who hasn't turned up?

- ○ TOMMY
- ○ ADA
- ○ THE RINGMASTER
- ○ HIS FATHER

31. The next morning, Grace visits the cemetery where Chief Inspector Campbell and his men have accounted for all but one of the guns. How does she react?

- ○ SHE EXPRESSES SURPRISE THAT ONE IS MISSING
- ○ SHE OFFERS TO STAY ON TO TRACK DOWN THE LAST GUN
- ○ SHE RESIGNS HER COMMISSION
- ○ SHE'S CONCERNED HER COVER WILL BE BLOWN

32. What does Chief Inspector Campbell produce next?

- ○ A BONUS PAYMENT
- ○ AN ENGAGEMENT RING
- ○ A LETTER OF COMMENDATION
- ○ A PASSAGE TO IRELAND

33. 'Do not despise the thief who steals to satisfy his _____.' Finish this quote from the Bible that Arthur Shelby Snr offers to his eldest son when confronted at the railway station.

- ○ HUNGER
- ○ STARVATION
- ○ THIRST
- ○ DREAMS

34. Drunk and distraught at his father's treachery, Arthur heads to the boxing warehouse. What happens to him there?

   ○ HE SPOILS FOR A FIGHT AND IS BEATEN UP
   ○ HE TAKES ON ALL CONTENDERS IN A BRAWL
   ○ HE FAILS IN HIS ATTEMPT TO HANG HIMSELF
   ○ HE VOWS TO SETTLE THE SCORE WITH HIS FATHER

35. With the guns no longer in his possession, and his bargaining power gone, Tommy heads to the Garrison to tell Grace he plans to lie low. What does she do when the police raid the pub?

   ○ URGES HIM TO GIVE HIMSELF UP OR BE KILLED
   ○ URGES HIM TO FLEE WITH HER
   ○ HIDES HIM IN THE BACK ROOM
   ○ HIDES HIM IN THE CELLAR

36. Hiding out in Grace's lodgings, Tommy asks her to dance. They do so without music. Why?

   ○ THEY DON'T WANT TO MAKE ANY NOISE AS THE SEARCH FOR HIM IS UNDERWAY
   ○ GRACE HAS NO GRAMOPHONE
   ○ THE GRAMOPHONE IS BROKEN
   ○ THE RECORD IS TOO SCRATCHED

37. From outside, Chief Inspector Campbell sees a silhouette of the couple and retreats into the night. In bed together later that night, what does Tommy say to Grace?

   ○ 'HE KNOWS I'M HERE.'
   ○ 'HE'LL BE WATCHING YOU.'
   ○ 'WE'LL HELP EACH OTHER.'
   ○ 'YOU'RE MEANT FOR ME, NOT HIM.'

SEASON ONE ▐ EPISODE FIVE

38. Tommy returns home the next morning to find Arthur alone. He notes the state of his older brother, aware that his father has swindled family money from him. What does Tommy do before he sits with him?

   ○ PUNCHES HIM
   ○ GRABS HIM BY THE THROAT
   ○ KISSES HIM ON THE FOREHEAD
   ○ SQUEEZES HIS SHOULDER

39. In a bid to focus him on a brighter future, Tommy shows Arthur the 'Shelby Brothers' business cards that he's just picked up from the printers. What is Arthur's job title?

   ○ ASSOCIATE BOOKMAKER
   ○ CHIEF BOOKMAKER
   ○ HEAD OF SECURITY
   ○ BETTING OFFICER

KILLER QUESTIONS

SEASON ONE ▮ EPISODE FIVE

40. When they meet in the Chinese quarter, Tommy hands Chief Inspector Campbell a Most Wanted flyer for Byrne. How much is the reward on offer for his capture?

   U £20
   U £50
   U £100
   U £200

41. Tommy proposes to deliver Byrne to the chief inspector. What does he ask for in return?

   U IMMUNITY FROM PROSECUTION
   U THE REWARD
   U WORD PUT OUT IN IRELAND THAT HE WAS NOT INVOLVED
   U PROTECTION FROM THE IRA

42. When Arthur Shelby Snr slams his eldest son against the wall at the railway station, what union notice is posted behind them?

   U UNITED SOCIETY OF BOILERMAKERS
   U UNION OF COMMUNICATION WORKERS
   U THE NATIONAL UNION OF RAILWAYMEN
   U TRANSPORT & GENERAL WORKERS UNION

1. Chief Inspector Campbell visits Zhang's dry cleaning den and brothel looking to buy company. What is Zhang doing as he arrives?

   ○ PRESSING A SUIT
   ○ HANGING THE SHELBY BROTHERS' SUITS ON A RAIL
   ○ COUNTING BANKNOTES
   ○ BRUSHING HIS TEETH

2. Preparing for a big day, Tommy enters the Garrison at first light. Arthur is at the desk in the office. What is he doing?

   ○ THE ACCOUNTS
   ○ COUNTING TAKINGS
   ○ SLEEPING
   ○ DRINKING

3. Where are John and new bride Esme when Tommy enters their house to summon him?

   ○ IN THE KITCHEN
   ○ IN THE PARLOUR
   ○ IN BED
   ○ BY THE FIRE

4. What is Polly doing when Tommy informs her that a family meeting is about to take place so he can lay out his plan for the day?

   ○ EATING BREAKFAST AT THE TABLE
   ○ PRAYING FOR TOMMY AND HIS BROTHERS
   ○ OPENING UP THE BETTING OFFICE
   ○ READING THE EVENING DISPATCH

5. Chief Inspector Campbell is seeking solace, having discovered that Grace is with Tommy. What does the prostitute call him?

   ○ A MAN WHO SEEMS SO LOST
   ○ A SPECIAL, SPECIAL CUSTOMER
   ○ AN ESTEEMED CUSTOMER
   ○ A MAN WITH A BROKEN HEART

6. Grace makes her way to a final meeting with Chief Inspector Campbell. Waiting for her instead is Sergeant Moss, who knows about her and Thomas. What does he call her on handing her a note from Campbell?

   ○ A FRAUD
   ○ A LIAR
   ○ A WHORE
   ○ A HEARTBREAKER

7. Following a tip-off from Zhang, Thomas finds Chief Inspector Campbell as he prepares to leave the brothel. Who does he say he is due to meet that morning?

   ○ GRACE BURGESS
   ○ ARTHUR SHELBY SNR
   ○ WINSTON CHURCHILL
   ○ BILLY KIMBER

8. 'You are I are opposites. _____.' Chief Inspector Campbell tells Tommy before he leaves. Complete the sentence.

   ○ '... WE WILL NEVER UNDERSTAND ONE ANOTHER.'
   ○ '... WE CANNOT BE ON THE SAME SIDE.'
   ○ '... WITH ONE IN DARKNESS AND THE OTHER IN LIGHT.'
   ○ '... BUT ALSO JUST THE SAME.'

SEASON ONE ▮ EPISODE SIX

9. While helping Ada tend to the baby, Polly talks about her own two children, Sally and Michael Gray. What age were they respectively when Polly was forced to give them up for adoption?

- ○ THREE AND FIVE
- ○ FOUR AND FIVE
- ○ TWO AND THREE
- ○ ONE AND FOUR

10. What crime had Polly committed that led to the adoption of her children?

- ○ SHE'D BEEN ARRESTED FOR ATTEMPTED MURDER
- ○ SHE'D BEEN CAUGHT WITH A HOME-MADE SPIRIT STILL FOR MAKING GIN
- ○ SHE'D BEEN CHARGED WITH MONEY-LAUNDERING
- ○ SHE'D ENCOURAGED YOUNG MICHAEL TO BECOME A PICKPOCKET

11. 'He never usually smiles,' observes Winston Churchill during his meeting with Chief Inspector Campbell. With whom has he shared the happy news that the stolen guns have been retrieved?

- ○ KING GEORGE V
- ○ THE PRIME MINISTER
- ○ THE HOME SECRETARY
- ○ THE BRITISH ARMY CHIEF

12. How does Churchill suggest Campbell will be recognised for his success?

- ○ A GOLDEN HANDSHAKE
- ○ A NEW YEAR'S HONOUR
- ○ A PROMOTION
- ○ AN AUDIENCE WITH THE KING

13. At the family meeting, Tommy reveals his plan
to take down Billy Kimber. Then, with the family
business on a legitimate footing, what association
does he intend to join?

   ○ THE ASSOCIATION OF LICENSED BETTING OFFICES
   ○ THE RACECOURSE BETTING ASSOCIATION
   ○ THE NATIONAL ASSOCIATION OF RACECOURSE BOOKMAKERS
   ○ THE NORTHERN BOOKMAKERS PROTECTION ASSOCIATION

14. Tommy explains that Billy Kimber is expecting the
Peaky Blinders to join forces with his men to fight
the Lees, unaware that the two families are now
united through John and Esme's marriage. At what
racecourse will this power grab take place?

   ○ UTTOXETER
   ○ WOLVERHAMPTON
   ○ STRATFORD-UPON-AVON
   ○ WORCESTER

15. Polly introduces a new family member to the
meeting. She opens the door and Ada appears with
her new baby. She tells everyone he's named after a
famous communist leader. What is his name?

   ○ JOSEPH
   ○ KARL
   ○ LEV
   ○ NESTOR

16. Ada returns to the family fold because Tommy has
arranged for a police van carrying Freddie Thorne
to be ambushed. Who does he entrust to rescue his
brother-in-law?

   ○ DANNY WHIZZ-BANG
   ○ CHARLIE STRONG
   ○ CURLY
   ○ LOVELOCK

17. Before they head off to the racecourse, Tommy gets a round for the Peaky Blinders on the house. What are they each permitted?

- ○ A PINT
- ○ A PINT AND A CHASER
- ○ A SHOT
- ○ TWO PINTS

18. Where does Grace draw breath to confess her past to Tommy, only to be interrupted by news that Kimber's men are heading for Small Heath?

- ○ THE BETTING SHOP DOORWAY
- ○ OUTSIDE THE GARRISON
- ○ IN THE SNUG
- ○ IN THE BACK ROOM BEHIND THE BAR

19. Tommy rushes to tell Ada to take the baby and hide in public. Where does he suggest?

- ○ THE PARK
- ○ THE PUBLIC LIBRARY
- ○ CITY HOSPITAL
- ○ THE BULL RING MARKET

20. In the Garrison, after the Peaky Blinders have rushed out to confront Billy Kimber's men, Polly confronts Grace about her true identity. What does Polly draw as a weapon?

- ○ A PISTOL
- ○ A GARROTTE
- ○ A HAIRPIN
- ○ A BROKEN BOTTLE

21. Polly and Grace sit down to talk. Grace asks what Tommy was like before the war. What does Polly tell her?

  ○ HE WANTED TO BE A MECHANIC
  ○ HE WANTED TO WORK WITH HORSES
  ○ HE WANTED TO GO TO SEA
  ○ HE WANTED TO BE A GUNSMITH

22. Polly's mood then darkens considerably. She threatens to kill Grace unless she's gone from the city by when?

  ○ THE HOUR
  ○ SUNDOWN
  ○ THE NEXT DAY
  ○ THE END OF THE WEEK

23. John brings further word on the approach of Kimber and his men. Who has he heard this from?

  ○ SMITH AT YARDLEY
  ○ NIPPER AT HAY MILLS
  ○ FORRESTER AT ALUM ROCK
  ○ JONES AT WAKE GREEN

24. Tommy gathers his troops. They're outnumbered but determined to win the fight. What vehicles are said to be approaching?

  ○ TWO MORRIS COWLEYS
  ○ THREE NAPIERS
  ○ TWO RILEY VANS
  ○ ONE CORBITT TRUCK

25. Tommy estimates that without the Lee family they are outnumbered. By how much?

  ○ THREE TO ONE
  ○ EIGHT TO ONE
  ○ TEN TO ONE
  ○ FIFTEEN TO ONE

SEASON ONE ▮ EPISODE SIX

26. Before his men take up arms, he calls them by a
    name from their war days. What is it?

    ○ SMALL HEATH GUNNERS
    ○ SMALL HEATH RIFLES
    ○ BLACK COUNTRY BRIGADE
    ○ BIRMINGHAM WARRIORS

27. Sergeant Moss expresses surprise when Chief
    Inspector Campbell requests that Kimber's men
    should not be stopped. Who handed Campbell the
    information he needed about Tommy's plan and
    alerted Kimber?

    ○ FREDDIE THORNE
    ○ GRACE BURGESS
    ○ MR ZHENG
    ○ ADA SHELBY

28. Minutes before the showdown with Kimber and his
    men, who gives Tommy pause for thought by saying
    about the Peaky Blinders: 'You're bad men, but you're
    our bad men.'

    ○ CURLY
    ○ SERGEANT MOSS
    ○ ESME SHELBY
    ○ HARRY FENTON

29. As the stand-off takes shape with Billy Kimber and
    his men, who steps up with the missing machine gun
    to ensure the Peaky Blinders have the upper hand?

    ○ FINN SHELBY
    ○ CURLY
    ○ POLLY GRAY
    ○ FREDDIE THORNE

30. 'I believe you boys call this No-Man's Land.' Who comes between the two sides?

    ○ POLLY GRAY
    ○ ADA SHELBY
    ○ ARTHUR SHELBY SNR
    ○ CHIEF INSPECTOR CAMPBELL

31. Billy Kimber breaks the silence that follows by shooting Tommy in the shoulder. He pulls the trigger one more time. Who rushes in to take the bullet for Tommy?

    ○ FREDDIE THORNE
    ○ DANNY WHIZZ-BANG
    ○ CHARLIE STRONG
    ○ JEREMIAH JESUS

32. Tommy fires just one shot, which kills Billy Kimber and marks the end of the dispute. Where does the bullet strike Billy?

    ○ THE HEART
    ○ THE STOMACH
    ○ THE NECK
    ○ THE HEAD

33. Why does Grace visit Chief Inspector Campbell one more time?

    ○ TO ASK HIM WHAT HE SAID TO TOMMY
    ○ TO ASK HIM TO SPARE TOMMY
    ○ TO REQUEST THAT HE MAKE NO FURTHER CONTACT WITH HER
    ○ TO DEMAND THAT HE LEAVE FOR LONDON STRAIGHT AWAY

34. 'I still have the knack!' Who declares this, having extracted the bullet from Tommy's shoulder and dropped it in a glass?

    ○ JEREMIAH JESUS
    ○ JOHNNY DOGS
    ○ FREDDIE THORNE
    ○ ARTHUR SHELBY

SEASON ONE ▮ EPISODE SIX

35. 'To Danny Whizz-Bang,' says Tommy in proposing a toast to his fallen comrade. Complete the sentence.

   ○ '... MAY HE REST IN PEACE AT LAST.'
   ○ '... YOUR WAR IS FINALLY OVER.'
   ○ '... MAY WE ALL DIE TWICE.'
   ○ '... THE ONLY MAN TO VISIT HIS OWN GRAVE.'

36. 'It's just uniform,' reasons Grace about her actions when Tommy finds her packing at her lodgings. She hands him an address and asks him to join her within the week. Where is it?

   ○ LONDON
   ○ DUBLIN
   ○ BELFAST
   ○ GLASGOW

37. Tommy returns to the Garrison, where Polly, Arthur and John are waiting for him. What drink does he suggest?

   ○ WHISKEY
   ○ RUM
   ○ GIN
   ○ CHAMPAGNE

38. With the Lee family taking over the racecourse pitches in the absence of Billy Kimber and his men, Shelby Brothers is now the third-largest legal race track operation in the country. Along with the Sabinis, what other gang stands in their way for the top spot?

   ○ THE WHITES
   ○ THE SOLOMONS
   ○ THE GREENS
   ○ THE MULLINS

39. In writing a letter to Grace about their future, what
    method of decision-making does Tommy say he used
    to favour?

    ○ TOSSING A COIN
    ○ TALKING TO POLLY
    ○ CONSULTING HIS LATE MOTHER
    ○ TAKING A VOTE WITH HIS BROTHERS

KILLER QUESTIONS

40. On the blackboard behind Tommy when he briefs the Peaky Blinders on his plan to take down Billy Kimber, who is the favourite at the forthcoming race at Worcester?

   O SMOKING GUN
   O KINGSMAN
   O BAY RUM
   O APOLLO

41. When Jeremiah brings word that Kimber's men are heading for the Garrison, what road does he say they're on?

   O COVENTRY ROAD
   O HOLYHEAD ROAD
   O TYBURN ROAD
   O STRATFORD ROAD

42. What is the brand of typewriter that Tommy uses to compose his letter to Grace, unaware that the spurned Chief Inspector Campbell is set to raise his gun to her as she prepares to depart the city?

   O UNDERWOOD
   O BARLET
   O ROYAL
   O SMITH

SEASON TWO

1. The season opens on the railway station platform.
   Grace is staring down the barrel of Chief Inspector
   Campbell's pistol. He's heartbroken at her rejection
   of his engagement proposal, and enraged that she's
   tangled up with Tommy. What happens next?

   O SHE TURNS AND RUNS
   O SHE SHOOTS HIM DEAD WITH THE PISTOL CONCEALED IN HER
     HANDBAG
   O HE TURNS THE GUN ON HIMSELF
   O SHE WOUNDS HIM WITH THE PISTOL CONCEALED IN HER
     HANDBAG

2. In what year does Season 2 take place?

   O 1919
   O 1921
   O 1923
   O 1925

3. Two women in billowing black dresses leave bombs
   outside the Garrison doors. What are the explosives
   concealed inside?

   O PACKAGES
   O PRAMS
   O MILK CRATES
   O BARRELS

4. Meanwhile the Peaky Blinders have gathered at a
   cemetery graveside, where Tommy says a few words.
   Who are they burying?

   O JOHNNY DOGS
   O FREDDIE THORNE
   O ZILPHA LEE
   O HARRY FENTON

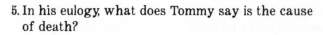
5. In his eulogy, what does Tommy say is the cause of death?

○ PLAGUE
○ PESTILENCE
○ A FALL
○ A HEART ATTACK

6. On leaving the cemetery, Ada talks to Tommy about his new-found wealth. She points out how unfair it is that half the country is starving while he owns what?

○ SIX RACEHORSES
○ FOUR BUGATTIS
○ A ROLLS-ROYCE
○ A BUTLER

7. Why does Tommy ask Ada to move out of London and back to Birmingham?

○ TO RUN THE BETTING OFFICE
○ TO MANAGE THE GARRISON
○ FOR PROTECTION WHILE HE EXPANDS THE BUSINESS INTO THE CAPITAL
○ SO POLLY CAN HELP WITH KARL

8. Tommy suspects the IRA are behind the bombing. Why?

○ POLLY FINDS GREEN CONFETTI ON THE FLOOR OF THE GARRISON
○ POLLY DISCOVERS THE CHARRED REMAINS OF A LOYALIST POEM INSIDE
○ IRISHMEN HAD BEEN SEEN OUTSIDE THE PUB
○ TOMMY HEARS OF CELEBRATIONS IN SPARKHILL

9. 'I heard there was a bit of a bang in your part of town,' says the landlord of a Sparkhill pub that Tommy visits, a drinking den for Irish nationalists. He promptly refuses to accept his money for a drink. Who then appears to escort Tommy to the meeting?

   ○ A SMALL BOY
   ○ A SURLY IRISH NATIONALIST
   ○ A CORRUPT COPPER
   ○ A WOMAN IN A BILLOWING BLACK DRESS

10. Tommy follows his escort to an empty abattoir, where two men remove his cap and gun and check his coat for hidden weapons. What do they place over his head before leading him to the meeting?

   ○ A GARROTTE
   ○ A NOOSE
   ○ A HESSIAN SACK
   ○ A CLOAK

11. While John and Polly keep the betting office running, what is Arthur's task in the aftermath of the bombing?

   ○ PREVENTING LOOTERS FROM STEALING THE GARRISON'S WHISKEY
   ○ ORGANISING THE CLEAN-UP OPERATION
   ○ PROTECTING THE GARRISON'S WHISKEY FROM THE POLICE
   ○ OVERSEEING A WHISKEY-SMUGGLING OPERATION TO REPLENISH STOCKS AT THE PUB

12. 'She said we all look like we work in a factory under the ground. She said we look like ghosts.' The pressure of the Shelby business enterprise is getting to John, who shares his anxiety with Polly at the betting shop. Who made this observation to him about their appearance?

   ○ GRACE BURGESS
   ○ ADA THORNE
   ○ ESME SHELBY
   ○ LIZZIE STARK

SEASON TWO ▮ EPISODE ONE

13. Tommy finds himself facing two IRA representatives, who attempt to blackmail him into working for them. Tommy counters with background information on the leader, Irene O'Donnell, to demonstrate he knows exactly who he's facing. What does he tell her?

- ◯ SHE HAS A DAUGHTER WHO IS BLIND IN ONE EYE
- ◯ SHE HAS A SON WHO WEARS IRONS ON HIS LEGS
- ◯ HER MOTHER IS DYING OF TUBERCULOSIS
- ◯ SHE IS STAYING IN LODGINGS ACROSS FROM THE BOATYARD

14. Tommy leaves in a state of agitation. Against his will, Irene has found a way to bring him on board. On storming out, where does he find his coat?

- ◯ DUMPED ON THE FLOOR
- ◯ PLACED ON A STACK OF WOODEN CRATES
- ◯ HANGING FROM A MEAT HOOK
- ◯ SLUNG OVER A PIG CARCASS

15. Sergeant Moss is now in the pay of the Peaky Blinders. With his IRA mission in mind, Tommy asks him to keep the streets clear of coppers around the co-operative stables between what hours that night?

- ◯ 11.00PM TO 3.00AM
- ◯ 12.00AM TO 4.00AM
- ◯ 1.00AM TO 5.00AM
- ◯ 2.00AM TO 6.00AM

16. Sergeant Moss also brings news that 'an old friend' is back in Birmingham. Campbell has been promoted to Major, but what does Moss call the secret department he's now running?

- ◯ THE MAINLAND OFFICE
- ◯ THE UNIONIST MISSION
- ◯ SPECIAL OPERATIONS
- ◯ THE IRISH DESK

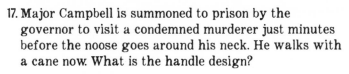

17. Major Campbell is summoned to prison by the governor to visit a condemned murderer just minutes before the noose goes around his neck. He walks with a cane now. What is the handle design?

   ○ A SILVER WOLF HEAD
   ○ A BRONZE COBRA HEAD
   ○ A GOLDEN EAGLE
   ○ AN IVORY PHOENIX

18. Inside the cell, the condemned man pleads desperately that he was carrying out orders from an intelligence officer matching Major Campbell's description. From the other side of the door, Campbell denies all knowledge to the governor, but what does he say to ensure his silence?

   ○ 'CARRY OUT THIS EXECUTION OR YOU'LL BE NEXT IN THE NOOSE.'
   ○ 'I KNOW WHERE YOU LIVE.'
   ○ 'DON'T MAKE ME LOOK INTO YOUR PERSONAL AFFAIRS.'
   ○ 'YOUR WAGE PACKET WILL BE THICKER THIS WEEK.'

19. Finn summons Arthur from the boxing club for a family meeting. He's fit, lean and driven, and turning a skipping rope furiously. Before he breaks off and responds to his youngest brother, how many skips does Arthur say he's completed?

   ○ ONE HUNDRED
   ○ FIVE HUNDRED
   ○ EIGHT HUNDRED
   ○ TWO THOUSAND

SEASON TWO ▐ EPISODE ONE

20. The family wait for Tommy to begin the meeting. Before he arrives, John shares his misgivings about Shelby Company Ltd's expansion south. He points out that there's no need because the gambling business is earning an average of how much each day?

O £80
O £100
O £150
O £400

21. Esme speaks up at the meeting, backing her husband. How does she describe London?

O HELL ON EARTH
O SMOKE AND TROUBLE
O A CURSED CAPITAL
O NO PLACE FOR SHELBYS

22. Tommy informs the family that 'the bang at the pub' has nothing to do with London, and that expansion into the capital begins the next day. He invites anyone who wants no part in it to walk out of the door. Who leaves?

O JOHN AND ESME SHELBY
O CHARLIE STRONG
O NOBODY
O JOHN SHELBY

23. Given her position in the company, Polly is annoyed that Tommy has made plans without her knowledge. What is her job title?

O GENERAL MANAGER
O COMPANY TREASURER
O GENERAL SECRETARY
O CHIEF FINANCE OFFICER

24. In disclosing his plan for London to Polly, Tommy explains that two gangs — the Jews and the Italians — are at war. How long have they been fighting?

- ○ THREE WEEKS
- ○ SIX MONTHS
- ○ EIGHTEEN MONTHS
- ○ TWO YEARS

25. Tommy intends to back the Jewish gang, who control North London, so he can begin his expansion plans. 'We need a foothold _____,' he tells Polly. Complete the sentence.

- ○ ... AND CAMDEN WILL PROVIDE THAT FOR US
- ○ ... AT THE SOUTHERN END OF THE GRAND UNION
- ○ ... BEFORE WE CAN TAKE LONDON
- ○ ... TO STAMP OUR AUTHORITY ON THE CITY

26. Before leaving for London, Tommy pays for time with Lizzie Stark. Afterwards, she tells him she's taken up a correspondence course. What is she learning?

- ○ INDEXING
- ○ TYPEWRITING
- ○ BOOKKEEPING
- ○ ADMINISTRATION

27. Polly takes part in a séance. Why?

- ○ TO SEEK FREDDIE THORNE'S BLESSING IN BRINGING ADA AND HIS SON BACK TO BIRMINGHAM
- ○ TO THANK DANNY WHIZZ-BANG FOR HIS SACRIFICE
- ○ TO ASK TOMMY'S MOTHER TO PROTECT HIM FROM THE GRAVE
- ○ TO FIND OUT IF THE DAUGHTER TAKEN FROM HER IS ALIVE OR DEAD

SEASON TWO ▮ EPISODE ONE

28. Tommy carries out a killing on behalf of the IRA. What is the profession of the man he shoots?

  ○ TANNER
  ○ FARRIER
  ○ BLACKSMITH
  ○ CARPENTER

29. 'They tell you what you already believe.' Esme reveals to Polly that the medium she visited is a charlatan. How does she say she knows?

  ○ SHE KNOWS HOW THEY 'PUSH THE GLASS'
  ○ THE ACCOMPLICE MASQUERADING AS A CLIENT IS ESME'S COUSIN
  ○ ESME HAS BEEN TRICKED HERSELF
  ○ ESME'S MOTHER ONCE PERFORMED THE SAME TRICK

30. En route to London, the Shelby brothers stop on a barren stretch of country road to relieve themselves. Afterwards, Tommy opens the boot. What's inside that needs to be buried?

  ○ A CHEST OF MONEY, SHOULD THEY NEED IT IN EMERGENCY
  ○ THE LAST MACHINE GUN FROM THE STOLEN CHEST
  ○ THE BODY OF THE MAN HE ASSASSINATED
  ○ A HAUL OF JEWELS

31. Tommy, Arthur and John visit the Eden Club in London, which is controlled by the Italians. 'It's a freak show,' observes Arthur as they take their seats amid the dancing, drinking and debauchery. When the owner asks them to leave, considering their presence to be a provocation, what sparks a brawl?

  ○ SOMEONE THROWS A BOTTLE OF WINE AT TOMMY
  ○ JOHN HEADBUTTS THE OWNER
  ○ ARTHUR SMASHES THE WHISKEY BOTTLE AND USES IT TO THREATEN THE BOUNCER
  ○ THE BOUNCER PRODUCES A HANDGUN

SEASON TWO ▮ EPISODE ONE

32. What brings the fight to an end, and allows Tommy to address everyone present with a clear message for Mr Sabini, who heads the Italian gang?

- ○ MARIO, THE CLUB MANAGER, SUMMONS THE POLICE
- ○ MARIO FIRES A RIFLE AT THE CEILING
- ○ TOMMY FIRES A RIFLE AT A MIRROR
- ○ THE OWNER HOLDS JOHN AT GUNPOINT

33. Major Campbell visits Winston Churchill at his office. What does he interrupt?

- ○ A TELEPHONE CONVERSATION WITH THE KING
- ○ AN ARGUMENT BETWEEN CHURCHILL AND HIS WIFE
- ○ A LIFE-DRAWING SESSION WITH A NUDE MODEL
- ○ A MOMENT OF INTIMACY BETWEEN CHURCHILL AND HIS SECRETARY

34. In updating Churchill on his activities in Birmingham, what does Major Campbell reveal?

- ○ HE IS AWARE OF AN IRA CELL PLOTTING A CAMPAIGN FROM THE CITY
- ○ HE IS BEHIND THE IRA OPERATION TO BLACKMAIL TOMMY, AND WISHES TO RECRUIT HIM FOR A BIGGER TASK
- ○ HE IS AWARE THAT THE PEAKY BLINDERS ARE EXPANDING THEIR BUSINESS SOUTH, AND PLANS TO STOP THEM
- ○ HE BELIEVES THAT TOMMY IS VOLUNTARILY WORKING IN LEAGUE WITH THE IRA

35. Major Campbell makes no secret of the fact that he wants to see Tommy Shelby dead. By what means?

- ○ SHOOTING
- ○ BURIED ALIVE
- ○ BURNING
- ○ HANGING

SEASON TWO ▮ EPISODE ONE

36. Back home, Tommy recruits Lizzy for discreet secretarial work. What test does she pass to be offered the job?

   ○ SHE CAN TYPE WHILE TOMMY COVERS HER EYES
   ○ SHE CAN TYPE FIFTY WORDS A MINUTE
   ○ SHE CAN TYPE SIXTY WORDS A MINUTE
   ○ SHE SPELLS 'AMBITION' CORRECTLY

37. Polly hands Tommy a telegram that's arrived from the Jewish gang. She's furious because it confirms that Tommy has picked a side in their war with the Italians. What does it say?

   ○ WE SHOULD PARLAY
   ○ TO A GOOD YEAR
   ○ MORE POWER TO YOU
   ○ LET US BREAK BREAD TOGETHER

38. That night, both Tommy and Ada are attacked. While Ada is dragged away in London, Tommy is beaten senseless in the dark, rain-drenched streets of Small Heath. Mr Sabini steps out of the shadows. What does he order his henchman to do?

   ○ EXTRACT A GOLD TOOTH FROM TOMMY'S MOUTH
   ○ SLICE OFF A FINGER
   ○ CUT OFF AN EARLOBE
   ○ BREAK AN ARM

39. Sabini issues the order to execute Tommy, only for who to come to his rescue?

   ○ ARTHUR AND JOHN SHELBY
   ○ ESME SHELBY
   ○ MAJOR CAMPBELL
   ○ SERGEANT MOSS

KILLER QUESTIONS

40. What is the name of the Sparkhill pub that Tommy visits before his meeting with the IRA kingpins?

   ○ CROSSKEYS
   ○ THE BLACK LION
   ○ THE GREEN DRAGON
   ○ KELLY'S

41. Before the expansion into London, according to Tommy in conversation with Polly, how many staff worked for Shelby Company Limited?

   ○ FIFTEEN
   ○ EIGHTEEN
   ○ TWENTY-TWO
   ○ TWENTY-FOUR

42. When Tommy pulls up in the street to collect Arthur and John for the trip to London, he confiscates a medicine bottle from his older brother because he wants to keep him 'sharp'. Later, what does Polly tell him it contained?

   ○ MORPHINE
   ○ OPIUM AND BROMIDE
   ○ BARBITURATES
   ○ COCAINE

SEASON TWO ▮ EPISODE ONE

1. Ada is rescued from Sabini's thugs by the Peaky Blinders. Instead of showing her gratitude, however, she's furious at her failure to escape from the Shelby reach. How does she respond to the man who saves her?

   ○ PUNCHING HIM ON THE NOSE
   ○ SLAPPING HIM ACROSS THE FACE
   ○ KNEEING HIM IN THE GROIN
   ○ STAMPING ON HIS FOOT

2. Bloodied and beaten senseless by Sabini's men, how do we see Tommy transported to hospital?

   ○ SLUNG OVER A HORSE
   ○ BY STRETCHER
   ○ BY CART
   ○ BY CAR

3. Major Campbell visits Tommy in hospital. What is Tommy's first request from him?

   ○ CLOSE THE CURTAINS
   ○ PASS HIS CIGARETTES
   ○ SHUT THE DOOR
   ○ POUR HIM A GLASS OF WATER

4. Before getting down to hard talk, Tommy tells Major Campbell that Grace is now married and living in America. The Major is aware, and knows her husband's profession. What it is?

   ○ A PROPERTY MAGNATE
   ○ A BANKER
   ○ A FARMER
   ○ A RANCHER

5. 'You are on my hook, Mr Shelby, and from this
moment on you belong to *me*!' How has Major
Campbell ensured that Tommy will work for him as
a spy?

   U THE MAJOR HAS THREATENED TO TAKE ADA INTO CUSTODY,
   WHICH WOULD MEAN SHE'D LOSE KARL
   U HE KNOWS THAT TOMMY CARRIED OUT A KILLING FOR THE IRA
   U HE HAS ENOUGH EVIDENCE AGAINST GRACE TO SEE HER HANG,
   SHOULD SHE RETURN FROM AMERICA
   U HE HAS THE POWER TO SHUT DOWN SHELBY BROTHERS LTD
   FOR CRIMINAL ACTIVITIES

6. Tommy discharges himself from hospital early and
staggers to Charlie Strong's boatyard. There, what
does he request for his injuries so that he can travel
by barge to London?

   U WILD COMFREY
   U CANOLA OIL
   U HORSE OIL
   U LANOLIN

7. How long does Charlie estimate the journey will
take?

   U THREE DAYS
   U FOUR DAYS
   U ONE WEEK
   U A FORTNIGHT

8. Tommy finally surfaces from below deck on the
barge, with one day left before reaching Camden
Town. Where does Curly say they are on the journey?

   U HEATHROW
   U SOUTHALL
   U HOUNSLOW
   U BERKHAMSTED

SEASON TWO ▌ EPISODE TWO

9. Tommy visits Jewish gang leader, Alfie Solomons, in his bakery. How many loaves does Alfie claim to bake each week?

   O TWO HUNDRED
   O FIVE HUNDRED
   O ONE THOUSAND
   O TWO THOUSAND

10. Alfie shows Tommy around the bakery and invites him to try a sample of 'bread'. What is he really producing here?

    O OPIUM
    O BEER
    O RUM
    O COCAINE

11. From across the desk in his office, Alfie bristles when Tommy suggests he is losing the gang war. In response, he talks about taking out an Italian soldier in the trenches during the war. What method of killing does he describe in gruesome detail?

    O HAMMERING A NAIL UP HIS NOSE
    O STABBING HIM THROUGH THE EYE
    O CUTTING HIS THROAT WITH A SERRATED KNIFE
    O PUSHING A BAYONET THROUGH THE BACK OF HIS NECK

12. Tommy attempts to strike a deal. As well as offering Alfie access to race tracks north of the border, what else can he provide him?

    O HORSE TRAINERS IN THE PAY OF THE PEAKY BLINDERS
    O POLICE IN THEIR PAY
    O ARMED MEN
    O BOARD AND LODGINGS IN BIRMINGHAM EN ROUTE TO THE RACES

13. Alfie pulls a gun on Tommy. He's heard enough. He threatens to shoot him and dispose of his body in barrels. Name one place he proposes to send a barrel.

   ○ CAIRO
   ○ MANDALAY
   ○ ISTANBUL
   ○ SYDNEY

14. Before the pair strike a deal, Alfie observes that he always thought that a man like Tommy Shelby would wear what kind of jewellery?

   ○ SILVER HOOPS THROUGH HIS EARS
   ○ A GOLD RING THROUGH HIS NOSE
   ○ A ROSE-GOLD INDEX RING
   ○ A ROSE-GOLD THUMB RING

15. Tommy stops Ada in the streets of London. He's anxious that she accepts protection in view of the Sabini threat, but Ada has taken steps of her own. What form does it take?

   ○ A BODYGUARD
   ○ A GUN CONCEALED IN HER PURSE
   ○ A KNIFE STRAPPED TO HER THIGH
   ○ SHE'S PAID THE COPPERS TO KEEP AN EYE ON HER

16. Still concerned for her safety, and keen to launder money from the shady side of the family business, what does Tommy hand his sister?

   ○ THE KEY TO A LONDON TOWNHOUSE
   ○ THE KEY TO A COUNTRY MANOR
   ○ THE KEY TO A SAFE HOUSE SHOULD SHE NEED TO VANISH IN A HURRY
   ○ THE NUMBER FOR A CHAUFFEUR TO DRIVE HER HOME TO BIRMINGHAM

SEASON TWO ▤ EPISODE TWO

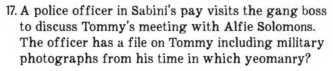

17. A police officer in Sabini's pay visits the gang boss to discuss Tommy's meeting with Alfie Solomons. The officer has a file on Tommy including military photographs from his time in which yeomanry?

   ○ SHROPSHIRE
   ○ WARWICKSHIRE
   ○ NORTHAMPTONSHIRE
   ○ LEICESTERSHIRE

18. Sabini suspects the police officer has been 'got at' by the Peaky Blinders, and therefore must rely on his own men to deal with them. How does he send the officer on his way?

   ○ BY WAVING A PISTOL AT HIM
   ○ BY THROWING A BAR STOOL AT HIM
   ○ BY HURLING A WINE BOTTLE AT HIM
   ○ BY KICKING THE CHAIR FROM UNDER HIM

19. Back in Birmingham, when Polly wakes from another disturbed sleep and rushes to get dressed, what does she slip inside her boot?

   ○ A PAIR OF SCISSORS
   ○ A KNIFE
   ○ A KNITTING NEEDLE
   ○ BANKNOTES

20. Polly walks into the betting shop, to be met by a round of applause. Why?

   ○ A HORSE SHE TIPPED HAS WON
   ○ THE WORKFORCE HAS JUST RECEIVED A BONUS, WHICH SHE DISTRIBUTED
   ○ IT'S HER BIRTHDAY
   ○ SHE HAS ORGANISED A HALF DAY OFF FOR THE STAFF

21. Tommy furthers his money-laundering activities by presenting Polly with a house of her own. It's a large suburban home and she questions how she'll fill it. How does Tommy plan to help her?

○ ORGANISING PARTIES FOR HIS BUSINESS ASSOCIATES WITH POLLY AS HOSTESS
○ FINDING A GOOD MAN TO MARRY
○ BRINGING HOME HER TWO CHILDREN, WHOM HE PLANS TO TRACK DOWN ON HER BEHALF
○ ENCOURAGING HER TO ADOPT A CHILD NOW SHE'S A RESPECTABLE AND WEALTHY WOMAN

22. Back at the office, Lizzie updates Tommy on the events of the day. Why have the decorators stopped working at the Garrison?

○ JOHN THREATENED TO CUT THEIR THROATS FOR DRINKING ON THE JOB
○ FINN HEARD THEM SPEAKING WITH HEAVY IRISH ACCENTS
○ ARTHUR PULLED A GUN ON THEM WHEN THEY SAID THEY NEEDED PAYING
○ THEY DIDN'T FEEL SAFE AROUND THE REGULARS

23. 'Dear Mr Churchill ...' Polly is taken aback when Tommy begins to dictate a letter. What is his purpose for writing?

○ REQUESTING IMMUNITY FROM PROSECUTION FOR HIS WORK AS AN AGENT OF THE CROWN
○ INFORMING CHURCHILL THAT MAJOR CAMPBELL HAS BEEN OPERATING OUTSIDE THE LAW
○ REQUESTING AN EXPORT LICENCE IN RETURN FOR HIS WORK AS AN AGENT OF THE CROWN
○ INFORMING CHURCHILL OF HIS VIEW THAT MAJOR CAMPBELL'S VENDETTA AGAINST HIM IS PERSONAL

SEASON TWO ▌ EPISODE TWO

24. 'With respect,' protests **Major Campbell** when **Churchill** shares the content of his letter, 'Thomas Shelby is a murdering, cut-throat, _____ gangster.' Fill in the blank.

  ○ ... REMORSELESS
  ○ ... MONGREL
  ○ ... LOW-LIFE
  ○ ... COLD-HEARTED

25. Tommy visits a cottage in the countryside that's home to Polly's seventeen-year-old son, Michael, since his forced adoption as a small boy. What is his adoptive name?

  ○ DANIEL
  ○ HENRY
  ○ PETER
  ○ STANLEY

26. Tommy hands Michael a note, despite protests from the boy's adoptive mother, who will be powerless to stop him from making his own decisions when he turns eighteen. What does Tommy say the note contains?

  ○ AN APOLOGY FROM HIS REAL MOTHER, POLLY
  ○ POLLY'S ADDRESS
  ○ THE GARRISON ADDRESS WITH A DATE FOR A FAMILY MEETING
  ○ TOMMY'S CONTACT DETAILS

27. At the boxing club, Arthur's inner rage gets the better of him and he accidently kills his opponent. Finn and Isaiah witness the scene. When Tommy asks for their account, on how many occasions does his youngest brother say that Arthur has lost his self-control?

  ○ NEVER
  ○ ONCE, JUST AFTER RETURNING FROM THE WAR
  ○ SIX OR SEVEN TIMES
  ○ EVERY OTHER DAY

28. Arthur is a broken man, unsure if he can trust himself not to take his own life. What does he ask Tommy to do?

○ TAKE HIS GUN
○ ASSIGN SOMEONE TO WATCH OVER HIM
○ HAVE HIM COMMITTED
○ FETCH A DOCTOR WHO CAN MEDICATE HIM

29. Tommy responds harshly. What does he say?

○ 'MARCH ON FROM THE WAR! MARCH ON.'
○ 'THE WAR IS DONE! SHUT THE DOOR ON IT.'
○ 'THE WAR IS OVER! THE WAR IS DONE.'
○ 'THIS WAR IN YOUR HEAD MUST END!'

30. 'A single stroke of mustard. That's the thing!' Major Campbell is touched that Sergeant Moss has remembered this detail in his favourite sandwich. What's in it?

○ CORNED BEEF
○ COLD LAMB
○ TONGUE AND PICKLE
○ EGG AND SARDINE

31. Campbell's mood then darkens considerably. What has he discovered about Moss?

○ HE'S LOOKING FOR A TRANSFER AWAY FROM CAMPBELL
○ HE'S ON THE PAYROLL OF THE PEAKY BLINDERS
○ TOMMY HAS GIVEN HIM A POCKET WATCH
○ HE'S BEEN SEEN DRINKING IN THE GARRISON

32. Tommy has news for Polly about her two children. Sadly, her daughter, Anna, has passed away 'of something called Spring Fever'. Where did she die?

○ STAFFORDSHIRE
○ BIRMINGHAM
○ AUSTRALIA
○ APPALACHIA

SEASON TWO ▮ EPISODE TWO

33. Though Tommy reveals that her son, Michael, is alive, he asks Polly to wait for him to reach out to her. What does she do before storming from the room?

- ○ KICKS OVER A CHAIR
- ○ SWIPES A BOTTLE OF WINE ACROSS TOMMY'S DESK
- ○ FIRES A GUN INTO THE CEILING
- ○ SPITS ON THE FLOOR

34. Renovations are complete at the Garrison and preparations underway for the reopening. Why does Finn visit Arthur at home beforehand?

- ○ TO MAKE SURE HE'S DRESSED FOR THE OCCASION
- ○ TO GET HIM DRUNK BEFORE THE BIG NIGHT
- ○ TO INTRODUCE HIM TO COCAINE AS A PICK-ME-UP
- ○ TO GIVE HIM A REPEAT PRESCRIPTION FOR THE SEDATIVE TOMMY TIPPED AWAY

35. The Garrison is rammed at the reopening. Tommy absorbs the atmosphere, but what does he caution Finn about?

- ○ DRINKING WHISKEY
- ○ GAMBLING
- ○ SMOKING CIGARS
- ○ CONSORTING WITH A PROSTITUTE

36. Alone, Tommy places an envelope on the table that he's been carrying for some days. Who is it from?

- ○ CHURCHILL
- ○ GRACE BURGESS
- ○ ADA THORNE
- ○ IRENE O'DONNELL

37. What does he do with the envelope?

- ○ RETURNS IT TO HIS POCKET
- ○ READS THE LETTER INSIDE
- ○ BURNS IT
- ○ SCREWS IT UP AND TOSSES IT IN THE BIN

38. Ada makes a surprise appearance at the reopening. Why has Tommy persuaded her to attend?

- SO THE SHELBYS ARE REUNITED AS A FAMILY
- IN THE HOPE THAT ADA CAN SMOOTH THINGS BETWEEN TOMMY AND POLLY
- BECAUSE IT'S SAFER FOR HER IN BIRMINGHAM THAN IN LONDON
- TO TALK TO ARTHUR ABOUT MANAGING HIS TEMPER

39. Polly escapes her troubles by throwing herself into the party. Where does she end up?

- WEEPING AT THE CANAL-SIDE
- IN A POLICE CELL
- IN BED WITH A MAN
- PASSED OUT IN THE SNUG

40. The next morning, a mess after the night before, Polly wanders home to be stopped by whom?

- MAJOR CAMPBELL
- TOMMY SHELBY
- MICHAEL GRAY
- ADA THORNE

KILLER QUESTIONS

41. According to Major Campbell, when he visits Tommy in hospital, what happened in the Co-operative Stables in Montague Street?

○ A KIDNAPPING
○ A MURDER
○ A HORSE THEFT
○ A MUGGING

42. During his first meeting with Alfie Solomons, what brand of unfiltered cigarettes does Tommy smoke?

○ WOODBINE
○ ECKSTEIN
○ SWEET AFTON
○ CHESTERFIELD

43. 'Insanity and _____'. Complete the headline in the newspaper that Sabini is reading when the police visit him to discuss Tommy's London activities.

○ CORRUPTION
○ REVOLUTION
○ CRIME
○ PROHIBITION

1. What happens in the opening scene, while children watch a shadow puppet theatre production?

    ○ A CHILD IS KIDNAPPED
    ○ A MAN IS GARROTTED IN THE BACKGROUND
    ○ A WOMAN HAS HER BAG SNATCHED
    ○ A PERFORMER IN THE WINGS IS KNIFED

2. Major Campbell and Sergeant Moss are looking over a report of the incident at the theatre, which has Irish links. What paper does the Major recommend that Moss reads in order to broaden his mind?

    ○ THE TIMES
    ○ THE TELEGRAPH
    ○ THE LONDON GAZETTE
    ○ THE DAILY MAIL

3. The Major intends to spend some time in Birmingham for operational purposes. What help does he request from Sergeant Moss?

    ○ ORGANISING LODGINGS
    ○ ARRANGING A DRIVER
    ○ ASSIGNING A POLICE OFFICER AS PERSONAL PROTECTION
    ○ RECRUITING A SECRETARY WHO CAN BE TRUSTED NOT TO LEAK INFORMATION

4. In the snug at the Garrison, Tommy, Arthur and John are interviewing men in turn. They're looking for fall guys to be jailed voluntarily for gambling offences they didn't commit. Why?

    ○ TO TAKE UP POLICE TIME SO THE BUSINESS CAN OPERATE FREELY
    ○ SO THE POLICE MEET THEIR QUOTA AND LEAVE SHELBY BROTHERS LTD ALONE
    ○ TO SETTLE A BET BETWEEN THE BROTHERS THAT THEY CAN RECRUIT SOMEONE WILLING TO BE JAILED
    ○ TO PROVOKE THE GOVERNMENT INTO TIGHTENING GAMBLING LAWS TO DISADVANTAGE LEGITIMATE COMPETITION

SEASON TWO ▮▮ EPISODE THREE

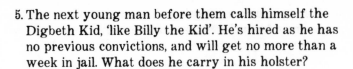

5. The next young man before them calls himself the Digbeth Kid, 'like Billy the Kid'. He's hired as he has no previous convictions, and will get no more than a week in jail. What does he carry in his holster?

Ⓣ A LOADED GUN
Ⓣ A DECOMMISSIONED GUN
Ⓣ A GUN LOADED WITH BLANKS
Ⓣ A WOODEN GUN

6. 'They didn't fight, so they're different,' says Tommy, when Arthur chuckles at the latest hiring. Complete his observation.

Ⓣ 'WE SHOULD ENVY THEM.'
Ⓣ 'THEY STAY KIDS.'
Ⓣ 'THEY LIVE IN A DREAM.'
Ⓣ 'THEY HAVE NO IDEA ABOUT LIFE.'

7. 'I've got about a million questions.' Over breakfast, Michael faces his real mother for the first time. Polly struggles to take in the fact that the well-spoken young man at her table is her son. What complimentary word does he use, confirming his middle-class upbringing, that she repeats?

Ⓣ SUPER
Ⓣ SMASHING
Ⓣ ACE
Ⓣ TERRIFIC

8. Their conversation is interrupted when the Shelby brothers spill into the house. Arthur remembers his cousin because he used to throw him out of the window for John to catch. John recalls putting the little boy in a shoebox and doing what?

Ⓣ KICKING HIM DOWN WATERY LANE
Ⓣ HIDING HIM IN A CUPBOARD
Ⓣ SEEING IF HE WOULD FLOAT IN THE CANAL
Ⓣ THROWING STONES AT HIM

9. Tommy meets a gang leader, ex-soldier and brother-in-arms from the Black Country called Billy Kitchen. Tommy recruits him to head up a new brigade of warehousemen, seeking assurance that he'll give the Peaky Blinders free passage on the waterway to London. Billy is currently recovering from a bullet wound. Where was he shot?

○ THE LEG
○ THE CHEST
○ THE SHOULDER
○ THE HAND

10. 'You're Polly's son, all right.' Michael has just told Tommy what he will do if he's made to go back to village life with his adoptive family. What is it?

○ HE'LL KNOCK OUT HIS ADOPTIVE FATHER
○ HE'LL BLOW UP THE WISHING WELL ON THE VILLAGE GREEN
○ HE'LL SMASH UP THE VILLAGE HALL
○ HE'LL BURN DOWN THE VILLAGE PUB

11. Billy Kitchen's men arrive by barge in Camden Town. They file into Alfie Solomon's office to be registered and issued documentation as what?

○ MILLERS
○ STEVEDORES
○ BAKERS
○ WAREHOUSEMEN

12. Initially, where will the men be staying while working in London?

○ THE WAREHOUSE ON THE OTHER SIDE OF THE CUT
○ THE BAKERY
○ LODGINGS ACROSS CAMDEN
○ THE STREETS

SEASON TWO ▇ EPISODE THREE

13. Why does Tommy advise them not to touch 'the bread'?

   ○ IT'S LIKELY TO EXPLODE
   ○ ALFIE WILL CUT OFF THEIR HANDS
   ○ THEY WOULD HAVE TO PAY A FINE
   ○ ALFIE WILL CUT OUT THEIR TONGUES

14. Alfie Solomons steps in to say his piece. Which of these rules does he issue the men?

   ○ EATING IS NOT PERMITTED ON THE PREMISES
   ○ FIREARMS ARE BANNED
   ○ JEWISH WOMEN ARE OFF THE MENU
   ○ THE MEN SHOULD WASH THEIR HANDS BEFORE ENTERING THE BAKERY

15. Why is Ada surprised to see Tommy at her London townhouse?

   ○ HE SHOULD BE AT THE RACES
   ○ SHE DIDN'T REALISE HE HAD A SPARE KEY
   ○ SHE THOUGHT HE WAS IN BIRMINGHAM
   ○ SHE UNDERSTOOD HE WAS STILL IN HOSPITAL

16. 'What is it that you want, Tommy?' Why does Ada refuse to help him find rentals to buy with the last £800 of his property money?

   ○ SHE'S DEVOTED TO CARING FOR HER SON FULL-TIME
   ○ SHE KNOWS HE'LL PROVIDE SQUALID LIVING CONDITIONS
   ○ SHE TELLS HIM HER LATE HUSBAND WOULDN'T APPROVE
   ○ SHE ADVISES HIM TO INVEST IN RACEHORSES INSTEAD

17. When Polly brings Michael to visit her suburban townhouse, she hopes they'll spend the week together. Who has she hired in preparation?

   ○ A COOK
   ○ A DRIVER
   ○ A MAID
   ○ A GARDENER

18. They arrive by car. What make is the vehicle?

O SWIFT
O AUSTIN
O VAUXHALL
O HUMBER

19. When Arthur opens up the Garrison for the day, who is first through the door to confront him?

O BILLY KIMBER'S WIDOW
O THE MOTHER OF THE BOXER HE KILLED IN THE RING
O THE WIDOW OF THE IRISHMAN THAT TOMMY ASSASSINATED
O DANNY WHIZZ-BANG'S SON

20. Tommy visits Charlie Strong at the yard. Business is flowing from Birmingham down to London. How many boats does Tommy tell him will be leaving the next day?

O TWO
O FOUR
O SIX
O EIGHT

21. Why does Charlie complain that the new 'manufactured' cargo, such as car parts and water pumps for export, isn't like the cigarettes and alcohol he's used to smuggling?

O THE CRATES ARE HEAVY
O THE CONTENTS AREN'T SECURED PROPERLY INSIDE
O THEY TAKE UP TOO MUCH SPACE
O THERE'S NOTHING HE CAN HELP HIMSELF TO ON THE JOURNEY

SEASON TWO ▮ EPISODE THREE

22. Major Campbell is unpacking at the lodging recommended by Sergeant Moss. He pauses for a moment, having taken a wallet from his case containing what?

   ○ HIS GOVERNMENT PASS
   ○ TOMMY'S MILITARY PHOTOGRAPH
   ○ GRACE'S POLICE IDENTITY CARD
   ○ AN IRA MEMBERSHIP CARD

23. Name one of the sandwiches his landlord, Mrs Ross, offers to prepare for Major Campbell before he decides to get some air instead.

   ○ SHRIMP PASTE
   ○ EGG AND CRESS
   ○ FRUIT JAM
   ○ BEEF JELLY

24. Major Campbell finds Tommy waiting for him in the shadows. Why is he surprised at his presence?

   ○ CAMPBELL UNDERSTOOD HE NOW SPENT ALL HIS TIME IN LONDON
   ○ THEIR AGREED MEETING IS NOT UNTIL SUNDAY
   ○ THEY HAVEN'T ARRANGED A MEETING
   ○ CAMPBELL PREFERS TO STAGE THEIR MEETINGS UNDER COVER OF DARKNESS

25. What does Tommy tell Major Campbell 'in the spirit of friendship and cooperation'?

   ○ GRACE HAS WRITTEN A LETTER FROM AMERICA
   ○ HIS LODGINGS ARE IN FACT A BROTHEL
   ○ HIS LODGINGS ARE A COMMUNIST STRONGHOLD
   ○ THE IRA KNOW WHERE HE'S STAYING

26. In on the Peaky Blinders' scam, Sergeant Moss is booking the Digbeth Kid for being an illegal bookmaker. What profession does he suggest the Kid should adopt for the purpose of the booking sheet?

- ○ BOTTLE WASHER
- ○ UMBRELLA MAKER
- ○ BOOT POLISHER
- ○ RETAIL CLERK

27. Mr Sabini believes that Tommy is fixing his races by 'bewitching' his horses. He wishes to send out a message to the Shelbys. What is his right-hand man, George Sewell, dispatched to organise?

- ○ THE KIDNAP OF ADA'S SON, KARL
- ○ THE MURDER OF THE DIGBETH KID IN JAIL
- ○ BURNING DOWN THE SHELBY'S BETTING SHOP
- ○ KILLING A SOLOMON GANG MEMBER AND FRAMING TOMMY

28. 'I only wanted proof, not satisfaction.' Having thrown coins on the bed, what had Major Campbell asked his landlady to do?

- ○ FETCH HIM A NEWSPAPER
- ○ SHOW HIM HER GUEST BOOK
- ○ REMOVE HER CLOTHES
- ○ CANCEL HIS LODGINGS

29. Tommy calls a family meeting the morning after the Digbeth Kid is found in his cell with his throat cut. As well as wishing to start a fund for the boy's family, what is his concern?

- ○ SABINI WILL BE COMING FOR HIM NEXT
- ○ HIS MEN NEED TO FEEL PROTECTED
- ○ THE MURDER WILL ATTRACT POLICE ATTENTION INTO HIS BUSINESS AFFAIRS
- ○ ALFIE SOLOMON WILL GET SPOOKED AND PULL OUT OF THE DEAL

SEASON TWO ▮ EPISODE THREE

30. Tommy orders Scudboat to get himself arrested and take out the prison killer. He suggests breaking a few windows will be sufficient. What crime does Scudboat propose so he can at least benefit from it?

- ○ STEALING A CAR
- ○ SAFE BREAKING
- ○ A JEWELLERY SNATCH
- ○ PICKPOCKETING

31. 'What do we want with a thousand-dollar horse?' asks Polly, who learns from Tommy that it'll give the Peaky Blinders access to Sabini in the Winner's Enclosure at what prestigious race?

- ○ THE GRAND NATIONAL
- ○ THE EPSOM DERBY
- ○ THE CHELTENHAM GOLD CUP
- ○ THE EPSOM OAKS

32. Who joins the meeting late and uninvited?

- ○ CURLY
- ○ MICHAEL GRAY
- ○ CHARLIE STRONG
- ○ ESME SHELBY

33. At Polly's suburban house, Michael asks about his father. Polly tells him he died drunk, but how?

- ○ TRAMPLED BY A HORSE
- ○ SQUEEZED BETWEEN A BOAT AND A CANAL LOCK
- ○ SUFFOCATED ON HIS OWN VOMIT
- ○ FELL AND HIT HIS HEAD

34. Michael is dressed like his Peaky Blinder cousins, ready to join them on a trip to the horse auction. Whose old clothes is he wearing?

    ○ MICHAEL'S LATE FATHER'S
    ○ JOHN'S
    ○ TOMMY'S
    ○ ARTHUR'S

35. When Thomas and his brothers pull up outside the house, and blow the horn, what does Polly send her son off with?

    ○ A GUN
    ○ SANDWICHES
    ○ A KNIFE
    ○ A PRAYER

36. 'Why do people come late to these things?' When the Peaky Blinders arrive at the auction, Tommy's presence is noted by widow and racehorse breeder May Carleton. She is accompanied by her father. How does he respond?

    ○ BECAUSE THEY'VE COME A LONG WAY
    ○ BECAUSE THEY KNOW WHAT THEY WANT
    ○ BECAUSE THEY'RE NOT SERIOUS BUYERS
    ○ BECAUSE THEY HAVE NO RESPECT FOR CONVENTION

37. When May Carleton joins in the bidding against Tommy, which opens at 800 guineas, what price does he end up paying for the horse?

    ○ 1,750 GUINEAS
    ○ 1,800 GUINEAS
    ○ 2,000 GUINEAS
    ○ 2,050 GUINEAS

SEASON TWO ▮ EPISODE THREE

38. With the auction over and the horse in Tommy's ownership, May introduces herself. As they talk, what does Tommy tell her that he does?

    ○ 'FORTUNE TELLING.'
    ○ 'BAD THINGS.'
    ○ 'HONEST WORK.'
    ○ 'SECURITY.'

39. On leaving, as Tommy pockets May's business card, the Peaky Blinders are accosted by George Sewell. He's here to kill Tommy for Mr Sabini, but hasn't banked on Arthur's brutal rage. Michael looks on in horror at the beating that ensues. What are his first words to Tommy in the aftermath?

    ○ 'I DON'T WANT TO BE HERE.'
    ○ 'TAKE ME HOME.'
    ○ 'I DIDN'T SEE THIS.'
    ○ 'I'M ALL RIGHT TO DRIVE.'

SEASON TWO ▮ EPISODE THREE

KILLER QUESTIONS

40. What is the name of the newspaper that Arthur is reading when the brothers interview candidates willing to be 'stood up' and jailed for gambling offences?

   ○ RACING FORM
   ○ ILLUSTRATED SPORTING & DRAMATIC NEWS
   ○ THE WINNING POST
   ○ SPORTS BUDGET

41. When Tommy visits Ada in her townhouse and she pulls a gun on him, what is on the table in front of her?

   ○ A PACKET OF CIGARETTES
   ○ A TEACUP AND SAUCER
   ○ A TEDDY BEAR
   ○ A VASE OF ROSES

42. When Sabini summons George Sewell to the club, the gang boss is casually eating lunch off his lap in a blood-spattered boxing ring. What is the motif on the floor?

   ○ SPIDER
   ○ SCORPION
   ○ STAG
   ○ SNAKE

1. The grieving mother of the Digbeth Kid hangs his home-made gun holster over the gravestone. What is his name?

   ○ JAMES WILCOX
   ○ BILLY JOHNSON
   ○ HAROLD HANCOX
   ○ HENRY COPSALE

2. Tommy approaches the dead boy's mother and his sister, who leaps at him with slaps and scratches. What does he offer them afterwards?

   ○ FLOWERS
   ○ AN EMBRACE
   ○ HIS CONDOLENCES
   ○ A PAY-OFF

3. 'You might think this is a curious place for me to arrange a meeting,' says Major Campbell when Tommy finds him in a monastic seminary, 'but the surprises have only just begun.' Why are Irene O'Donnell and her associate in the next room?

   ○ IRENE O'DONNELL IS WORKING WITH THE CROWN TO ASSASSINATE THE SAME MAN
   ○ IRENE O'DONNELL IS BLACKMAILING MAJOR CAMPBELL
   ○ MAJOR CAMPBELL IS BLACKMAILING IRENE O'DONNELL
   ○ IRENE O'DONNELL IS AN IRA INFORMER

4. Tommy initially declines the mission and marches out of the room. Why?

   ○ HE DEMANDS A FEE AND BOTH SIDES REFUSE
   ○ HE REFUSES TO MURDER A SERVING MILITARY MAN
   ○ HE KNOWS THAT IRENE'S ASSOCIATE IS A SPY
   ○ TOMMY FOUGHT WITH THE MILITARY FIGURE TARGETED FOR ASSASSINATION

5. At Camden Town lock, Arthur checks in with Billy Kitchen about the ongoing warehouse operation, when a copper approaches them. What happens next?

- ○ ARTHUR WALKS AWAY
- ○ ARTHUR PAYS OFF THE COPPER
- ○ ARTHUR STARES AT THE COPPER, WHO PROMPTLY WALKS ON
- ○ BILLY PAYS OFF THE COPPER

6. Mob-handed, the Peaky Blinders visit the Eden Club to take over the place. Who does Arthur target?

- ○ MARIO THE MANAGER
- ○ GEORGE SEWELL
- ○ THE JAZZ BAND
- ○ THE BARMAN

7. Who accompanies Arthur and his boys?

- ○ MICHAEL THORNE
- ○ BILLY KITCHEN
- ○ THE LEE FAMILY
- ○ ALFIE SOLOMONS

8. How does Arthur celebrate the club takeover?

- ○ SWIGGING CHAMPAGNE ON THE DANCE FLOOR
- ○ SNORTING COCAINE AT THE BAR
- ○ CAVORTING WITH TWO WOMEN IN A BATHTUB
- ○ LOBBING WINE BOTTLES FROM THE BALCONY

9. After Major Campbell takes care of his concerns about the planned assassination, Tommy studies the target's file at his desk. What disturbs his concentration?

- ○ THE TELEPHONE RINGS
- ○ HE RUNS OUT OF CIGARETTES
- ○ HE TOUCHES A RECENT CUT ON HIS TEMPLE AND NOTES BLOOD ON HIS HANDS
- ○ THE INK ON HIS FINGERTIPS LEAVE A PRINT ON THE DOCUMENTS

SEASON TWO ▮ EPISODE FOUR

10. Michael visits Tommy, seeking employment at Shelby Brothers Ltd in what role?

   U ASSISTANT SECRETARY
   U PORTFOLIO MANAGER
   U BOOKKEEPER
   U ACCOUNTS CLERK

11. Michael points out that, like Lizzie, he knows what the company does. He is also aware that Polly is working towards making the business 80% legal. What time frame has Tommy put on this?

   U SIX MONTHS
   U ONE YEAR
   U THREE YEARS
   U TEN YEARS

12. 'I want to be proud of my family,' states Michael to finish his pitch. Tommy offers him the job, but what must he do first?

   U AGREE TO A SIX-WEEK PROBATION PERIOD
   U TELEPHONE POLLY TO KEEP HER INFORMED
   U REMOVE THE ADVERT FROM THE NEXT EDITION OF THE PAPER
   U INFORM LIZZIE SO SHE CAN DRAFT A LETTER OF EMPLOYMENT

13. Why does Thomas invite horseracing trainer May Carleton to visit him at the betting shop rather than his office?

   U TO KEEP THE LOCATION OF HIS OFFICE A SECRET FROM HER
   U TO INTIMIDATE HER
   U BECAUSE SHE HAS ALWAYS WANTED TO SEE AN AUTHENTIC GAMBLING DEN
   U SO THAT ESME CAN JUDGE HER CHARACTER FOR HIM

14. As Esme and May wait for Thomas, they discover a shared love of horses. What term do they use to describe themselves?

   ○ BORN IN THE SADDLE
   ○ HORSE MAD
   ○ BORN RIDING
   ○ HORSE CRAZY

15. 'Curly is the best horseman in England,' says Tommy as he escorts May to the boatyard to inspect the thoroughbred. May counters that she has a man who would argue the point. What is his name?

   ○ BILLY
   ○ SAMUEL
   ○ EDWARD
   ○ ALBERT

16. Tommy takes May to the Garrison and pours her a large gin. May is surprised he doesn't add tonic. When she asks, he finds none behind the bar. Playing up to her expectations, what does he use instead?

   ○ WATER
   ○ CORDIAL
   ○ GINGER ALE
   ○ SODA

17. Having sensed that Tommy is playing with her, May asks exactly what he wants. What is his reply?

   ○ A HORSE THAT DOUBLES ITS VALUE WITHIN A YEAR
   ○ A HORSE THAT WILL PAY OUT AT EPSOM ON AN EACH-WAY BET
   ○ A HORSE THAT WON'T LET HIM DOWN
   ○ A HORSE THAT WILL WIN THE DERBY THIS YEAR AND THE NEXT

SEASON TWO EPISODE FOUR

18. May asks Tommy what the horse will be called. What does he name her?

- ○ FOREVER GRACE
- ○ GRACE'S SECRET
- ○ AMAZING GRACE
- ○ GRACE'S MEMORY

19. At first, Polly refuses to allow Michael to work for the family business. What changes her mind?

- ○ POLLY DOESN'T LIKE THE YOUNG MAN TOMMY PLANS TO HIRE INSTEAD
- ○ TOMMY SUGGESTS MICHAEL WILL MOVE TO LONDON AND LOSE CONTACT
- ○ MICHAEL CONSIDERS EMIGRATING
- ○ POLLY WORRIES THAT MICHAEL WILL FIND WORK WITH ALFIE SOLOMONS

20. When Polly comes around, having agreed a wage for Michael on his behalf, how does she seal the deal with Tommy?

- ○ BY REMINDING HIM THAT HE'LL BE CURSED SHOULD HE BREAK HIS WORD
- ○ SPITTING INTO THEIR PALMS AND SHAKING ON IT
- ○ POURING A DRINK AND PROPOSING A TOAST
- ○ DRAWING UP A CONTRACT AND SIGNING IT

21. 'Welcome to the business.' What gift does Tommy give to Michael on his eighteenth birthday?

- ○ A GUN
- ○ A GOLD WATCH AND CHAIN
- ○ A CAP WITH A RAZOR TUCKED IN IT
- ○ A SILVER FOUNTAIN PEN

22. Having established a secure passage from Birmingham to the warehouse in Camden, Tommy extends his transport channel to which docks?

- ○ MILLWALL
- ○ POPLAR
- ○ EAST INDIA
- ○ ROYAL VICTORIA

23. 'Motor cars are the future.' Tommy sets out his export plans to Polly, Arthur and John. He announces that the first crate, containing car parts, will be bound for Nova Scotia. Why is Polly so certain that Tommy actually intends to smuggle whiskey?

- ○ ALCOHOL IS PROHIBITED IN NOVA SCOTIA, AND AT A PREMIUM ON THE BLACK MARKET
- ○ THE WAREHOUSE IS FULL OF CRATES OF WHISKEY
- ○ POLLY ORDERED A CRATE OF CAR PARTS TO BE OPENED AT THE BOATYARD SO SHE COULD SEE WHAT IT ALSO CONTAINED
- ○ MICHAEL HAD WORKED IT OUT AND TOLD HER

24. Billy Kitchen has made sure the Camden warehouse is secure, as per Tommy's instruction. He asks what Tommy is really exporting. What is Tommy's response?

- ○ HAPPINESS
- ○ TEMPTATION
- ○ HOPE
- ○ SOLACE

25. At the club, Tommy inspects the books and remarks to Arthur than an entry for £600 looks like a cover for illicit activity. What has the money – from drug dealing – been set against?

- ○ CANDLES
- ○ OLIVES
- ○ COASTERS
- ○ MATCHES

SEASON TWO ▊ EPISODE FOUR

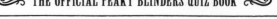

26. What reason does Tommy give to Arthur for letting the dealers sell the cocaine and just taking a cut?

  ○ A CLUB WITH A REPUTATION FOR DRUGS ATTRACTS THE WRONG CROWD
  ○ SELLING DRUGS DIRECTLY IS TOO RISKY AS THE GOVERNMENT IS CRACKING DOWN
  ○ A CLUB WITH A REPUTATION FOR DRUGS ATTRACTS RIVAL DEALERS
  ○ THE CLUB IS INTENDED TO LAUNDER MONEY, NOT CREATE MORE ILLEGITIMATE FUNDS

27. In preparation for his mission for Major Campbell, Tommy pulls up outside the address of his target. It's guarded by police. What is the purpose of this dry run?

  ○ TO BRIBE THE OFFICER TO TURN A BLIND EYE
  ○ TO TIME HOW LONG IT TAKES FOR THE OFFICER TO ASK WHAT PURPOSE HE HAS HERE
  ○ TO IDENTIFY THE OFFICER AND MENACE HIS FAMILY SO HE TURNS A BLIND EYE
  ○ TO ESTABLISH AN ESCAPE ROUTE

28. Putting his affairs in order, Tommy visits Ada because he's set up a trust fund for her son and John's children in the event of his death. A man called James answers her door. Who is he?

  ○ ADA'S BOYFRIEND
  ○ THE LODGER
  ○ A TRADESMAN
  ○ HER ASSISTANT

29. Calling a truce, Mr Sabini visits Alfie Solomons. Alfie presents him with a basket of bread and salt. In what traditional Italian way does Sabini respond?

  ○ HE KISSES ALFIE ON THE CHEEK THREE TIMES
  ○ HE PRESENTS ALFIE WITH A BOTTLE OF OLIVE OIL
  ○ HE KISSES ALFIE ON THE CHEEK FOUR TIMES
  ○ HE EMBRACES ALFIE AND CLAPS HIM ON THE BACK

SEASON TWO ▮ EPISODE FOUR

30. The two kingpins sit down to talk. Alfie wants the line between the Jews and the Italians redrawn to Farringdon Road. Where does Sabini insist it goes?

- ○ WARREN STREET
- ○ CAMDEN ROAD
- ○ CLERKENWELL ROAD
- ○ EUSTON ROAD

31. In return for his help in ridding London of the Peaky Blinders, what else does Sabini concede to Alfie?

- ○ HIS BOOKIES CAN RETURN TO EPSOM
- ○ THE JEWS CAN DISTRIBUTE RUM IN ITALIAN TERRITORY
- ○ ALFIE CAN SELL BREAD IN ITALIAN TERRITORY
- ○ HIS BOOKIES CAN RETURN TO KEMPTON

32. 'Nice house.' Tommy visits May Carleton's palatial country residence in Newmarket. She shows him the report on the horse, and comments that Mickey's opinion is that it has the lungs of what animal?

- ○ A PANTHER
- ○ AN ELEPHANT
- ○ A RHINO
- ○ A CHEETAH

33. What ground does the report say the horse favours?

- ○ HARD TO FIRM
- ○ FIRM
- ○ GOOD TO SOFT
- ○ HEAVY

SEASON TWO ▮ EPISODE FOUR

34. 'When anyone sees a lighthouse they steer clear.'
Why does May tell Tommy that she's not a woman
that men are usually drawn to?

   ○ SHE DOESN'T EASILY LET PEOPLE COME CLOSE
   ○ SHE'S STILL COMING TO TERMS WITH WIDOWHOOD
   ○ HER WEALTH MAKES HER INTIMIDATING
   ○ SHE CONSIDERS THE EMOTIONAL WATERS AROUND HER TO BE
     TREACHEROUS

35. Thomas responds that at midnight he's going to
come to her room and knock on her door. What does
he request in order to get there?

   ○ A MAP
   ○ A CANDLE LIGHT
   ○ A COMPASS
   ○ DIRECTIONS

36. Michael and Isaiah are finishing the accounts for
the week. It's payday. Isaiah is keen to get going. In
which pub does he say the BSA secretaries drink?

   ○ THE GARRISON
   ○ THE FOX & GRAPES
   ○ THE MARQUIS
   ○ THE CROWN

37. The pair head out together, only to attract trouble
when a drinker picks on Isaiah for the colour of his
skin. A fight breaks out. What brings it to an end?

   ○ MICHAEL HOLDS A BROKEN BOTTLE TO THE MAN'S THROAT
   ○ ISAIAH KNOCKS OUT AN ASSAILANT
   ○ THE POLICE ARRIVE AND BREAK IT UP
   ○ THE BARMAN MAKES THE MAN AWARE THAT MICHAEL IS THE
     SON OF POLLY GRAY

38. 'We did it for the good name of the company,' John tells Michael and Isaiah after seeking vengeance for the attack on the pair. What have they done?

- ○ CLOSED DOWN THE PUB
- ○ BURNED DOWN THE PUB
- ○ TAKEN OVER THE PUB
- ○ CRIPPLED THEIR ATTACKER

39. Tommy is brooding. His involvement with Major Campbell is jeopardising his plans. He sits alone in his office, reads a telegram and then makes a call to the Ritz in London. A voice answers and he ends the call. Who was it?

- ○ MAY CARLETON
- ○ GRACE'S AMERICAN HUSBAND
- ○ MR SABINI
- ○ GRACE

SEASON TWO ▐▐▌ EPISODE FOUR

KILLER QUESTIONS

40. What is the rank of the military figure Tommy must assassinate?

   ○ WING COMMANDER
   ○ GROUP CAPTAIN
   ○ BRIGADIER
   ○ FIELD MARSHALL

41. John refers to the luxury car that Esme has left unattended outside the betting shop. What make is it?

   ○ WOLSELEY
   ○ RILEY
   ○ BENTLEY
   ○ ROLLS-ROYCE

42. What is the only drink that Finn is permitted to drink at the Garrison?

   ○ WATER
   ○ MILD
   ○ CORDIAL
   ○ WHISKEY AND WATER

1. The episode opens at six o'clock. Major Campbell is having sex with his landlady at his lodgings while Sabini and his men are dining at a restaurant. At the bakery, what is Alfie Solomons leading towards a long table set for dining?

   ○ A DOG
   ○ A GOAT
   ○ A DONKEY
   ○ A SHEEP

2. Arthur and Billy Kitchen make their way to the bakery. Why have they been invited here by Alfie?

   ○ TO SIGN A CONTRACT
   ○ TO CELEBRATE PASSOVER
   ○ TO SAMPLE A NEW RUM
   ○ TO PLOT SABINI'S DOWNFALL

3. How does Arthur greet Alfie?

   ○ 'HELLO.'
   ○ 'GOOD EVENING.'
   ○ 'I RESPECT A RELIGIOUS MAN.'
   ○ 'SHALOM.'

4. Inspector Moss is at the wheel of a police car outside Polly's suburban house. Major Campbell is in the back seat eating a sandwich. What does Moss remind him?

   ○ EATING IS FORBIDDEN IN POLICE CARS
   ○ EATING ON DUTY IS FORBIDDEN
   ○ MOSS IS THE COMMANDING OFFICER ON THIS OPERATION
   ○ AS AN OBSERVER, CAMPBELL IS NOT PERMITTED TO CARRY A WEAPON

SEASON TWO ▮ EPISODE FIVE

5. Inside the house, Polly and Michael are sitting for supper. Polly says grace before they begin. What does she have to remind her son?

○ TO USE HIS NAPKIN
○ TO SAY 'AMEN'
○ TO EAT MORE
○ TO RELAX IN HIS OWN HOME

6. At the bakery table, Alfie Solomons is holding forth about this history of his people. Billy looks edgy when Alfie's men close the doors. How does Alfie address Billy when he asks if he needs to use the 'little boy's room'?

○ TREACLE
○ SQUIRE
○ DUCK
○ SWEETIE

7. Alfie summons the goat for ritual sacrifice. With a knife to its throat, he tells Arthur that he's named the animal. What is it called?

○ SABINI
○ ARTHUR SHELBY
○ TOMMY SHELBY
○ BILLY KITCHEN

8. The sacrifice marks the moment that Alfie and his men pounce. As Arthur struggles with a garrotte around his neck, what happens to Billy?

○ HE'S STABBED TO DEATH
○ HE'S SHOT THROUGH THE HEAD
○ HE'S STRANGLED TO DEATH
○ HE'S SHOT THROUGH THE HEART

9. At the same time that Arthur is fighting for survival, the police raid Polly's home. Meanwhile, what operation are Sabini and his men undertaking?

   ○ SEIZING JOHNNY DOGS AND TAKING HIM HOSTAGE
   ○ RECLAIMING THE EDEN CLUB FROM THE PEAKY BLINDERS
   ○ SURROUNDING THE BAKERY
   ○ SCUPPERING THE BARGES FROM BIRMINGHAM

10. 'Tell your Gypsy King that London gives its response.' Sabini has outmanoeuvred the Peaky Blinders. How does his right-hand man, George Sewell, make his mark on one of Tommy's men?

   ○ BLINDING HIM
   ○ SLICING HIS FACE WITH A RAZOR
   ○ BREAKING HIS NOSE
   ○ SPITTING IN HIS FACE

11. Before knocking him out on the bakery floor, how does Alfie make his mark on Arthur?

   ○ DAUBING HIS FACE IN BILLY KITCHEN'S BLOOD
   ○ ANOINTING HIS FACE IN WINE
   ○ SPITTING IN HIS FACE
   ○ DAUBING HIS FACE IN BLOOD FROM THE SACRIFICED GOAT

12. Alfie's men unlock the doors and the police enter. What does Alfie tell them?

   ○ BILLY KITCHEN GOT INTO A FIGHT WITH ARTHUR BEFORE TAKING HIS OWN LIFE
   ○ ARTHUR SHOT BILLY BEFORE ALFIE'S MEN OVERPOWERED HIM
   ○ HE JUST FOUND THE TWO MEN LIKE THIS
   ○ ARTHUR SHOT BILLY BEFORE TRIPPING AND HITTING HIS HEAD

SEASON TWO █ EPISODE FIVE

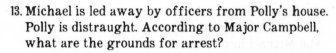

13. Michael is led away by officers from Polly's house. Polly is distraught. According to Major Campbell, what are the grounds for arrest?

   ○ MICHAEL'S ADOPTIVE MOTHER HAS REPORTED HIS INVOLVEMENT IN ILLEGAL GAMBLING
   ○ MICHAEL WITNESSED THE BEATING OF A MAN AT THE HORSE AUCTION
   ○ MICHAEL'S INVOLVEMENT IN THE PUB FRACAS AND THE RETRIBUTION THAT FOLLOWED
   ○ MICHAEL HAS BEEN ACCUSED OF BEATING THE MAN AT THE HORSE AUCTION

14. Tommy inspects his horse at May's stable. He tells her that her horseman, Billy, has been wasting his money on worming powder. What does he tell him to put in the trough as an effective and more economical preventative?

   ○ VINEGAR
   ○ GOLDFISH
   ○ GARLIC
   ○ CASTOR OIL

15. How do May's house servants show that they know that Tommy is spending the nights with her during his stay?

   ○ BY ASKING IF THEY SHOULD LIGHT A FIRE IN THE GUEST ROOM
   ○ BY ENQUIRING IF THEY SHOULD PREPARE THE BED IN THE GUEST ROOM
   ○ BY LEAVING A CANDLE LIGHT AND MATCHES OUTSIDE HIS DOOR
   ○ BY LEAVING A POT OF TEA AND TWO CUPS OUTSIDE MAY'S BEDROOM IN THE MORNING

16. 'To make sure your dog obeys you, you have to show it the stick.' Why has Major Campbell taken Arthur and Michael into custody?

- ○ HE BELIEVES TOMMY MAY TIP OFF HIS TARGET BEFORE THE ASSASSINATION ATTEMPT
- ○ KNOWING TOMMY IS UNAFRAID TO DIE, HE NEEDS FURTHER LEVERAGE TO ENSURE HE CARRIES OUT HIS MISSION
- ○ HE EXPECTS TOMMY TO FOCUS ON THIS MISSION AND NOT HIS BUSINESS AFFAIRS
- ○ HE WANTS TOMMY TO FEAR HIM

17. With the pressure mounting on Tommy, he receives a phone call back in his office. Who wants to arrange a meeting with him?

- ○ ALFIE SOLOMONS
- ○ GRACE
- ○ MR SABINI
- ○ THE SHELBY FAMILY LAWYER

18. Tommy calls a family meeting, where John reports on recent events. They've lost the club and the warehouse is in police control. Why is the canal no longer a viable channel for delivering goods to London?

- ○ CHARLIE STRONG'S BARGES HAVE BEEN SCUPPERED
- ○ BILLY KITCHEN'S GANG, WHO CONTROL THE WATERWAY, BELIEVE ARTHUR KILLED THEIR MAN
- ○ THE POLICE HAVE BEEN BRIEFED TO SEARCH ALL BARGES COMING INTO CAMDEN
- ○ SABINI HAS PLEDGED TO DESTROY TOMMY'S EXPORT BUSINESS

19. 'This life is bad.' Polly is not happy that Tommy is attending to business issues before family. What does she pledge to do on Michael's release?

- ○ TAKE HIM AWAY FROM THE FAMILY
- ○ RETURN HIM TO HIS ADOPTIVE FAMILY
- ○ FIND HIM RESPECTABLE WORK ELSEWHERE
- ○ BUY HIM A PASSAGE TO AMERICA

20. With Tommy's business affairs in ruins, who does Esme offer to speak to about recruiting Lee family men to bolster his numbers?

- ○ ZILPHA LEE
- ○ QUEEN MARY LEE
- ○ JOHNNY DOGS
- ○ QUEEN VICTORIA LEE

21. Where is the gypsy camp where Esme would seek this permission?

- ○ THE BLACK PATCH
- ○ HOCKLEY BROOK
- ○ THE BLACK PATCH
- ○ BOUNDARY BROOK

22. 'I'm talking about a simple transaction here.' What does Major Campbell request from Polly to secure Michael's freedom from prison?

- ○ INFORMATION ON SHELBY FAMILY BUSINESS
- ○ CONFIRMATION THAT GRACE IS BACK IN ENGLAND
- ○ TO SLEEP WITH HER
- ○ FOR HER TO BECOME AN INFORMANT

23. Ada is staying with Polly, who finds her aunt in the tin bath, following her traumatic encounter with Campbell. She tells Ada she's had 'a glass or two of rum at the Spotted Dog in Digbeth.' How many does Ada suggest she's had?

- ○ THREE
- ○ FOUR
- ○ FIVE
- ○ SIX

24. The next morning, Polly is waiting for Michael outside the prison gates. Why is Michael cool with her?

   ○ HE FEELS HE'S DISAPPOINTED HER
   ○ THE GUARDS TOLD HIM WHAT SHE'D DONE TO SECURE HIS RELEASE
   ○ HE HAD THOUGHT SHE'D GET HIM OUT SOONER
   ○ HE HAD EXPECTED TOMMY TO BAIL HIM OUT

25. 'To remind myself who I'd be if I wasn't who I am,' Tommy tells Curly, when asked what he's doing at the stable yard. What task has he undertaken?

   ○ SHOVELLING HORSE MANURE
   ○ WASHING THE HORSES
   ○ SWEEPING THE FLOOR
   ○ CLEANING THE SADDLES

26. Afterwards, what does Tommy ask Curly to load into his car?

   ○ TWO CANS OF MOTORING OIL
   ○ SIX CANS OF PETROL
   ○ FOUR MILK BOTTLES FILLED WITH PETROL
   ○ A SPARE TYRE AND CAR JACK

27. In London, ahead of her liaison with Tommy, who does Grace tell her American husband that she's visiting?

   ○ HER HALF-BLIND AUNTIE
   ○ HER HALF-DEAF UNCLE
   ○ HER NIECE OVER FROM DUBLIN
   ○ HER COUSIN DOWN FROM LIVERPOOL

SEASON TWO ▮ EPISODE FIVE

28. After a frosty start, Tommy takes Grace to meet Charlie Chaplin at a private function. What is the connection between the two men?

   ○ TOMMY AND CHAPLIN SHARE THE SAME LONDON TAILOR
   ○ TOMMY KNOWS CHAPLIN'S BODYGUARD
   ○ TOMMY KNOWS CHAPLIN'S BROTHER
   ○ TOMMY HAS PAID CHAPLIN'S MANAGER FOR AN INVITATION TO THE EVENT

29. Why does Tommy call Major Campbell from the event?

   ○ TO DEMAND ARTHUR'S IMMEDIATE RELEASE AS HE'S NOT SAFE IN JAIL
   ○ TO TAUNT HIM BY LETTING HIM KNOW THAT HE'S ABOUT TO SLEEP WITH GRACE
   ○ TO LET HIM KNOW THAT, FOLLOWING THE ARREST OF ARTHUR AND MICHAEL, HE'S A MAN ON BORROWED TIME
   ○ TO SUGGEST THAT THE IRA ARE ALSO PLANNING TO ASSASSINATE CAMPBELL

30. Before Grace leaves Tommy that evening, she discloses the reason she's in the UK with her husband. What is it?

   ○ THEY'RE BUYING A HOUSE
   ○ THEY'RE SEEKING FERTILITY TREATMENT AT HARLEY STREET
   ○ HER HUSBAND IS UNDERGOING CANCER TREATMENT AT HARLEY STREET
   ○ SHE'S ACCOMPANYING HER HUSBAND ON A BUSINESS TRIP

31. 'Here he is, the king of London Town.' John visits Arthur in prison. Facing the noose, his older brother is in a melancholy mood. What pastime does Arthur say he wished he'd pursued when he had the chance?

   ○ RIDING HORSES
   ○ DRAWING HORSES
   ○ TRAINING HORSES
   ○ PAINTING HORSES

32. John assures Arthur that Tommy has a plan. The first stage is in John's hands. What does he have to do?

   ○ POST A LETTER BOMB THROUGH THE DOOR OF THE MILITARY FIGURE THAT TOMMY MUST ASSASSINATE
   ○ CONSTRUCT A LETTER BOMB FOR TOMMY TO POST THROUGH THE DOOR
   ○ LOB A BOMB FROM THE STREET THROUGH AN UPSTAIRS WINDOW
   ○ LEAVE A PACKAGE UNDER THE FRONT WINDOW CONTAINING A BOMB ON A TIMER

33. Tommy visits **May** to tell her about Grace and end the relationship. May has several reasons why she can't let him go. Name one.

   ○ SHE LOVES HIM
   ○ HIGH SOCIETY HAVE ALREADY PREDICTED THE RELATIONSHIP WILL CRASH AND BURN
   ○ SHE'S TOLD HER STAFF TO PREPARE THE GUEST ROOM
   ○ HER FATHER HAS MISGIVINGS ABOUT TOMMY AND SHE DOESN'T WANT TO PROVE HIM RIGHT

34. Major Campbell visits the offices of Shelby Brothers Ltd. What drink does Lizzie offer him, which he curtly declines?

   ○ WHISKEY
   ○ GIN
   ○ TEA
   ○ CHAMPAGNE

35. Lizzie leaves the Major alone in Tommy's office. What is he doing when Tommy arrives?

   ○ LEAFING THROUGH A FILE ON HIS DESK
   ○ TRYING OUT HIS CHAIR FOR SIZE
   ○ TESTING HIS LOCKED DESK DRAWERS
   ○ POURING HIMSELF A DRINK

36. What is behind Tommy's desk that reflects his business ambition?

   ○ A TROPHY CABINET
   ○ A SAFE
   ○ A GLOBE
   ○ A STACK OF FINANCIAL TIMES NEWSPAPERS

37. Major Campbell is wise to the fact that Tommy is behind the bombing of his military target's residence. What is Tommy's response?

   ○ HE ADMITS IT WAS A FAILED ASSASSINATION ATTEMPT
   ○ HE DENIES ALL KNOWLEDGE THAT HE WAS BEHIND IT
   ○ HE REALISED THE HOUSE IS SO HEAVILY GUARDED THAT ANY ATTEMPT TO ASSASSINATE THE MAN AT HIS PLACE OF RESIDENCE WILL GUARANTEE HIS OWN DEATH
   ○ HE REALISED THE HOUSE IS SO HEAVILY GUARDED THAT REACHING THE TARGET IS IMPOSSIBLE

38. Tommy promises to carry out the assassination, but states that he will do so at Epsom racecourse on Derby Day. What does he require Major Campbell to organise?

   ○ HE MUST ENSURE THE TARGET RECEIVES AN INVITATION TO THE GRANDSTAND
   ○ HE MUST ENSURE THE TARGET RECEIVES AN INVITATION TO THE VIP ENCLOSURE
   ○ HE NEEDS TO MAKE SURE THE TARGET HAS ENJOYED A FEW DRINKS FIRST
   ○ HE NEEDS TO ENSURE THE TARGET'S SECURITY OFFICERS ARE DISTRACTED

39. 'You tell him he'll have to trust me,' says Tommy. Who does Major Campbell have to visit when this meeting concludes?

   ○ WINSTON CHURCHILL
   ○ SERGEANT MOSS
   ○ THE HOME SECRETARY
   ○ ARTHUR SHELBY

KILLER QUESTIONS

40. 'They'll let you _____,' Esme tells Tommy in the betting shop, encouraging him to return to his roots and start a new life in France. Complete this traditional gypsy phrase.

   ○ ... DISAPPEAR
   ○ ... GET LOST
   ○ ... BE REBORN
   ○ ... START AGAIN

41. When Tommy introduces Grace to Charlie Chaplin, he mentions something about the great actor that is believed to be rooted in truth. Which one of these real-life rumours does Tommy share?

   ○ CHAPLIN IS NOT HIS BIRTH NAME
   ○ CHAPLIN WAS BORN IN FRANCE
   ○ CHAPLIN IS SAID TO HAVE BEEN BORN IN BLACK PATCH, HOME TO THE CITY'S GYPSY COMMUNITY IN THE LATE 1800S
   ○ CHAPLIN'S FATHER WAS A LION TAMER

42. At May Carleton's stable yard, how many goldfish can be seen swimming in the water when Thomas inspects the horse trough?

   ○ TWO
   ○ THREE
   ○ FIVE
   ○ SIX

SEASON TWO ▮ EPISODE FIVE

1. 'Today I'm going to kill a man.' On the morning of the Derby, Tommy writes a confession to be opened in the event of his death. Who does he implicate in it?

   ○ MAJOR CAMPBELL AND WINSTON CHURCHILL
   ○ MAJOR CAMPBELL ONLY
   ○ MR SABINI AND ALFIE SOLOMONS
   ○ WINSTON CHURCHILL ONLY

2. The letter is addressed to the editor of which newspaper?

   ○ THE NEW YORK TIMES
   ○ THE LONDON TIMES
   ○ THE DAILY MAIL
   ○ THE NEW YORK HERALD

3. What is Ada doing before Tommy seals the letter and hands it to her for safe keeping, to be sent in the event of his death?

   ○ POURING TWO WHISKEYS
   ○ MAKING A POT OF TEA
   ○ WASHING UP
   ○ DRYING CROCKERY

4. In a bid to ease her rising concern, what does he tell her the letter is about?

   ○ POLICE CORRUPTION
   ○ BETTING SCAMS
   ○ INSURANCE
   ○ HORSE DOPING

5. 'He'll get you killed!' Ada is horrified to discover that her lodger, James, is leaving with Tommy to accompany him on a side mission. What reason does he give for accompanying him?

- ○ 'THE CHANCE TO BE SOMEBODY.'
- ○ 'THE GOOD OLD CAUSE.'
- ○ 'THE CHANCE TO BE AN ANARCHIST AT LAST.'
- ○ 'TO MAKE A DIFFERENCE.'

6. John also prepares for a big day. What items are on his desk before he rallies the troops in the betting shop?

- ○ CAR KEY AND A GUN
- ○ BOTTLE OF WHISKEY AND A GUN
- ○ BOTTLE OF WHISKEY AND A CLIP OF MONEY
- ○ CLIP OF MONEY AND A CAR KEY

7. The prison governor visits Arthur in his cell to tell him that all charges have been dropped. Fearing he is about to be set upon, however, what does Arthur hide behind his back?

- ○ A TOOTHBRUSH WITH A SHARPENED HANDLE
- ○ A COMB WITH A SHARPENED EDGE
- ○ A SHARD OF WOOD
- ○ AN EATING UTENSIL

8. 'You need to make a telephone call. It's all part of Tommy's plan, apparently.' Who is waiting to collect Arthur outside the prison gates?

- ○ JOHN SHELBY
- ○ JOHNNY DOGS
- ○ CHARLIE STRONG
- ○ MICHAEL GRAY

SEASON TWO ▉ EPISODE SIX

9. Tommy receives the call from Arthur while sitting across the desk from Alfie Solomons in his bakery. What does this signal?

- O ARTHUR IS FREE TO SEEK VENGEANCE AGAINST ALFIE, WHO TOMMY ADVISES TO GO TO GROUND
- O ALFIE HAS HONOURED HIS PART OF A DEAL BY WITHDRAWING WITNESS STATEMENTS AGAINST ARTHUR
- O TOMMY MUST NOW PAY AN AGREED SUM OF MONEY TO ALFIE FOR GETTING HIS OLDER BROTHER OFF THE HOOK
- O THE CHANCE TO BREAK BREAD WITH ALFIE AND MAKE A FRESH START

10. In negotiating with Alfie, what security measure does Tommy claim he has put in place to ensure he is not killed?

- O HE HAS PLANTED A GRENADE WITH A WIRE TRIP BEHIND A BARREL IN THE BAKERY
- O HE HAS BOOBY-TRAPPED THE LOADING BAY
- O HE HAS PLANTED A GRENADE WITH A WIRE TRIP IN ALFIE'S OFFICE
- O HE HAS BOOBY-TRAPPED THE MAIN DOORS

11. Tommy tells Alfie that his associate, James, is outside the bakery, and will detonate the bomb at what time if Tommy doesn't reappear?

- O 7.00AM
- O 7.30AM
- O 8.00AM
- O 8.30AM

12. In order to convince Alfie, he tells him that James is '___ _____ from Kentish Town'. Fill in the blanks.

- O ... A TERRORIST
- O ... AN ANARCHIST
- O ... A COMMUNIST
- O ... A HIRED KILLER

13. Alfie bets that Tommy is lying. What odds does he initially give?

   ○ 50:1
   ○ 100:1
   ○ ODDS ON
   ○ DEAD CERT

14. When Alfie's right-hand man, Ollie, begins to stress about time running out, Alfie slaps him around the face and orders him to do what?

   ○ LEAVE THE ROOM
   ○ QUIT THE BUSINESS
   ○ CALL THE POLICE
   ○ SIT IN THE CORNER

15. Tommy calls Alfie's bluff and the pair strike a deal. Rather than agreeing to hand over 100% of his business to Alfie, how much does he agree to give?

   ○ 25%
   ○ 35%
   ○ 50%
   ○ 65%

16. 'I need you today, brother.' Where are Tommy and Arthur reunited?

   ○ OUTSIDE THE BAKERY
   ○ OUTSIDE EPSOM RACECOURSE
   ○ OUTSIDE ADA'S HOUSE
   ○ ROADSIDE EN ROUTE TO THE DERBY

17. All the Peaky Blinders have gathered for the day's mission. Tommy tells Finn that his role is limited to what?

   ○ DRIVING
   ○ LOOKOUT
   ○ RUNNER
   ○ SCOUT

SEASON TWO ▌ EPISODE SIX

18. 'Take the money, get a train and start a new life.'
Where has Polly found the money to give to Michael?

- ○ SHE TOOK MAJOR CAMPBELL'S WALLET
- ○ SHE'S EMPTIED THE BETTING SHOP SAFE
- ○ SHE'S EMPTIED THE GARRISON'S TILL
- ○ SHE'S EMPTIED HER PERSONAL SAFE AT HOME

19. 'Behold, today's rabbit.' With a picture in hand,
Major Campbell meets three men tasked with killing
Tommy once he's carried out the assassination. What
is their allegiance?

- ○ COMMUNIST PARTY
- ○ MR SABINI'S GANG
- ○ ULSTER VOLUNTEER FORCE
- ○ IRA

20. 'I hope you've all obeyed instructions and brought
loaded firearms with you.' Tommy and his men pull
up in the truck en route to Epsom for a final briefing.
Where do they gather?

- ○ A VILLAGE GREEN
- ○ A PUB
- ○ A TEA ROOM
- ○ A COUNTRYSIDE VERGE

21. Tommy intends to undertake his secret mission in the
owners' enclosure at 3pm sharp. What must his men
do at the same time?

- ○ STEAL A RACEHORSE
- ○ KILL SABINI'S MEN
- ○ TAKE OVER SABINI'S PITCHES
- ○ CREATE AN ALIBI FOR TOMMY

22. How many years in prison will any of them face if they're caught by the police with a weapon at the race track?

- ○ 3 YEARS
- ○ 10 YEARS
- ○ 20 YEARS
- ○ LIFE

23. How does Tommy reassure them?

- ○ THE POLICE WILL BE DISTRACTED BY AN INCIDENT IN THE OWNERS' ENCLOSURE
- ○ IF ARRESTED, HE GUARANTEES THEY WILL BE RELEASED WITHOUT CHARGE
- ○ THE POLICE HAVE BEEN INSTRUCTED TO TURN A BLIND EYE
- ○ IN THE PANIC FOLLOWING THE INCIDENT, THEY'LL BE ABLE TO GET AWAY

24. As a final gesture, what horse does Tommy suggest they place a bet on because 'I hear she's going to win'?

- ○ IRISH BATTLE
- ○ NOM DE GUERRE
- ○ TAMAR
- ○ VILLARS

25. At the racecourse, Tommy finds May Carleton with Grace's Secret. Why is she briefly concerned?

- ○ THE HORSE HAS THROWN A SHOE
- ○ THE HORSE IS RESTLESS
- ○ THE HORSE APPEARS TO BE LAME
- ○ THE HORSE IS OFF HER FOOD

SEASON TWO ▮ EPISODE SIX

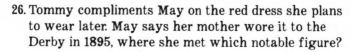
26. Tommy compliments May on the red dress she plans to wear later. May says her mother wore it to the Derby in 1895, where she met which notable figure?

○ THE MARQUESS OF SALISBURY
○ HG WELLS
○ QUEEN VICTORIA
○ THOMAS HARDY

27. Grace appears at the race, taking Tommy by surprise as he tails his target. What news does she bring?

○ SHE'S LEAVING FOR NEW YORK
○ SHE'S PREGNANT
○ SHE'S LEFT HER HUSBAND
○ SHE KNOWS ABOUT TOMMY'S RELATIONSHIP WITH MAY

28. Tommy is pressed because he can't afford to lose his target. Where does Grace arrange to wait for him?

○ WHERE THE VIPS ARE GATHERED
○ WHERE THE DRINKS ARE SERVED
○ WHERE THE BETS ARE LAID
○ WHERE THE WINNINGS ARE PAID OUT

29. 'It's how the soldiers know.' With reluctance, Lizzy agrees to distract Tommy's target and take him to a quiet place. She requests a piece of chalk from Tommy. Why?

○ TO WRITE A NOTE SHE CAN DISCREETLY HAND OVER
○ TO WRITE HER PRICE ON THE PALM OF HER HAND
○ TO WRITE HER PRICE ON THE TABLECLOTH
○ TO WRITE HER PRICE ON THE SOLE OF HER SHOE

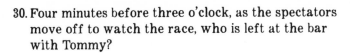

30. Four minutes before three o'clock, as the spectators move off to watch the race, who is left at the bar with Tommy?

- ⏼ GRACE
- ⏼ MAJOR CAMPBELL
- ⏼ MR SABINI
- ⏼ ARTHUR SHELBY

31. Tommy makes his way towards the toilet stalls where Lizzie has led his target, only to be stopped by the police and told to go around. Why?

- ⏼ THE AREA IS FOR RACE OFFICIALS ONLY
- ⏼ IT'S CORDONED OFF AS A VIP IS RECEIVING MEDICAL ATTENTION
- ⏼ THE AREA IS ACCESSIBLE TO VIPS ONLY
- ⏼ IT'S CORDONED OFF AS THE KING WILL SHORTLY BE IN THE VICINITY

32. In the amorous clutches of his target, Lizzie is in trouble when Tommy finally races in. He takes aim with his gun. What happens next?

- ⏼ TOMMY MISSES
- ⏼ THE GUN FAILS TO FIRE
- ⏼ TOMMY'S TARGET MOVES AND LIZZIE IS WOUNDED
- ⏼ TOMMY STUMBLES AND HIS TARGET KNOCKS THE GUN FROM HIM

33. A struggle ensues between Tommy and his target, who is finally killed when Tommy turns his own pistol on him. Having urged Lizzie to flee, what does he do with the pistol?

- ⏼ PLACES IT IN THE DEAD MAN'S HAND
- ⏼ FIRES IT INTO THE AIR THREE TIMES
- ⏼ POCKETS IT
- ⏼ TOSSES IT INTO A TOILET STALL

SEASON TWO ▮ EPISODE SIX

34. Hurrying out, Tommy tells the incoming police officer that he'd been in one of the stalls when he heard an argument and then gunshot. What accent does he claim to have heard?

   ○ SCOTTISH
   ○ IRISH
   ○ WELSH
   ○ AMERICAN

35. As the sound of police whistles fills the air, drawing officers away, the Peaky Blinders make their move on Sabini's pitches. What does Arthur gleefully set light to?

   ○ A BOOKMAKER'S TRACK PREMISES LICENCE
   ○ A BOOKMAKER'S RECORD OF BETS PAID IN AND OUT
   ○ A RACING NEWSPAPER
   ○ A WAD OF BETTING SLIPS

36. 'Where are our coppers?' On finding Tommy Shelby waiting for him in the owners' enclosure, it dawns on Mr Sabini that he's lost control. Why does Tommy advise him not to pull a gun here?

   ○ TOMMY HAS A GUN AIMED AT HIM UNDER THE TABLE
   ○ MR SABINI WILL BE CONSIDERED TO BE 'THE KING'S ASSASSIN'
   ○ MR SABINI WILL BE IMPLICATED IN THE RACECOURSE KILLING
   ○ TOMMY HAS MEN WATCHING WHO WILL SHOOT HIM DEAD

37. 'There's business and there's love.' Tommy is taken away by Major Campbell's UVF men masquerading as coppers, leaving May and Grace at the racetrack. When they talk, why is May so sure that the new betting licences will be awarded to Tommy?

   ○ LIKE GRACE, SHE HAS COME TO REALISE THAT TOMMY IS COMPLETELY UNCOMPROMISING
   ○ SHE HAS INFLUENCE ON THE BOARD
   ○ MR SABINI'S BOOKMAKERS WILL BE TOO SCARED TO RETURN TO THE TRACK
   ○ MR SABINI IS A DEAD MAN WALKING

38. Where does Polly find Major Campbell, before holding him at gunpoint?

    ○ AT THE BAR
    ○ IN A TELEPHONE BOOTH
    ○ BEHIND THE GRANDSTAND
    ○ OUTSIDE THE RACECOURSE EXIT

39. 'Comrade, we have our orders ...' Tommy awaits his execution before a makeshift grave in a ploughed field. Before the gun goes off, what are his final words?

    ○ 'IN THE BLEAK MIDWINTER.'
    ○ 'I CAME SO CLOSE.'
    ○ 'LET'S GET IT DONE.'
    ○ 'I NEARLY GOT EVERYTHING!'

SEASON TWO ▮ EPISODE SIX

KILLER QUESTIONS

40. At the bakery, what is written in chalk on the barrel where Tommy stops to tie a shoelace and plant a grenade?

   ○ HUBERMAN CHRISTMAS
   ○ HAMILTON PASSOVER
   ○ HAMILTON CHRISTMAS
   ○ HUBERMAN PASSOVER

41. When John and Arthur are first seen at the racecourse, entering a marquee, what is the name of the sponsor?

   ○ CLIPPER BATH
   ○ BRIGHTON MILD
   ○ PORTSMOUTH BRIGHT
   ○ HAPPY BRISTOL

42. In the celebration at the Garrison, Arthur raises a toast to the Lee boys, the Peaky Blinders and whom?

   ○ THE RED RIGHT HAND
   ○ THE SMALL HEATH RIFLES
   ○ NOM DE GUERRE
   ○ LIZZY STARK

SEASON THREE

1. Who has plans for Tommy after he escapes execution at the hands of the UVF?

   ○ THE IRA
   ○ THE KING
   ○ WINSTON CHURCHILL
   ○ MR SABINI

2. In what year does Season 3 take place?

   ○ 1921
   ○ 1922
   ○ 1923
   ○ 1924

3. It's Tommy's wedding day. Grace arrives by horse-drawn carriage. The colour of her dress and veil signifies she is a widow remarrying. What is the colour?

   ○ WHITE
   ○ BLACK
   ○ LILAC
   ○ GOLD

4. What is the hymn sung by the choir that precedes the bride's arrival?

   ○ AMAZING GRACE
   ○ GUIDE ME, O THOU GREAT REDEEMER
   ○ IN THE BLEAK MIDWINTER
   ○ O COME, ALL YE FAITHFUL

5. 'Dearly Beloved, we are gathered here today to join in holy matrimony, Thomas _____ Shelby and Grace Helen Burgess.' What is Tommy's middle name?

   ○ ARTHUR
   ○ MICHAEL
   ○ DAVID
   ○ JOHN

SEASON THREE ▐ EPISODE ONE

6. The wedding party move on to Arrow House, Tommy and Grace's grand manor. What has Tommy counted to be sure that none are stolen by the Lee girls?

O VASES
O DECANTERS
O PAINTINGS
O SILVER TRAYS

7. Tommy gathers the Peaky Blinders in the kitchen. Tensions are rising high, because members of the bridal party have contravened the dress code, and he wants to make sure there's no fighting. What are they wearing that's deemed provocative?

O OLD SCHOOL TIES
O REGIMENTAL UNIFORM
O MEMORIAL POPPIES
O IRISH UNIONIST LAPEL BADGES

8. Tommy and Grace have a son. What is his name?

O MICHAEL
O CHARLES
O ARTHUR
O THOMAS

9. In a moment away from the party, Grace is upset with Tommy. She knows something's on his mind, but he won't tell her what it is. In a bid to ease the tension between them, he jokes that something is frightening him. What is it?

O ARTHUR'S SPEECH
O JOHN'S TABLE MANNERS
O FINN'S DRINKING
O POLLY'S MOOD

SEASON THREE EPISODE ONE

10. Downstairs, Polly catches the eye of not one but two men. As one approaches, Lizzie Stark whispers to her that it must be down to what gift Tommy brought her back from New York?

   ○ FALSE EYELASHES
   ○ LIPSTICK
   ○ EYESHADOW
   ○ BLUSHER

11. The man's name is Anton Kaledin. He introduces himself as a Russian émigré and businessman. What raises Polly's guard?

   ○ KALEDIN JOKES THAT THE MARRIAGE CANNOT LAST
   ○ HE KNOWS HER ADDRESS
   ○ KALEDIN WISHES TO TALK BUSINESS AT A WEDDING
   ○ HE KNOWS HER NAME

12. Lizzy is upset with Michael because her Italian restaurateur boyfriend hasn't shown up. Michael reasons that he has a shady background with 'connections to the Naples boys'. How did the Peaky Blinders scare him off?

   ○ ARSON ATTACK AT HIS RESTAURANT
   ○ INTIMIDATION OF HIS KITCHEN STAFF
   ○ DEMANDING PROTECTION MONEY
   ○ PAYING OFF FOOD SUPPLIERS TO STAY AWAY

13. 'But first a few words from the heart ...' Hesitantly, Arthur begins his best man's speech in front of the wedding party and his own new wife, Linda. Why does Tommy step in and propose a toast?

   ○ ARTHUR FREEZES AND CAN'T GO ON
   ○ ARTHUR HAS ADOPTED LINDA'S RELIGIOUS CONVICTIONS, CAUSING LAUGHTER AMONG THE FAMILY
   ○ DESPITE GIVING UP ALCOHOL, ARTHUR IS VISIBLY DRUNK
   ○ ARTHUR IS ABOUT TO BLURT OUT THAT GRACE'S FIRST HUSBAND KILLED HIMSELF

SEASON THREE ▌ EPISODE ONE

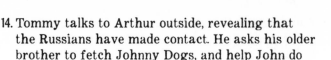

14. Tommy talks to Arthur outside, revealing that the Russians have made contact. He asks his older brother to fetch Johnny Dogs, and help John do what?

O DISTRIBUTE THE GUNS
O MARSHAL THE LEE BOYS
O LOCK THE DOORS
O SOBER UP

15. Polly approaches Kaledin. She says a codename had been agreed before the Russians made contact with Tommy. What codename does he give?

O VOLGA
O IVAN
O CONSTANTINE
O ODESSA

16. In order to speak to Kaledin undisturbed, Tommy asks Johnny Dogs to stage a horse race to distract the guests. How does Johnny know that the horse backed by Grace's family will lose?

O IT'S LAME
O HE'S TIGHTENED THE BLINKERS SO THE HORSE CANNOT SEE
O IT'S RECOVERING FROM ILLNESS
O HE'S DRUGGED THE HORSE WITH A MIXTURE OF MORPHINE AND WATER

17. Tommy insists the money must go to his charity dedicated to helping the poor people of Birmingham. What is its name?

O THE SHELBY FOUNDATION CHARITY
O THE PEAKY BLINDERS MISSION
O THE SHELBY BROTHERS FOUNDATION CHARITY
O THE SMALL HEATH MISSION

SEASON THREE | EPISODE ONE

18. Which Peaky Blinder rides one of the horses?

- ○ ISAIAH JESUS
- ○ FINN SHELBY
- ○ MICHAEL GRAY
- ○ CURLY

19. Arriving in the stable for his meeting with Tommy, Kaledin is frisked by John and Arthur. 'Why does he trust his _____ more than his brothers?' he asks them provocatively. Fill in the blank.

- ○ ... INSTINCT
- ○ ... WIFE
- ○ ... HOUSEMAID
- ○ ... AUNT

20. 'You have made very powerful enemies,' Kaledin tells Tommy, and reveals that every aspect of his life is under surveillance. As well as members of the British Government, who else does the émigré claim is watching him?

- ○ THE POLITBURO
- ○ THE SOVIET EMBASSY
- ○ THE ROYAL FAMILY
- ○ THE SOVIET FOREIGN DEPARTMENT

21. As well as contact from this foreign agent, representing the interests of Russian monarchists in the fight against Bolsheviks, Tommy is expecting a cash payment. According to Kaledin, 'the duke's niece' is travelling to Birmingham by train with $10,000 for him. Why has this individual been entrusted to bring Tommy the money?

- ○ THE DUKE ONLY TRUSTS FAMILY
- ○ THE DUKE'S NIECE IS ON A EUROPEAN TOUR
- ○ SHE SPEAKS FLUENT ENGLISH
- ○ SHE IS AUTHORISED TO NEGOTIATE ON BEHALF OF THE DUKE

SEASON THREE ▪ EPISODE ONE

22. Tommy insists that he send someone to pick her up. Who?

- ○ SERGEANT MOSS
- ○ JOHN SHELBY
- ○ MICHAEL SHELBY
- ○ JOHNNY DOGS

23. Following the meeting, with the horse race underway, Tommy instructs Johnny Dogs and his boys to light a fire in the woods 'big enough _____'. Complete the sentence.

- ○ ... TO LIGHT UP THE NIGHT SKY
- ○ ... TO TAKE MEAT
- ○ ... TO COOK GAME
- ○ ... TO BURN UNTIL DAYBREAK

24. Michael settles in a room with a young debutante called Charlotte. He declines her offer of cocaine, but what does she call it?

- ○ CHIBA
- ○ TOKYO
- ○ KYOTO
- ○ SAGA

25. 'Royalist Russians buying weapons to fight the Bolsheviks in Georgia.' Grace tells Polly that she knows about Tommy's business matter with the Russian. What is Polly filling her glass with as she listens?

- ○ CHAMPAGNE
- ○ PUNCH
- ○ WHISKEY
- ○ GIN

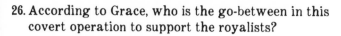

26. According to Grace, who is the go-between in this covert operation to support the royalists?

- ◌ THE PRIME MINISTER
- ◌ THE FOREIGN SECRETARY
- ◌ THE SECRETARY OF STATE FOR WAR
- ◌ WINSTON CHURCHILL

27. 'Get this business done and get away from things like this.' As they take the floor for the first dance, Grace sets out her vision to Tommy for their legitimate new life. What does she see herself running?

- ◌ THE FOUNDATION CHARITY
- ◌ THE HOUSEHOLD
- ◌ THE SHELBY BROTHERS OFFICE
- ◌ THE NIGHTCLUBS

28. On the dance floor, Tommy makes her a vow. What is it?

- ◌ NO GUNS IN THE HOUSE
- ◌ NO FIGHTING ON THE GROUNDS
- ◌ NO SWEARING IN FRONT OF THEIR SON
- ◌ NO MORE RISK-TAKING

29. With the Duke's niece due to arrive with the money, where do Tommy and his brothers head for the handover?

- ◌ THE DRIVE
- ◌ THE GATEHOUSE
- ◌ THE LODGE HOUSE
- ◌ THE MAIN GATES

30. What is the title of the Duke's niece, Tatiana Petrovna?

- ◌ PRINCESS
- ◌ DUCHESS
- ◌ GRAND DUCHESS
- ◌ COUNTESS

SEASON THREE ▮ EPISODE ONE

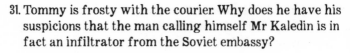

31. Tommy is frosty with the courier. Why does he have his suspicions that the man calling himself Mr Kaledin is in fact an infiltrator from the Soviet embassy?

- ○ HIS STORY IS INCONSISTENT
- ○ HE GAVE THE WRONG CODENAME
- ○ HE'S ASKED TOO MANY QUESTIONS
- ○ HE DOESN'T MATCH THE DESCRIPTION OF THE MAN TOMMY WAS EXPECTING

32. The other wedding guest who has been paying attention to Polly makes his move. His name is Ruben Oliver, an artist. The military members of Grace's family have been giving him the cold shoulder, and so he makes a confession. What is it?

- ○ HE HAD AN AFFAIR WITH A FAMILY MEMBER
- ○ HE WAS A CONSCIENTIOUS OBJECTOR
- ○ HE EMBARRASSED THE FAMILY AT THE LAST WEDDING
- ○ HE SLEPT WITH THE WIFE OF ONE OF THE COLONELS WHO SAT FOR HIM

33. 'There's just some shit that goes with it.' Tommy confesses to Arthur that the covert work he's expected to undertake extends beyond breaking into a factory. This begins with killing Mr Kaledin. How does Tommy refer to him?

- ○ A RED
- ○ A SPY
- ○ A COMMUNIST
- ○ ENEMY OF THE STATE

34. In talking Arthur round, Tommy promises that the work will bring them a fortune. What purchase does he intend to make in America with the initial $10,000?

- ○ A PACKING PLANT IN NORFOLK HARBOUR
- ○ A WHARF AT BOSTON DOCKS
- ○ A DOCK AT BALTIMORE PORT
- ○ A WAREHOUSE IN NEW JERSEY

35. Back inside the manor, Tommy is keen that the party remain in full swing while the Peaky Blinders carry out their work for the evening. What music does he instruct the band to play?

   O FOXTROT
   O DIXIELAND
   O RAGTIME
   O JAZZ

36. Mr Kaledin is alone with Ada, just before Arthur joins them to escort him on what will be his final moments. Kaledin observes that her family are close. What phrase does Ada use to describe their relationship?

   O 'PERMANENTLY AT BOILING POINT.'
   O 'NEVER FAR FROM TROUBLE.'
   O 'ALWAYS WITHIN PUNCHING DISTANCE.'
   O 'PRACTICALLY HANDCUFFED TOGETHER.'

37. Arthur is tasked with shooting Mr Kaledin, which he does with reluctance in the cellar. What rowdy event has John staged in the grounds to serve as a cover for the noise?

   O A DOG FIGHT
   O A BARE-KNUCKLE BOXING FIGHT
   O A COCKEREL FIGHT
   O A MASS BRAWL

38. From his bedroom window that night, with Grace at his side, Tommy sees Arthur perched on the side of the cart transporting Kaledin's body away to be burned. Who is at the reins?

   O CURLY
   O JOHNNY DOGS
   O JOHN SHELBY
   O CHARLIE STRONG

SEASON THREE ▌ EPISODE ONE

149

39. The Shelbys leave the manor at first light and drive to Small Heath in a fleet of cars. What's Tommy's first task in sweeping into the betting shop?

   ○ TOASTING HIS NEW WIFE
   ○ HANDING OUT BONUSES TO THE STAFF
   ○ STASHING THE $10,000 IN THE WALK-IN SAFE
   ○ STASHING KALEDIN'S RINGS IN THE SAFE

KILLER QUESTIONS

40. In the family wedding photograph, taken outside the church, Tommy stands with a cigarette in his mouth. Who else is smoking in the picture?

   ○ ARTHUR SHELBY
   ○ CHARLIE STRONG
   ○ MICHAEL GRAY
   ○ JOHN SHELBY

41. What is Arthur eating in the kitchen during Tommy's 'no fighting' speech?

   ○ WEDDING CAKE
   ○ SHORTBREAD
   ○ A CARROT
   ○ A SANDWICH

42. 'He's a red,' say Tommy, referring to Mr Kaledin. He's explaining to Arthur that he's been tasked by Churchill to illicitly acquire military hardware to influence a fight-back in Russia against the ruling party. 'We're being paid by the whites.' Who are the whites?

   ○ ANARCHISTS
   ○ EURO-SLAVISTS
   ○ ANTI-COMMUNIST FORCES
   ○ PRO-COMMUNIST FORCES

SEASON THREE ▮ EPISODE ONE

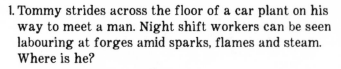

1. Tommy strides across the floor of a car plant on his way to meet a man. Night shift workers can be seen labouring at forges amid sparks, flames and steam. Where is he?

   ○ EXCELSIOR MOTOR COMPANY
   ○ LANCHESTER MOTOR COMPANY
   ○ CALTHORPE MOTOR COMPANY
   ○ WOLSELEY MOTORS LIMITED

2. Tommy has come to see a man called Connor Nutley, who greets him with disdain because 'your brothers came to my house'. Who is Nutley?

   ○ THE SHOP STEWARD
   ○ THE COMPANY DIRECTOR
   ○ THE FOREMAN
   ○ THE UNION LEADER

3. 'What is it you want from a simple working man?' Tommy turns to a blueprint layout of the factory on the wall. What is his answer?

   ○ THE KEYS TO THE SIDE ENTRANCE
   ○ THE KEYS TO BAY SIX
   ○ THE SKELETON KEYS
   ○ THE KEYS TO THE PAINT SHOP

4. In return for the key, Tommy hands Nutley an envelope of money. He declines to accept it initially. What does he suggest that Tommy do with the money instead?

   ○ 'RETURN IT TO THOSE YOU STOLE IT FROM.'
   ○ 'I DON'T ACCEPT BLOOD MONEY.'
   ○ 'GIVE IT TO YOUR CHARITY.'
   ○ 'PUT IT IN THE HARDSHIP BOX.'

5. Tommy makes his way to a dark, quiet quarter of the factory. In the shadows, he finds a fleet of armoured cars. What are some of the vehicles covered in?

   ○ RUST
   ○ TARPAULINS
   ○ WEBBING
   ○ BRITISH ARMY INSIGNIA

6. Before climbing into the cab of one of the cars, what does he do?

   ○ STRIKE A MATCH
   ○ LIGHT A LAMP
   ○ SWITCH ON AN INTERIOR LIGHT
   ○ WAIT FOR THE MOON TO APPEAR FROM BEHIND A CLOUD

7. At Charlie Strong's yard, Tommy meets a priest called Father Hughes, who is his go-between in the supply of military vehicles for the Russia mission. Tommy expected Hughes to arrive with a shadowy establishment group called 'Section D', comprising 'MPs, _____ and army officers.' Fill in the blank.

   ○ ... BUSINESSMEN
   ○ ... MERCENARIES
   ○ ... HIGH-RANKING POLICE
   ○ ... FOREIGN AGENTS

8. As they wait, Hughes enquires about Tommy's charity for children. He tells him that he and an MP called Patrick Jarvis intend to 'drop by in the evenings after a few drinks'. Disgusted at the intimation, how does Tommy react?

   ○ HE DRAWS HIS GUN TO SILENCE HIM
   ○ HE FACES HIS CHAIR AWAY FROM HUGHES
   ○ HE ORDERS HIM TO STOP TALKING
   ○ HE WALKS AWAY

SEASON THREE ▐ EPISODE TWO

9. As the clock strikes, Father Hughes tells him the meeting is cancelled. Section D have better things to do. Having visited the factory, as per their instruction, what information does Tommy ask Hughes to relay to them?

   ○ HE HAS COUNTED THE MILITARY ITEMS THEY REQUIRE
   ○ HE BELIEVES THE ITEMS ARE FIT FOR NOTHING MORE THAN SCRAP
   ○ HE HAS BEEN UNABLE TO LOCATE THE ITEMS THEY REQUIRE
   ○ HE BELIEVES THE ITEMS ARE TOO HEAVILY GUARDED FOR THEIR PLAN TO PROCEED

10. Before leaving, Hughes hands Tommy a scrap of paper with a name on it, and tells him to head to London immediately. At which hotel in London is he expected to meet this new contact?

   ○ CLARIDGE'S
   ○ THE RITZ
   ○ THE SAVOY
   ○ THE CONNAUGHT

11. Grand Duke Leon Petrovich Romanov awaits his breakfast tea at Wilderness House in Hampton Court. A solo musician keeps him company. What instrument is he playing?

   ○ FLUTE
   ○ VIOLIN
   ○ PIANO
   ○ HARPSICHORD

12. The Duke's butler goes through his appointments for the day. He has just one, to discuss automobiles with Mr Thomas Shelby. How many social engagements have been cancelled around this meeting?

   ○ ONE
   ○ TWO
   ○ THREE
   ○ FOUR

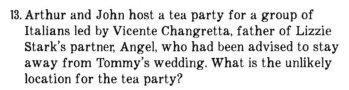

13. Arthur and John host a tea party for a group of Italians led by Vicente Changretta, father of Lizzie Stark's partner, Angel, who had been advised to stay away from Tommy's wedding. What is the unlikely location for the tea party?

○ THE UNDERGROUND BOXING RING
○ CHARLIE STRONG'S YARD
○ THE CEMETERY
○ THE CHINESE QUARTER

14. Changretta points out that he obeys all of Tommy's rules, but that his son should be free to date any woman. What does John suggest might happen to Angel if he continues to see Lizzy?

○ A BULLET IN EACH KNEE
○ TWO BROKEN ARMS
○ BLINDED IN ONE EYE
○ A BROKEN FOOT

15. Changretta and his men walk away in disgust. John has gone too far, and even Arthur knows it. What is Vicente's final gesture?

○ HE SMASHES A CHAIR
○ HE SPITS IN THE MUD
○ HE SMASHES THE TEAPOT
○ HE UPENDS THE TABLE

16. Tommy visits Ada at her library workplace. With his secret mission in mind, he's interested in books about the Russian Revolution. Ada hands him two books, one of which she describes as 'A list of the _____ who ran away.' Fill in the blank.

○ ... COWARDS
○ ... BASTARDS
○ ... ROYALISTS
○ ... SCUM

17. Why does Ada say her brother can't rip out the entry for Petrovich Romanov?

   ○ ADA BELIEVES ALL BOOKS ARE SACRED
   ○ THE BOOK IS PROPERTY OF THE PEOPLE
   ○ IT'S THE LIBRARY'S ONLY COPY
   ○ THE BOOK HAS JUST BEEN REQUESTED FOR LOAN

18. Polly approaches John in the betting shop. She's not happy, because one of the Lee brothers got drunk and shared a drug intended for the racehorses with his cousins instead. What drug?

   ○ MORPHINE
   ○ COCAINE
   ○ HEROIN
   ○ OPIUM

19. 'We own the city … but we don't want rebellions.' Speaking on Arthur's behalf, Polly asks John to apologise to Angel Changretta or compromise and ask Lizzie to do so for him. Who does John blame for what he perceives as a climbdown?

   ○ JEREMIAH JESUS
   ○ GRACE SHELBY
   ○ LINDA SHELBY
   ○ TOMMY SHELBY

20. Tommy arrives at the hotel for his meeting with Romanov. What problem does he encounter at reception, and solve with a roll of banknotes?

   ○ THE HOTEL DOES NOT PERMIT THE WORKING CLASS
   ○ TOMMY'S CAP CONTRAVENES THE DRESS CODE
   ○ ROMANOV HAS DEFAULTED ON HIS BILLS
   ○ TOMMY HASN'T MADE A RESERVATION AND THE DINING ROOM IS FULL

SEASON THREE ▮▮▮ EPISODE TWO

21. Over lunch, which is effectively a huge pile of caviar for the Russian exile, Tommy listens impassively to Romanov's account of his journey to England. What does he claim to have lost in hostile conditions in the Crimea?

   ○ A FINGER
   ○ HIS WIFE
   ○ A TOE
   ○ HIS FORTUNE

22. When Tommy reminds him that there is a high price for work he's expected to undertake in support of his cause, what jewel does Romanov offer him?

   ○ A WHITE OPAL
   ○ A BLUE SAPPHIRE
   ○ A GREEN EMERALD
   ○ A CRIMSON RUBY

23. Along with Romanov's wife, who else helped him smuggle family jewels into England?

   ○ ROMANOV'S NIECE
   ○ CHURCHILL
   ○ ROMANOV'S BUTLER
   ○ THE KING'S FOOTMAN

24. John ambushes Angel Changretta to show him who's in charge. Where does he jump him?

   ○ THE ITALIAN QUARTER
   ○ THE CHINESE LAUNDRY
   ○ ANGEL'S RESTAURANT
   ○ LIZZIE'S LODGINGS

SEASON THREE ▮ EPISODE TWO

25. 'Remember, these are the bastards that wanted Danny Whizz-Bang dead.' How does Tommy propose to stamp out a rebellion by the Italians, despite misgivings from Arthur and Polly?

   ○ INCREASING PROTECTION PAYMENTS ACROSS THE ITALIAN QUARTER
   ○ TAKING SEVERAL PUBS CONTROLLED BY THE CHANGRETTAS
   ○ TAKING ANGEL'S RESTAURANT
   ○ KILLING ANGEL

26. At Wilderness House, Grand Duke Leon Petrovich Romanov is summoned to the drawing room by his wife. She's sickly, but clearly calls the shots. What does she hand him, followed by the warning that Mr Shelby may have to be killed when his work is done?

   ○ THREE HANDWRITTEN LETTERS
   ○ A JEWEL TO REPLACE THE ONE HE GAVE TO TOMMY
   ○ AN UNPAID BILL
   ○ A TELEGRAM FROM THE WHITES IN GEORGIA

27. When Tommy returns home at the end of a long day, he finds Grace in a state of excitement about the Shelby Foundation. What news does she share with him?

   ○ HER BID TO PURCHASE A BUILDING TO HOUSE THE ORPHANAGE HAS BEEN ACCEPTED
   ○ BIRMINGHAM CITY COUNCIL HAVE MADE A SIZEABLE DONATION
   ○ THE LEADER OF BIRMINGHAM CITY COUNCIL HAS ACCEPTED HER INVITATION TO THE FOUNDATION DINNER
   ○ THE FOUNDATION'S CHARITABLE STATUS HAS BEEN OFFICIALLY CERTIFIED

28. What has Tommy done with the jewel that Romanov gave him?

   ○ DELIVERED IT TO THE JEWELLERS TO HANDCRAFT A BROOCH
   ○ HAD IT MADE INTO A NECKLACE FOR GRACE, WHICH HE
     PRESENTS TO HER
   ○ DELIVERED IT TO THE JEWELLERS TO HANDCRAFT A NECKLACE
   ○ HAD IT MADE INTO A BROOCH FOR GRACE, WHICH HE
     PRESENTS TO HER

29. 'Working in the dark is for the devil, we said.' Linda pressures Arthur not to go out to attend to business. What does he tell her needs to be done?

   ○ CONTRACT WORK
   ○ PAPERWORK
   ○ A NEGOTIATION
   ○ A REVIEW

30. 'I thought you boys were too big for this kind of thing these days?' En route to crush the Changretta rebellion, with the rain sweeping down, Arthur slips Moss some money so the police turn a blind eye. What does Moss suggest is motivating Tommy here that makes his brother uneasy?

   ○ POWER
   ○ WEALTH
   ○ AUTHORITY
   ○ SPORT

31. The next day, Tommy strides into the betting shop to find John having sex with Esme. He reminds them that they have a house. 'Yeah, it's full of ...' Esme retorts. Fill in the blank.

   ○ ... STAFF
   ○ ... DECORATORS
   ○ ... KIDS
   ○ ... FAMILY

SEASON THREE █ EPISODE TWO

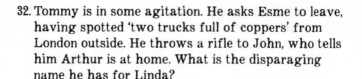

32. Tommy is in some agitation. He asks Esme to leave, having spotted 'two trucks full of coppers' from London outside. He throws a rifle to John, who tells him Arthur is at home. What is the disparaging name he has for Linda?

○ THE QUAKER WIFE
○ THE MADONNA OF MOSELEY
○ THE SISTER OF SPARKHILL
○ THE NUN OF NECHELLS

33. Officers from Special Branch burst in, dragging Esme with them. Tommy and John are forced to surrender. Later, Father Hughes visits Tommy in his cell. What does he bring to intimidate him and make sure he complies with the mission?

○ TWO ARMED OFFICERS
○ A CROWBAR
○ A DOBERMAN
○ A NOOSE

34. Tommy is not easily intimidated when Hughes tells him Ada's association with Russian activists puts her life at risk. What does Hughes say that seizes Tommy's attention?

○ HE INTIMATES THAT THE SHELBY FOUNDATION WILL BECOME A MAGNET FOR SEXUAL PREDATORS
○ HE CLAIMS TO HAVE VISITED HIS SON'S NURSERY AT SPARK HALL
○ HE TELLS HIM GRACE IS NOT SAFE
○ HE THREATENS TO HAVE EVERY MEMBER OF HIS FAMILY KILLED

35. Rushing back to Arrow House, Tommy finds a business card for a funeral home with his son's name handwritten on it. 'You promised,' says Grace, sensing his alarm. 'Everything's _____,' he replies. Fill in the blank.

    U ... GONE WRONG
    U ... IN HAND
    U ... GONE TO HELL
    U ... FINE

36. The artist, Ruben Oliver, looks on in wonder at Polly when she appears in the dress she wants to wear for her portrait. 'Made in Paris,' he offers. What is Polly's response?

    U 'HANDED DOWN FROM MY MOTHER.'
    U 'I MADE IT MYSELF.'
    U 'AND STOLEN IN BIRMINGHAM.'
    U 'IT BELONGS TO ADA.'

37. The great and the good assemble for the Shelby Foundation Fundraising Dinner. Tommy's mood sours when Father Hughes appears with the MP, Patrick Jarvis. Taking Tommy aside, Jarvis tells him the Duke's niece wishes to inspect the military vehicles at the factory. Why does Tommy say it's not possible?

    U THE FACTORY IS CLOSED UNTIL MONDAY
    U UNION CONVENORS WILL BE WATCHING
    U AN INSPECTION RISKS THE FOREMAN REPORTING HIM
    U HER PRESENCE WILL AROUSE SUSPICIONS FROM THE FACTORY OWNER

SEASON THREE ▮ EPISODE TWO

38. Returning to the throng, Tommy finds the duchess in conversation with Grace, who senses they have met. In a moment alone, what does Tatiana disclose about the Russian jewel his wife is wearing?

- ○ IT'S FAKE
- ○ IT'S FLAWED
- ○ IT'S STOLEN
- ○ IT'S CURSED

39. As the guests move to the dining hall, an assassin hired by the Changretta family takes aim at Tommy. What is the assassin dressed as?

- ○ A WAITER
- ○ A CHEF
- ○ THE TOASTMASTER
- ○ A DOORMAN

KILLER QUESTIONS

40. On our first visit to Wilderness House, a grand painting hangs in the drawing room where Grand Duke Leon Petrovich Romanov reads his newspaper. What does the painting depict?

   ◡ A LION
   ◡ A STAG
   ◡ A HORSE
   ◡ AN EAGLE

41. When Tommy returns to the office, he finds Michael behind his desk. Michael introduces him to Charlotte Murray from the wedding. What shape is the big window behind Tommy's desk?

   ◡ SQUARE
   ◡ TRIANGULAR
   ◡ ROUND
   ◡ HALF ROUND

42. What is the name of the company on the business card Tommy finds tucked inside his son's crib?

   ◡ SMALL HEATH UNDERTAKERS
   ◡ THE CO-OPERATIVE CREMATORIUM
   ◡ SPARKHILL FUNERAL HOME
   ◡ ST JUDE'S ORPHANAGE

SEASON THREE ▮ EPISODE TWO

1. We find Tommy at daybreak, grieving the loss of his wife. Since Grace's death with a bullet intended for him, where has he taken to sleeping?

   ○ IN THE STABLES
   ○ UNDER THE STARS
   ○ IN A GYPSY WAGON
   ○ ON A BARGE

2. According to Ada, for what reason does Tommy come back to the house each morning?

   ○ TO MAKE BREAKFAST
   ○ TO SEE HIS SON
   ○ TO WORK AT HIS DESK
   ○ TO WASH

3. Tommy summons Michael and Polly for a business update. What does John report?

   ○ THE SAFE ARRIVAL OF A SHIPMENT OF WHISKEY TO AMERICA
   ○ AN INCREASE IN DONATIONS TO THE SHELBY FOUNDATION CHARITY
   ○ A DECREASE IN TAKINGS FROM THE RACECOURSES
   ○ THE SETTLEMENT OF A TAX DISPUTE

4. Michael also informs Tommy that a councillor has suggested a name for the new children's school to be run by the charity. What is it?

   ○ THE GRACE SHELBY SCHOOL
   ○ SHELBYS
   ○ THE GRACE SHELBY INSTITUTE
   ○ THE GRACE SHELBY SCHOOL FOR UNDERPRIVILEGED CHILDREN

5. John and Arthur are next to be summoned into Tommy's office. Polly asks them to help get their brother back on his feet. Why? Because Alfie Solomons and Mr Sabini have each sent something that spells trouble. What is it?

- ○ GIFT BASKETS
- ○ AN INVITATION TO THE RACES
- ○ FLOWERS
- ○ AN INVITATION TO PARLAY

6. Tommy asks for an update on Angel Changretta's well-being. What does Arthur report?

- ○ THEY'VE RUN HIM OUT OF BIRMINGHAM
- ○ THEY'VE CUT HIS THROAT AND HE'S DEAD
- ○ HE'S BEEN DISCHARGED FROM HOSPITAL
- ○ HE'S GONE TO GROUND

7. Angel's father, Vicente, has fled to Liverpool. Arthur reports that he's waiting to board a liner to New York. Tommy pledges to bring the man to justice using his connections with which shipping company?

- ○ AMERICAN LINE
- ○ CUNARD
- ○ DOMINION
- ○ RED STAR LINE

8. Tommy instructs Arthur and John to shoot Vicente's wife before bringing him back to Birmingham. Why are the pair reluctant to do so?

- ○ SHE'S DEEPLY RELIGIOUS
- ○ SHE TAUGHT THE BOYS AT SCHOOL
- ○ SHE RUNS A CHARITY FOR THE POOR
- ○ SHE WAS GOOD FRIENDS WITH THEIR MOTHER

9. Handing them a list of instructions, Tommy requests that they burn it afterwards and don't communicate by phone. Who does he suspect could be eavesdropping?

   ○ THE CHANGRETTA FAMILY
   ○ THE SECRET SERVICE
   ○ ALFIE SOLOMON'S GANG
   ○ MR SOLOMON'S ORGANISATION

10. Before leaving, John is upset that Michael had been summoned before his own brothers. What reason does Tommy give for this?

   ○ MICHAEL IS NEWEST TO THE FAMILY, AND IN SHOCK
   ○ MICHAEL IS YOUNGEST IN THE FAMILY BUSINESS, AND REQUIRES GUIDANCE
   ○ MICHAEL DEALS WITH LEGITIMATE BUSINESS, WHICH IS A PRIORITY SINCE GRACE'S DEATH
   ○ MICHAEL HAD ARRIVED ON TIME, AND TOMMY REWARDS PUNCTUALITY

11. In the kitchen after their briefing from Tommy, Arthur and John are angry that they've been treated like 'foot soldiers' while Michael has been entrusted with business matters. How does Polly diffuse the situation?

   ○ BY PROPOSING A TOAST
   ○ WITH A ROUND OF TEA
   ○ BY ORDERING ARTHUR TO GET SOME FRESH AIR
   ○ BY SENDING MICHAEL BACK TO WORK

12. Finn brings news that Tommy has taken off with his son, Charles, in a horse and wagon. They find a note from him to say he'll be back in three days. Who else has he left with?

   ○ CHARLIE STRONG
   ○ JOHNNY DOGS
   ○ CURLY
   ○ JEREMIAH JESUS

13. Where are they heading?

   O SCOTLAND
   O CORNWALL
   O WALES
   O CUMBRIA

14. 'She'll be with us in our hearts.' Tommy muses over his loss with his son, Charles. Looking out over water, chewing on mint leaves together, what aspect of her affairs does he pledge to sort out?

   O HER WILL AND TESTIMONY
   O HER PHOTOGRAPHS AND CLOTHES
   O HER LETTERS AND JEWELLERY
   O HER TREASURED POSSESSIONS

15. Following a day of whiskey drinking, John and Arthur teach Michael how to fire a gun. 'It's like _____ when you cock that trigger,' Arthur tells him. Fill in the blanks.

   O ... PREPARING TO RAISE HELL
   O ... WAKING UP A GIRL
   O ... THE WORLD STOPS TURNING
   O ... DEMANDING ATTENTION

16. When Michael turns the gun on John, encouraged by Arthur to see how it feels, John slurs that it 'jumps on the hammer', suggesting it could go off accidentally. What make is the gun?

   O COLT
   O LUGER
   O WEBLEY
   O MAUSER

SEASON THREE ▮ EPISODE THREE

17. 'We're just educating the boss here on our side of the business,' growls Arthur when Polly cools the moment. What does she order Michael to do that prompts him to remind her that he's not a kid any more?

   ○ GO TO HIS ROOM
   ○ HAND THE GUN BACK
   ○ EMPTY THE CHAMBER OF BULLETS
   ○ GO TO THE HOUSE

18. The next day, Arthur and John meet the foreman, Connor Nutley, at the vehicle factory. He's convinced the plan is doomed, and informs them that a woman in a fur coat – Tatiana Petrovna – had visited asking about armoured cars. What does he say she looked like?

   ○ CATHERINE THE GREAT
   ○ A PRINCESS
   ○ THE QUEEN OF SHEBA
   ○ QUEEN VICTORIA

19. The Shelby brothers hand a list to Nutley. It contains names of all the workers on the night shift who are aligned to what party?

   ○ COMMUNIST
   ○ ANARCHIST
   ○ CONSTITUTIONALIST
   ○ NATIONALIST

20. Nutley is shocked when Arthur instructs him to take care of these workers in a particular way. What does he ask Nutley to do?

   ○ SACK THEM
   ○ LOCK THEM OUT ON A CERTAIN DATE
   ○ SET THEM UP FOR CRIMES THEY DIDN'T COMMIT
   ○ PLACE THEM ON PROBATION

21. The brothers have deliberately left one name off the list to see if Nutley will offer it to them. When he doesn't, Arthur and John promise to watch him closely. What rattles Nutley?

○ THEY KNOW HIS HOME ADDRESS
○ THEY KNOW THE NAMES OF HIS CHILDREN
○ THEY KNOW HIS WIFE'S NAME
○ THEY KNOW WHERE HIS MOTHER LIVES

22. Polly is posing for her portrait by Ruben Oliver. In getting to know each other, he asks what books she likes to read. He guesses riding, flower arranging and what?

○ THE CLASSICS
○ EMBROIDERY
○ COOKING
○ HOMEMAKING

23. 'You'd be surprised at the things I know,' says Polly, before making a personal confession that forces her to contain her emotions. What is it?

○ SHE'S UNCOMFORTABLE IN HIGHER SOCIAL CIRCLES
○ SHE'S NOT EDUCATED
○ SHE'S FRIGHTENED OF LOVE
○ SHE BELIEVES ALL MEN COME TO FEAR HER

24. Ruben offers his reasons for wanting to paint her portrait, telling her she has 'a face full of _____.' Complete the sentence.

○ ... SADNESS
○ ... JOY
○ ... CONTRADICTIONS
○ ... SECRETS

25. 'The second motivation is that I am planning to seduce you eventually.' How does Polly respond to Ruben's candid admission?

   U SHE KISSES HIM
   U SHE RETURNS TO HER POSE
   U SHE MAKES HER EXIT
   U SHE PRETENDS NOT TO HEAR

26. 'I need to get some sleep.' To ease his guilt, Tommy arranges a roadside meeting with an old gypsy woman called Bethany Boswell. He needs to know whether the Russian jewel Grace was wearing on the night she was shot is really cursed. Once Bethany tells him what he needs to hear, what happens to the jewel?

   U BETHANY BOSWELL TAKES IT
   U TOMMY AND BETHANY BURY IT
   U TOMMY THROWS IT IN THE WATER
   U BETHANY REMOVES THE CURSE

27. At the docks in Liverpool, Vicente Changretta and his wife are queuing nervously to board the ship. A boarding officer asks all passengers to check the date on their tickets. What does he advise those who can't read?

   U BRING THE TICKET TO HIM
   U FIND SOMEONE WHO CAN
   U GO TO THE INFORMATION DESK
   U GO TO THE BACK OF THE QUEUE

28. Vicente senses danger as two men approach. He appeals for assistance from a police officer, pressing money on him. What does one of the men say to him as the officer leads him away?

   U 'DO YOU NEED HELP WITH YOUR BAGGAGE?
   U 'CAN WE SEE YOUR TICKET?
   U 'HAVE YOU GOT A LIGHT?'
   U 'WE NEED TO SPEAK TO YOU.'

29. As the officer leads Vicente and his wife under a jetty, what does Tommy do with a framed photograph of Grace and Charles back in his office?

○ PLACES IT IN A DRAWER
○ FACES IT OUTWARDS ON HIS DESK
○ LIES IT FACE DOWN
○ SMASHES IT ON THE FLOOR

30. 'How many times I looked the other way because of your sweet smile?' Changretta's wife is horrified to see Arthur and John approach. They are disobeying Tommy's orders by not shooting her. How does she try to stop them taking Vicente?

○ BLOCKS THEIR PATH
○ WRAPS HER ARMS AROUND HIM
○ FALLS TO HER KNEES
○ GRABS ARTHUR'S HANDS

31. As Vicente surrenders, led away by Arthur, John is left to offer a little consolation to his distraught wife. 'America,' he says. _____ Fill in the blank.

○ '... A CHANCE FOR LIFE.'
○ '... YOUR ONLY CHANCE.'
○ '... AMERICA OR DEATH.'
○ '... A NEW LIFE.'

32. 'I'm going to keep you alive until it gets light.' Tommy faces Vicente in a dark, bare and empty space. Vicente is stripped to his waist and tied to a chair. What is he doing as Tommy addresses him?

○ BEGGING FOR HIS LIFE
○ CURSING THE PEAKY BLINDERS
○ PLEADING WITH TOMMY TO SPARE HIS WIFE
○ RECITING THE LORD'S PRAYER IN ITALIAN

SEASON THREE ▮ EPISODE THREE

171

33. What is the last thing that Tommy wants Vicente to hear, reminding him that his wife will never hear it again?

   O THE BLACKBIRD SINGING
   O THE SKYLARK SINGING
   O THE GOLDFINCH SINGING
   O THE DAWN CHORUS

34. Having detailed the ordeal he plans to put Vicente through, Tommy's nerve wavers. He wheels away to compose himself. What happens next?

   O VICENTE ATTEMPTS TO ESCAPE AND ARTHUR SHOOTS HIM DEAD
   O ARTHUR SHOOTS VICENTE DEAD TO SPARE HIM AND TOMMY FURTHER TORMENT
   O JOHN CUTS VICENTE'S THROAT TO SPARE HIM AND TOMMY FURTHER TORMENT
   O TOMMY TURNS AND SHOOTS VICENTE DEAD

35. John admits that they didn't kill Mrs Changretta, defying Tommy's orders. What is Arthur's reasoning?

   O 'WE'RE BETTER THAN THAT.'
   O 'WE'RE NOT THAT SORT OF MEN.'
   O 'WE'RE NOT MONSTERS.'
   O 'WE NEED TO LIVE WITH OURSELVES, TOO.'

36. Back home, Ada gives Tommy the name of a communist associate – James Monkland – who is receiving information about Tommy's secret government mission and feeding it to the Soviet Embassy. In return, Tommy offers Ada an American post in Shelby Company Ltd. Where would it take her?

   O BOSTON
   O NEW YORK
   O NEW JERSEY
   O PHILADELPHIA

37. Tommy presses Monkland for the name of his informant in the powerful establishment group to which Father Hughes belongs. Tommy refers to them as 'The Economic League, The _____ Committee, The Odd Fellows, Section D.' What is the missing word?

   ○ SURVEILLANCE
   ○ VIGILANCE
   ○ PROTECTION
   ○ DEFENCE

38. Arthur has just stepped out of the shower when Linda breaks the news that she's pregnant. After a moment to take it in, and process what this means, he suggests what drink?

   ○ WHISKEY
   ○ GIN
   ○ TEA
   ○ RUM

39. Thomas visits the Grand Duke, the Grand Duchess and Tatiana as they dine with the MP, Patrick Jarvis, and Father Hughes. He outlines the plan for the armoured vehicle theft before handing a note on a napkin to the Grand Duchess that will ultimately expose Hughes as the informant. What does the note say?

   ○ 'TATIANA MUST LEAVE WITH ME.'
   ○ 'YOU ARE NOT SAFE.'
   ○ 'SAY NOTHING TO HUGHES.'
   ○ 'I HAVE SECRETS.'

SEASON THREE ▮ EPISODE THREE

KILLER QUESTIONS

40. In the kitchen at Tommy's house, when Arthur and John are brooding at being relegated to 'binmen' by their brother, what does Polly ask Finn to fetch?

   ○ WHISKEY
   ○ FRESH BREAD
   ○ CIGARETTES
   ○ FRESH MILK

41. Before being seized by the Peaky Blinders, what class ticket were Vicente Changretta and his wife travelling under?

   ○ VIP
   ○ FIRST CLASS
   ○ STEERAGE PASSENGERS
   ○ THIRD CLASS

42. What is Arthur wearing when Linda tells him she's pregnant?

   ○ A SUIT
   ○ A TOWEL AROUND HIS WAIST
   ○ BOXING SHORTS
   ○ PYJAMAS

1. The episode opens with Tommy and the boys on a hunting party near Arrow House. What is in their rifle sights?

   ○ A HARE
   ○ A STAG
   ○ A FOX
   ○ A DEER

2. Over a fire in a clearing, Tommy summons just his brothers to inform them that their father, Arthur Shelby Snr, has been killed in a bar. In what city did he die?

   ○ LONDON
   ○ BOSTON
   ○ NEW YORK
   ○ DUBLIN

3. The brothers recall one fond memory they had growing up with him. What song does John say he drunkenly sang 'about a hundred times'?

   ○ THE PREACHER AND THE BEAR
   ○ SILVER DAGGER
   ○ A BIRD IN THE GILDED CAGE
   ○ BEDELIA

4. 'So, his name _____,' Tommy says to finish, having consulted with his brothers. Complete the sentence.

   ○ ... HAS NO FURTHER PLACE IN THE FAMILY
   ○ ... DIES
   ○ ... WILL NEVER BE SPOKEN OF AGAIN
   ○ ... BECOMES A MEMORY, AND NOTHING MORE

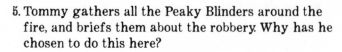

5. Tommy gathers all the Peaky Blinders around the fire, and briefs them about the robbery. Why has he chosen to do this here?

- ○ THERE ARE WORKMEN IN THE HOUSE
- ○ HE DOESN'T TRUST THE MAIDS
- ○ THE STABLE LADS MIGHT CHATTER
- ○ THE GROUNDSMAN HAS FAMILY AT THE VEHICLE FACTORY

6. Polly goes to church to make a confession, where the priest tells her she's come on the wrong day. How does Polly persuade him?

- ○ MAKES A DONATION
- ○ TAKES HIM BY THE ELBOW AND LEADS HIM TO THE BOOTH
- ○ TELL HIM SHE'S A SHELBY
- ○ PRESSES ON HIM THAT IT CAN'T WAIT

7. Polly has been drinking, struggling with her conscience over the death of Major Campbell. She tells the priest about a voice in her head. What does Polly claim the voice calls her?

- ○ KILLER
- ○ MURDERER
- ○ ASSASSIN
- ○ SINNER

8. 'Look it up. Look who did it,' Polly tells the priest in defence of what she considers the just taking of a human life. 'Moses. Samson. _____.' What is the missing name?

- ○ NAPOLEON
- ○ LENIN
- ○ LORD KITCHENER
- ○ HANNIBAL

9. What else does Polly allude to in the confessional?

 ○ CHURCHILL'S HAND IN TOMMY'S SECRET MISSIONS
 ○ A PLOT TO KILL A PRIEST
 ○ THE ARMOURED VEHICLE HEIST
 ○ THE CIRCUMSTANCES BEHIND THE DISAPPEARANCE OF
   VICENTE CHANGRETTA

10. Polly heads for the betting shop, where Esme is complaining about being left to deal with the customers while John and the Shelby boys enjoy a hunt. 'Without men here,' she says, 'they'd be like _____.' Complete the sentence.

 ○ ... RATS IN A SHIP'S HOLD
 ○ ... DOGS PISSING UP THE WALL
 ○ ... COCKS IN A FIGHTING RING
 ○ ... VERMIN RUNNING WILD

11. While Polly's confessional at church brought her little solace, what admission does Lizzie make to her and Esme so there are no secrets?

 ○ SHE'S CHANGED THE LOCK ON THE SAFE TO PROTECT TOMMY
   FROM HIMSELF
 ○ SHE'S SLEEPING WITH TOMMY
 ○ SHE'S MOVED MONEY FROM THE SAFE TO ANOTHER SECURE
   PLACE TO PROTECT THE COMPANY
 ○ SHE'S READ THE LETTER TOMMY RECEIVED ABOUT THE DEATH
   OF THEIR FATHER

12. Tommy shares the plan to steal the armoured cars with his men. Charlie Strong wants to know who would want to do such a thing. What is Tommy's response?

 ○ 'A DEAD MAN.'
 ○ 'A FOOLISH MAN.'
 ○ 'A WEALTHY MAN.'
 ○ 'A MAN WITH NO OTHER CHOICE.'

SEASON THREE ■ EPISODE FOUR

13. '£150,000. Cash, diamonds and sapphires.' The reward is hard to resist as Tommy sells it to his men. What does he propose they do with the majority of it?

- ○ BUILD SEVERAL RACECOURSES
- ○ ACQUIRE PROPERTY IN AMERICA
- ○ OPEN A CASINO AND HOTEL
- ○ PLOUGH IT BACK INTO SMALL HEATH AND LIFT THE PEOPLE OUT OF POVERTY

14. 'Part of the reason for doing this last job,' Tommy tells them, 'is so you'll be set up when you do decide to walk away.' Arthur is uneasy, having already vowed to give up his illegitimate activities. Whom did he make the promise to?

- ○ POLLY
- ○ LINDA
- ○ JOHN
- ○ MRS CHANGRETTA

15. Linda shows up at the betting shop to help out. She offers to make tea and empty ashtrays, but what do her religious beliefs prevent her from doing?

- ○ DEAL WITH CUSTOMERS WHO ARE DRUNK
- ○ HANDLE MONEY OR SLIPS
- ○ DEAL WITH CUSTOMERS WHO SWEAR
- ○ STEP IN TO HALT ANY FIGHTS

16. Linda also brings a message from a female shop steward called Jessie Eden. Among many reasons, why is Jessie encouraging women in the workplace to go on strike on this particular day?

- ○ IT'S WAGES DAY
- ○ IT'S A HOLY DAY
- ○ IT'S THE KING'S BIRTHDAY
- ○ IT'S A SATURDAY

17. The strike is due to take place at 9.00am. Where will the march be heading?

- ○ THE CHAMBERS OF COMMERCE
- ○ THE BULL RING
- ○ THE TOWN HALL
- ○ THE WORKERS' UNION BUILDING

18. 'I'm not in the mood today,' says Polly before downing tools. What does Esme declare?

- ○ 'PRAISE BE!'
- ○ 'AMEN!'
- ○ 'HALLELUJAH!'
- ○ 'THANK YOU, LORD!'

19. The hunting party return to the manor on horseback. Tatiana is waiting for Tommy in his office. What does she request?

- ○ A CHANCE TO STUDY THE FACTORY BLUEPRINT
- ○ SUPPER WITH TOMMY
- ○ PROOF THAT THE PRIEST IS A SOVIET INFORMANT
- ○ EVIDENCE THAT WORKERS WITH COMMUNIST LEANINGS AT THE CAR FACTORY ARE BEING DISMISSED

20. John interrupts to bring news of the strike. According to reports, what has Polly been heard calling for during the march?

- ○ A GENERAL STRIKE
- ○ REVOLUTION
- ○ DOWNFALL OF THE GOVERNMENT
- ○ OVERTHROW OF THE KING

SEASON THREE EPISODE FOUR

21. Much to Tatiana's surprise, Tommy asks John to go outside to Tatiana's Bentley in the drive and 'put a nail in its tyre'. Why?

- ◯ TO REMIND HER THAT HE WILL SEEK RETRIBUTION SHOULD SHE RENEGE ON PAYMENT FOR THE FACTORY HEIST
- ◯ SO SHE WILL HAVE TO STAY THE NIGHT
- ◯ TO SHOW HIS DISPLEASURE THAT SHE'S COME TO HIM UNINVITED
- ◯ TO SIGNAL THAT THERE IS A PRICE TO BE PAID FOR HIS TIME

22. Back at the betting shop, John catches Esme sneaking into the walk-in safe 'to take a tenner'. According to him, what does she need the money for?

- ◯ GAMBLING
- ◯ COCAINE
- ◯ PAYING OFF PERSONAL DEBTS
- ◯ SUPPORTING HER GYPSY KIN

23. 'If you feel cooped up we'll take the wagon, camp out by the ditch.' John knows Esme misses the travelling lifestyle. He proposes buying a big house with enough land to meet her needs. Where is the house?

- ◯ TAMWORTH
- ◯ LICHFIELD
- ◯ CANNOCK
- ◯ TELFORD

24. Tommy sleeps with the Duchess, and a conversation follows about power. In convincing Tommy that she sees through him, Tatiana grabs his gun and a chase ensues through the house. 'You break the law,' she says, 'but _____.' Complete the sentence.

- ◯ ... YOU'RE AFRAID OF THINGS OUT OF YOUR CONTROL
- ◯ ... YOU OBEY THE RULES
- ◯ ... YOU'RE SCARED OF YOURSELF
- ◯ ... POWERLESSNESS FRIGHTENS YOU

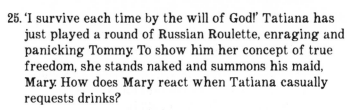

25. 'I survive each time by the will of God!' Tatiana has just played a round of Russian Roulette, enraging and panicking Tommy. To show him her concept of true freedom, she stands naked and summons his maid, Mary. How does Mary react when Tatiana casually requests drinks?

   ○ SHE ASKS TOMMY IF HIS GUEST REQUIRES A DOCTOR
   ○ SHE ASKS IF THEY WOULD LIKE WHISKEY
   ○ SHE TURNS AROUND AND WALKS AWAY
   ○ SHE BOWS HER HEAD AND ASKS TATIANA TO DRESS

26. What does Tatiana claim about a maid who answers the call of her master after midnight?

   ○ SHE'S SCARED OF HIM
   ○ SHE'S PLOTTING TO KILL HIM
   ○ SHE'S IN LOVE WITH HIM
   ○ SHE'S STEALING FROM HIM

27. Tommy follows Tatiana to the master bedroom. What has she found there that belonged to Grace?

   ○ HER WEDDING RING
   ○ HER PERFUME
   ○ HER EARRINGS
   ○ HER LETTERS FROM TOMMY

28. 'From now on, you must do everything that you want.' What has Tatiana just given Tommy permission to do?

   ○ BE FREE FROM HIS GREATEST FEAR
   ○ FALL IN LOVE WITH HER
   ○ KILL THE PRIEST
   ○ MOVE ON FROM THE DEATH OF GRACE

SEASON THREE ▮ EPISODE FOUR

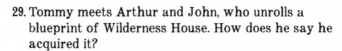

29. Tommy meets Arthur and John, who unrolls a blueprint of Wilderness House. How does he say he acquired it?

- ○ HE STOLE IT FROM THE COUNCIL OFFICES
- ○ ADA USED HER SCHOLAR'S PASS AT THE BRITISH LIBRARY
- ○ HE PAID A HOUSE SERVANT TO LOCATE IT
- ○ POLLY CALLED ON A PAST LOVER AT A SURVEYOR'S OFFICE

30. From the story Tatiana shared about her uncle, Tommy believes the Russians stash the family jewels in a cellar under the house. What does the blueprint reveal?

- ○ A SECRET TUNNEL TO THE CELLAR FROM THE NEIGHBOURING PROPERTY
- ○ A SECRET TUNNEL TO THE CELLAR FROM THE OTHER SIDE OF THE RIVER
- ○ A SECRET TUNNEL TO THE CELLAR FROM THE RIVER AT LOW TIDE
- ○ A SECRET TUNNEL TO THE CELLAR FROM THE GROUNDS

31. How does Tommy plan to gather more information about the family?

- ○ PURSUING A ROMANCE WITH TATIANA
- ○ PLANTING A RUSSIAN-SPEAKING ASSOCIATE INSIDE THE HOUSE AS A STAFF MEMBER
- ○ BLACKMAILING THE VIOLINIST TO SUBMIT DAILY REPORTS ON THEIR MOVEMENTS
- ○ INVITING THE GRAND DUKE TO DINNER AND GETTING HIM DRUNK

32. Lizzie knocks to inform Tommy that the women are ready to meet him to discuss their working conditions. How does she refer to them collectively?

- ○ THE UNION OF WOMEN BOOKMAKERS
- ○ THE UNITED FRONT OF FEMALE BOOKMAKERS AND ASSOCIATED TRADES
- ○ THE EXECUTIVE COMMITTEE OF THE UNION OF BOOKIES AND ALLIED TRADES
- ○ THE CONFEDERATION OF WOMEN IN GAMBLING SERVICES

33. Tommy is interested in knowing more about Jessie Eden, the female shop steward. What is Polly's view of her?

- ○ SHE'S TOO SOFT
- ○ SHE'S TOO QUIET
- ○ SHE'S TOO WELL SPOKEN
- ○ SHE LACKS AMBITION

34. Esme reveals that the women know Tommy is planning an armoured car robbery. How did they find out?

- ○ JOHN TOLD ESME
- ○ ARTHUR CONFIDED IN LINDA
- ○ CHARLIE STRONG GOT DRUNK AND TOLD THE GARRISON BARMAN
- ○ POLLY WORKED IT OUT FOR HERSELF

35. Who tips off Father Hughes that the Shelbys plan to kill him?

- ○ THE GRAND DUCHESS
- ○ THE PRIEST WHO HEARD POLLY'S CONFESSION
- ○ TATIANA
- ○ THE GRAND DUKE

36. 'No man is good enough.' Portrait artist Ruben Oliver identifies the expression on Polly's face that he wants to capture. He even sums it up in one word. What is it?

- ○ IMPOSING
- ○ IMPERIOUS
- ○ DETACHED
- ○ ABSOLUTE

SEASON THREE ▮ EPISODE FOUR

37. 'It's part of a bigger picture.' Tommy tracks Father Hughes to a village fete, only to be ambushed and savagely beaten by the priest's men. How do they take him away for an audience with Hughes and Jarvis?

   ◌ BY AMBULANCE
   ◌ BY CAR
   ◌ BY TRUCK
   ◌ BY HORSE AND CART

38. 'We have people in your life.' Hughes tells Tommy he's been feeding information to the Soviet Embassy with establishment consent, and must apologise to the Duke and Duchess or his son will be taken. What does Tommy do on reaching home?

   ◌ APPEALS TO WINSTON CHURCHILL FOR HELP
   ◌ PLACES HIS SON, CHARLES, IN LINDA AND ARTHUR'S CARE
   ◌ SACKS ALL THE FORMER SOLDIERS ON HIS STAFF
   ◌ ASSIGNS JOHN TO WATCH OVER CHARLES

39. 'My family are the ones to be sacrificed if you decide to blow up the train.' Having carried out Hughes's instructions, despite horrific injuries, Tommy staggers to Ada's townhouse and confesses all to a Soviet diplomat. The establishment are feeding them information so they commit a violent act on British soil to stop the robbery. Why?

   ◌ TO FORCE THE BRITISH GOVERNMENT TO BREAK OFF DIPLOMATIC RELATIONS
   ◌ TO INCITE A CONFLICT BETWEEN RUSSIA AND GREAT BRITAIN
   ◌ TO CREATE AN INTERNATIONAL DISTRACTION FROM UNPOPULAR DOMESTIC POLICIES
   ◌ TO INCREASE LEVERAGE IN TRADE NEGOTIATIONS

KILLER QUESTIONS

40. When Polly forgets the combination to the walk-in safe, Lizzie is on hand to remind her. What is it?

   ○ 22-2-29
   ○ 24-8-22
   ○ 20-6-25
   ○ 21-3-26

41. When Linda surprises Polly and Esme at the betting shop, offering to help out while the boys are on the shoot, what home-made drink does she bring in a basket to share?

   ○ ELDERFLOWER CORDIAL
   ○ LEMONADE
   ○ A FLASK OF TEA
   ○ GRAPE SODA

42. Lying half-conscious on the stairs at Ada's townhouse, Tommy mumbles that although his vision has failed he can see someone. Who?

   ○ VICENTE CHANGRETTA
   ○ HIS FATHER
   ○ FREDDIE THORNE
   ○ HIS WIFE

1. Tommy lies in a hospital bed, heavily medicated and experiencing strange dreams. What part of his body is caged in a brace?

   ○ LEG
   ○ ARM
   ○ CHEST
   ○ HEAD

2. During his long convalescence, Michael visits Tommy in hospital. Why does he ask if he can be the one to shoot Father Hughes?

   ○ AS REVENGE FOR TOMMY'S BEATING
   ○ TO PROTECT TOMMY'S SON, CHARLES, FROM FURTHER THREAT
   ○ BECAUSE HUGHES ABUSED MICHAEL AS A BOY
   ○ TO PROTECT ADA FROM FURTHER THREAT

3. How much time passes before Tommy is finally discharged home?

   ○ TWO MONTHS
   ○ THREE MONTHS
   ○ FOUR MONTHS
   ○ FIVE MONTHS

4. In a bid to return to form, what does Tommy pour down the sink?

   ○ WHISKEY
   ○ MORPHINE
   ○ RUM
   ○ LAUDANUM

5. Mary, the housekeeper, serves breakfast for Tommy, who dines alone at the end of his long banqueting table. What kind of eggs has she prepared for him?

   ○ POACHED
   ○ SCRAMBLED
   ○ BOILED
   ○ OMELETTE

6. Working with the Soviets, so they have no need to intervene during the heist to stop it, what do the Peaky Blinders remove from each of the armoured cars in the factory?

○ STARTER MOTOR
○ BATTERY
○ ALTERNATOR
○ FIRING PIN

7. 'I'm surrounded by maids and booze and food.' Johnny Dogs has made himself at home at Arrow House. Tommy points to a treeline that forms the perimeter of his grounds and calls it 'The border between Birmingham and _____.' Fill in the blank.

○ ... HEAVEN
○ ... PARADISE
○ ... SAFETY
○ ... PEACE

8. Tommy asks Johnny to set up camp with the Lees on land he's purchased as part of his tunnelling plans to access Wilderness House. Where is the land?

○ BEHIND THE GATEHOUSE
○ ON THE OPPOSITE SIDE OF THE RIVER
○ BESIDE THE TRADE ENTRANCE
○ ON THE OPPOSITE SIDE OF THE STREET

9. Alfie visits Tommy. In conversation, what does Tommy admit that he now relies upon as a result of his head injury?

○ A WALKING CANE
○ READING GLASSES
○ AN EAR TRUMPET
○ DARKENED GLASSES

10. In the kitchen, Michael has just told Johnny, Arthur and John that Charlotte, the young heiress he's been seeing, is pregnant. What's the main option he's considering?

    ○ GETTING MARRIED
    ○ TELLING POLLY
    ○ STOPPING CHARLOTTE FROM TELLING HER PARENTS
    ○ SEEKING AN ABORTION

11. 'Arthur, Shalom!' Tommy summons his brothers to join him and Alfie in the study. What is Arthur's first reaction on seeing the Jewish gang leader?

    ○ HE WALKS OUT
    ○ HE TAKES A SWING AT ALFIE
    ○ HE DRAWS HIS GUN
    ○ HE SPITS AT HIS FEET

12. 'Whatever happened between us back then, that was business.' Alfie persists and leads Arthur to a seat so that he can apologise for attempting to kill him. What physical gesture of conciliation does Alfie make throughout?

    ○ HE RESTS AN ARM AROUND ARTHUR
    ○ HE CLASPS ARTHUR'S HAND WITH BOTH HIS HANDS
    ○ HE PATS HIM ON THE KNEE
    ○ HE SQUEEZES HIS SHOULDER

13. 'I am Old Testament.' Arthur is struggling to hold back as Alfie gently taunts him for his new-found religious beliefs. What does Arthur reach for as if to use as a weapon?

    ○ A CRYSTAL DECANTER
    ○ A GLASS ASHTRAY
    ○ A DESK STATUE
    ○ A FIRE POKER

14. Tommy plans to rob the Russian exiles as he believes they'll renege on the deal to pay him for the armoured car heist. Why has he invited Alfie to discuss the plan to break into the treasury?

    ○ ALFIE HAS TWO DOZEN MEN AT HIS DISPOSAL
    ○ HE'S NEEDED TO ASSESS WHAT'S STORED INSIDE
    ○ ALFIE CONTROLS THE RIVER, AND TOMMY NEEDS HIS PERMISSION TO DIG UNDERNEATH
    ○ ALFIE ONCE SERVED AS A JEWEL BROKER FOR THE DUKE AND DUCHESS

15. 'Just remember they're fucking insane, and dangerous, and drunk on stuff we've never heard of.' Tommy arrives at Wilderness Hall with John and Arthur to select enough jewels to cover payment for the robbery. What do the Russian exiles station outside as a security measure?

    ○ A PRIVATE REGIMENT OF BRITISH MERCENARIES
    ○ A DETAIL OF ARMED COSSACKS
    ○ A SMALL TANK ON THE LAWN
    ○ MEN HIRED FROM MR SABINI'S MOB

16. Inside – as a security measure and because Tommy has already been through the process – why are John and Arthur expected to strip naked for the Duchess and Tatiana?

    ○ THE WOMEN WISH TO ASSESS THE PHYSICAL STATURE OF THE MEN EXPECTED TO CARRY OUT THE ROBBERY
    ○ TO CHECK FOR SIGNS OF ILLNESS OR DISEASE
    ○ TO CHECK FOR RUSSIAN TATTOOS THAT WOULD MARK THEM OUT AS ENEMIES
    ○ TO TEST HOW THE MEN REACT WHEN STRIPPED OF THEIR DIGNITY

SEASON THREE EPISODE FIVE

17. What item of clothing does Arthur keep on throughout the inspection?

   ○ HIS UNDERWEAR
   ○ HIS SHIRT
   ○ HIS SOCKS
   ○ HIS CAP

18. Polly and Michael visit Ada's townhouse so she can sign legal documents bringing her back into the family business. What is her new role?

   ○ DIRECTOR OF NEW BUSINESS
   ○ HEAD OF PROPERTY & ACQUISITIONS
   ○ SHELBY COMPANY LIMITED AMERICAN BUREAU CHIEF
   ○ EXPORT MANAGER

19. Michael presses to excuse himself from the table while she signs the document. In the hall he makes a phone call under an assumed surname. What is it?

   ○ WHITE
   ○ BARKER
   ○ SMITH
   ○ TURNER

20. Rattled at having made his call, Michael retires early to bed. Which bedroom has Ada given him?

   ○ THE ROOM BESIDE ADA'S
   ○ THE ROOM NEXT TO KARL'S
   ○ THE ATTIC ROOM
   ○ THE LODGER'S QUARTERS, AS HE'S AWAY

21. 'He's like a tiny bird pecking at me, and I think he's given up on me.' Polly leaves Ada to visit Ruben. On what pretext has he invited her round?

   ○ HE'S MISSING HER COMPANY
   ○ HER PORTRAIT IS FINISHED
   ○ HE HAS FINISHING TOUCHES TO MAKE TO THE PAINTING
   ○ HE'S HOSTING A DINNER PARTY

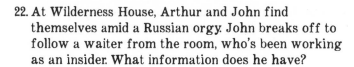

22. At Wilderness House, Arthur and John find themselves amid a Russian orgy. John breaks off to follow a waiter from the room, who's been working as an insider. What information does he have?

○ THE DUKE AND DUCHESS PLAN TO VANISH WITH THE JEWELS DURING THE ROBBERY
○ SPECIAL BRANCH HAVE THEIR OWN SPY IN THE HOUSEHOLD STAFF
○ TATIANA IS PLOTTING TO KIDNAP CHARLES SO TOMMY GOES THROUGH WITH THE PLAN
○ THE RUSSIAN EXILES INTEND TO KILL THE SHELBY BROTHERS DURING THE THEFT

23. Tatiana escorts Tommy to the Treasury so he can inspect the jewels. In sharing the 200-year-old history of the building with him, what reason does she give for the need for this stronghold?

○ IN CASE OF A PEOPLE'S UPRISING
○ IN CASE OF A FRENCH INVASION
○ IN CASE THE BUILDING COLLAPSES
○ IN CASE OF FIRE

24. Inside, the Duke and Duchess are waiting for Tommy, along with Alfie Solomons. 'The only jeweller that I trust in London.' What precaution have the Russian exiles taken?

○ HIS WRISTS ARE BOUND
○ HE IS WEARING A HOOD OVER HIS HEAD
○ HE IS FLANKED BY COSSACK SOLDIERS
○ THE DUKE HOLDS A PISTOL TO HIS NECK

25. Why is Alfie so hostile to the Russian exiles?

○ BECAUSE MANY ITEMS ARE STOLEN AND OF JEWISH ORIGIN
○ HIS MOTHER WAS PERSECUTED BY THE RUSSIAN RULING CLASS
○ BECAUSE THEY HOARDED THEIR RICHES RATHER THAN BRINGING THEM TO THE LONDON MARKET
○ HIS FATHER WAS DRIVEN FROM HIS HOME BY RUSSIAN ROYALTY

SEASON THREE ▮ EPISODE FIVE

26. Tatiana invites Alfie to select items of jewellery that will serve as a reward for the robbery. What is the agreed value?

- ○ £15,000
- ○ £50,000
- ○ £70,000
- ○ £140,000

27. As he gathers items, what fairy tale name does Alfie use to address the Duke?

- ○ PRINCE CHARMING
- ○ SINBAD
- ○ RUMPELSTILTSKIN
- ○ ALI BABA

28. Tommy and Alfie insist that the Russians include a Fabergé egg to bring the haul to the full value. Tatiana agrees, and presents them with one. Where does she claim to have brought it from?

- ○ ROSTOV-ON-DON
- ○ ODESA
- ○ CRIMEA
- ○ KRASHNODAR

29. 'I demand absolute honesty.' Ruben presents Polly with her portrait. She's overwhelmed, seeing herself anew, but words fail her. Before finally falling for the artist's charms, what does she tell him?

- ○ 'IT'S ME.'
- ○ 'IT'S GOOD.'
- ○ 'IT'S MORE THAN ME.'
- ○ 'WHAT DO YOU SEE IN ME?'

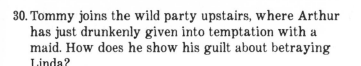

30. Tommy joins the wild party upstairs, where Arthur has just drunkenly given into temptation with a maid. How does he show his guilt about betraying Linda?

- O MUTTERS A PRAYER
- O MUTTERS AN APOLOGY TO HIS WIFE
- O TELLS HIMSELF TO WALK AWAY
- O REMOVES HIS WEDDING RING

31. Tatiana leads Tommy to a bedroom, where she talks him into submitting to erotic asphyxiation. What happens as he approaches unconsciousness?

- O HE KICKS HER AWAY
- O HE SEES A VISION OF GRACE
- O HE SEES GERMAN TUNNELLERS COME THROUGH THE WALL
- O SHE RELEASES HIM FROM HER GRIP

32. Across at Ruben's house, after sleeping with him, what does Polly suggest he should call her painting?

- O THE GREAT SEDUCTION
- O BOW DOWN TO ME
- O FUCK THEM ALL
- O GO TO HELL

33. 'Do you want to hear the wildest confession of them all?' Polly asks as they lie before her portrait. What does she tell him?

- O HER NEPHEWS WOULD TAKE OUT RUBEN'S EYES IF THEY KNEW HE HAD SEDUCED HER
- O SHE HAS KILLED A POLICEMAN
- O THE PARISH REMOVED HER CHILDREN FROM HER
- O HER FAMILY ARE PLOTTING TO STEAL ARMOURED CARS FOR THE STATE

SEASON THREE ■ EPISODE FIVE

34. 'We've had worse nights.' Tommy, Arthur and John leave Wilderness Hall at dawn. John taunts Arthur by telling him that there can be no secrets from Linda. Who does he claim will tell her everything?

   ○ ALFIE SOLOMONS
   ○ ARTHUR
   ○ TOMMY
   ○ TATIANA

35. A reunion takes place at Charlie Strong's yard between Tommy, his brothers and their fellow tunnellers from the war, 'The Tipton Clay Kickers'. According to Arthur, how many are left from the original band of 50?

   ○ 7
   ○ 10
   ○ 20
   ○ 22

36. Tommy shares the plan to rob the Armoury. Over the blueprint of Wilderness Hall, he explains to William Letso and his men that there are three cellars in total, 'wine, kitchen, _____'. Fill in the blank.

   ○ ... TOOLS
   ○ ... SEPTIC
   ○ ... STORAGE
   ○ ... STAFF

37. Polly finds the key for Michael's office. She's looking for an explanation as to why he's been so 'sour' lately, only to discover a bullet with Father Hughes's name inscribed across it. What is the bullet hidden inside?

   ○ A MATCHBOX
   ○ A BOX OF PAPERCLIPS
   ○ A JEWELLERY BOX
   ○ AN EMPTY INK BOTTLE

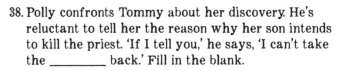
38. Polly confronts Tommy about her discovery. He's
reluctant to tell her the reason why her son intends
to kill the priest. 'If I tell you,' he says, 'I can't take
the _____ back.' Fill in the blank.

U ... KNOWLEDGE
U ... GUILT
U ... HORROR
U ... INFORMATION

39. Polly tells Tommy that if he allows Michael to pull
the trigger, there will be consequences. What does
she threaten to do?

U EXPOSE THE PLAN TO STEAL THE ARMOURED CARS
U BRING DOWN THE ORGANISATION
U DISASSOCIATE HERSELF FROM THE FAMILY
U MOVE AWAY AND TAKE MICHAEL WITH HER

SEASON THREE ■ EPISODE FIVE

KILLER QUESTIONS

SEASON THREE ▦ EPISODE FIVE

40. Tommy experiences vivid hallucinations on the medication he's been taking for his head injuries. He tells his maid, Mary, that he's seen her reading from the Bible naked at his bedside. What book does he say she's selected?

    ○ JUDGES
    ○ LEVITICUS
    ○ NUMBERS
    ○ EZEKIEL

41. Johnny Dogs is drinking in Tommy's staff kitchen when John and Arthur discuss Michael's issue with Charlotte. The bottle sits beside him. What is it?

    ○ WHISKEY
    ○ RUM
    ○ GIN
    ○ VODKA

42. When Tatiana places her hands around Tommy's neck, she explains that back home a priest performed the same move to induce a dangerous, ecstatic state. She describes it as 'a Siberian prayer'. What was it called?

    ○ KAYNYN
    ○ STRANNICK
    ○ ANANDA
    ○ KHLYSTY

1. The family arrive outside the building that houses Tommy's new charitable venture. What is the name on the sign at the entrance?

   ○ THE GRACE SHELBY INSTITUTE FOR ORPHANED CHILDREN
   ○ THE GRACE SHELBY SCHOOL FOR THE POOR
   ○ THE GRACE SHELBY FOUNDATION
   ○ THE GRACE SHELBY MEMORIAL SHELTER

2. What kind of hat is Tommy wearing?

   ○ FLAT CAP
   ○ BOWLER
   ○ FEDORA
   ○ HOMBURG

3. 'These children are now _____.' Tommy addresses the audience gathered to mark the opening. Fill in the blank.

   ○ ... THRIVING
   ○ ... PROTECTED
   ○ ... SAFE
   ○ ... RESCUED

4. Tommy also promises that in their care the children won't be 'shipped away' to where?

   ○ FOREIGN SHORES
   ○ THE COLONIES
   ○ ACROSS THE EMPIRE
   ○ DISTANT LANDS

5. Father Hughes makes an unwelcome appearance. He shows Tommy that he even has his own keys. What has he given himself as part of their 'broader arrangement'?

   ○ A SEAT ON THE BOARD OF GOVERNORS
   ○ AN OFFICE
   ○ A TEACHING POST
   ○ A COPY OF THE REGISTER

SEASON THREE ▮ EPISODE SIX

6. Hughes also informs Tommy that the operation to steal the armoured cars is imminent. When will he be expected to follow orders?

- ○ AFTER DARK
- ○ WITHIN THE NEXT TWENTY-FOUR HOURS
- ○ IN TWO DAYS' TIME
- ○ WITHIN THE WEEK

7. During the reception, John reports that there has been a delay with the tunnelling under the river. What have the men encountered?

- ○ HEAVY CLAY
- ○ A SEAM OF ROCK
- ○ LEAKAGE
- ○ A SHORTAGE OF LUMBER FOR SHORING

8. With the reception in full swing, what is the cast-iron model that the members of the Moseley War Widows Institute present to Tommy?

- ○ A BUST OF TOMMY
- ○ A MODEL OF TOMMY'S HORSE
- ○ A BUST OF GRACE
- ○ A MINIATURE REPRODUCTION OF THE BUILDING

9. Who takes Charles from Tommy and then vanishes with him?

- ○ FATHER HUGHES
- ○ A NURSE
- ○ MP PATRICK JARVIS
- ○ A POLICE OFFICER

10. As a frantic search of the building and grounds begins, Tommy scrambles to react. With Arthur and John covering the roads, what junction does he order Michael to cover?

   ○ COVENTRY ROAD
   ○ MAYPOLE
   ○ STRATFORD ROAD
   ○ SELLY OAK

11. 'We did warn you that your son would be in danger if you deviated from the plan.' Father Hughes reveals that he knows Tommy has gone behind their backs to stop the Soviets from blowing up the train. Where does this meeting take place?

   ○ OUTSIDE IN A THUNDERSTORM
   ○ OVER THE PHONE
   ○ INSIDE A CAR PARKED OUTSIDE THE OFFICE
   ○ SHELTERING IN A DOORWAY

12. 'It's always been about the explosion ... the bang. The outrage.' With Charles in his hands, Hughes expects Tommy to blow up the train himself. What does he give him to scatter in the wreckage to implicate the Soviets?

   ○ SOVIET BOMB PARTS
   ○ NOTES AND FRAGMENTS
   ○ CHARRED ROUBLES
   ○ RUSSIAN CIGARETTE STUBS

13. 'Our friends at _____ and The Daily Mail will do the rest,' the priest says to finish. What other newspaper will publicise the explosion, leading to the British Government severing ties with Russia?

   ○ THE EVENING STANDARD
   ○ THE TIMES
   ○ THE DAILY EXPRESS
   ○ THE DAILY TELEGRAPH

SEASON THREE ▦ EPISODE SIX

14. When Father Hughes discloses that he also knows about the tunnel, he specifically names the 1898 Fabergé egg that Tommy's men plan to steal. What is the name?

   ○ APPLE BLOSSOM
   ○ ROSE TRELLIS
   ○ LILY OF THE VALLEY
   ○ CHANTICLEER

15. If Tommy is to see Charles alive again, what is the final demand Hughes places on him?

   ○ TO HAND OVER THE FABERGÉ EGG AND ALL THE STOLEN JEWELS
   ○ TO KILL TATIANA
   ○ TO BOOBY-TRAP THE ARMOURY BEFORE THEY LEAVE
   ○ TO KILL THE DUKE AND DUCHESS

16. When Tommy returns to the office, why is Esme absent?

   ○ SHE'S RECRUITING THE LEE FAMILY TO HELP SEARCH FOR CHARLES
   ○ HER WATERS HAVE BROKEN
   ○ SHE HAS ACCOMPANIED MICHAEL TO THE JUNCTION
   ○ SHE HAS SUFFERED A DIZZY SPELL

17. Desperate to find out who has informed Hughes, Tommy demands to know who has spoken about the plan outside the family. Why is Michael in the clear?

   ○ TOMMY HASN'T TOLD HIM THAT HE NOTIFIED THE SOVIET EMBASSY OF THE PLAN
   ○ TOMMY NEVER MENTIONED THE EXISTENCE OF THE FABERGÉ EGG TO HIM
   ○ TOMMY KNOWS THAT MICHAEL'S ONLY INTEREST IN HUGHES IS TO KILL HIM
   ○ TOMMY DIDN'T TELL HIM THAT THE TUNNELLING WORK HAS BEGUN

18. 'I need 50 sticks of BSA dynamite, 300 yards of cable and six _____.' What is the final item Tommy requires from John and Arthur to blow up the train?

○ PRIMERS
○ GRENADES
○ DETONATORS
○ TRIP SWITCHES

19. Distraught, Polly slashes her portrait with a knife. Tommy has 'done the odds' on who is leaking information to Father Hughes, and pointed a finger at Ruben. According to him, what are the chances that the artist is responsible?

○ 5:1
○ EVENS
○ 2:1
○ 3:1

20. Tommy arranges a meeting with Alfie, paying him to supply a list of all the customers who would buy a Fabergé egg for their wives. On reading the list, which he'd already acquired from other London jewellers, how does he know that Alfie is the informant?

○ ANOTHER JEWELLER HAS POINTED THE FINGER AT HIM
○ HE'S LEFT ONE NAME OFF THE LIST TO PROTECT HIM
○ HE'S ADDED A FALSE NAME
○ HE KNOWS THAT ALFIE IS PLANNING TO VANISH WITH THE EGG

21. Tommy levels a gun at Alfie, just as Alfie's minder takes aim at Tommy. How does the minder end up with a bullet in his head?

○ POLLY SHOOTS HIM
○ MICHAEL SHOOTS HIM
○ ARTHUR SHOOTS HIM
○ ALFIE SHOOTS HIM

SEASON THREE ▮ EPISODE SIX

22. 'Why didn't you come?' Ruben visits the offices of Shelby Company Ltd, only to find himself staring down the barrel of Polly's gun. She'd read his absence as guilt, only to melt into his arms. What reason does Polly give for slashing the portrait?

   ○ SHE NO LONGER RECOGNISES HERSELF
   ○ SHE DOESN'T DESERVE TO BE IMMORTALISED ON CANVAS
   ○ SHE LOOKS TOO SURE OF HERSELF
   ○ SHE LOOKS FALSE

23. The prime suspect is bundled into a cell where John and Arthur are waiting. How do they extract the information they need?

   ○ PREPARE TO HANG HIM
   ○ THREATEN TO CUT HIS EYES OUT
   ○ SLICE OFF HIS EAR
   ○ HOLD A GUN TO HIS HEAD

24. As Tommy races to help dig the tunnel in time, Michael meets Arthur and Tommy. They hand him the address where Hughes is believed to be holding Charles. Arthur offers Michael his gun, which he declines as he has his own weapon holstered. What model is the gun he turns down?

   ○ KOLIBRI
   ○ BROWNING
   ○ COLT
   ○ SMITH & WESSON

25. Frantically, Tommy picks and shovels at the tunnel head. A cry goes up that one of the clay kickers 'has got the shakes', which was a hazard for World War I tunnellers. What's caused it?

   ○ LACK OF FOOD
   ○ OVERHEATING
   ○ CARBON MONOXIDE POISONING
   ○ CLAUSTROPHOBIA

SEASON THREE ▮▮ EPISODE SIX

26. As the train couples with the trucks at the factory carrying the armoured cars, and the Peaky Blinders gather in the shadows, why do John and Arthur volunteer themselves to rig the bomb on the tracks and detonate it?

   ○ THEY CAN'T TRUST ANYONE ELSE
   ○ THEY PICKED THE MEN ON BOARD WHO WILL PERISH IN THE EXPLOSION
   ○ THE MISSION IS POTENTIALLY FATAL
   ○ IF CAUGHT, THEY WILL HANG

27. Moments before Tommy presses ahead with the final push to break into the armoury, one of the clay kickers warns him the tunnel is in danger of collapse. What reason does he give?

   ○ THEY'RE NOT DEEP ENOUGH UNDER THE RIVERBED
   ○ IT'S TOO WET
   ○ IT'S FLOODING
   ○ IT'S TOO LONG

28. Father Hughes overpowers Michael, who had held him at gunpoint, and a desperate fight ensues. What weapon does Michael grab to regain the advantage?

   ○ A BRICK
   ○ A RAZOR
   ○ A GUN
   ○ A METAL TRAY

29. 'Who wants to go to heaven, eh?' With the train approaching, Arthur prepares to detonate the bomb. John offers to do it for him. What reason does Arthur give for taking responsibility?

   ○ AS THE ELDEST, IT FALLS TO HIM TO DO IT
   ○ ARTHUR TOLD TOMMY HE WOULD DO IT
   ○ ARTHUR SEES IT AS A MEANS OF MOVING ON FROM HIS WORLD WAR I EXPERIENCES
   ○ HE DOESN'T WANT JOHN TO SUFFER AS HE HAS SINCE THE WAR

SEASON THREE ▮ EPISODE SIX

SEASON THREE ▣ EPISODE SIX

30. Finn hurtles out of the darkness, desperate to stop Arthur and John from blowing up the train as it departs. Why?

   ○ A CRISIS OF CONSCIENCE
   ○ CHARLIE IS SAFE
   ○ THE STOKER ON BOARD IS A SCHOOL FRIEND
   ○ ANOTHER LOCOMOTIVE IS INBOUND

31. 'You go to bed. Good boy!' With the jewels in his possession, an exhausted Tommy stops at a phone box and calls the office to hear his son. What does he do on closing the call?

   ○ PRAYS
   ○ WEEPS
   ○ RAGES
   ○ TALKS TO GRACE

32. On a country lane at dawn, Tommy presents Tatiana with the stolen jewels. As part of a plan hatched between them before the heist, she takes the haul in exchange for money. Who is the man accompanying her?

   ○ A BODYGUARD
   ○ A RUSSIAN COSSACK
   ○ A FRENCH JEWELLER
   ○ A LOVER

33. What does Tommy require from her to complete the deal?

   ○ TATIANA MUST PROVIDE AN ALIBI TO COVER HIS TIME IN THE TUNNEL
   ○ HER SIGNATURE ON A CONTRACT TO LEGITIMISE THE SALE
   ○ A PROMISE THAT SHE'LL NEVER MAKE CONTACT WITH HIM AGAIN
   ○ EVIDENCE THAT THE DUKE AND DUCHESS HAVE FLED THE COUNTRY

34. Before her final surprise, one that causes Tommy to wheel around with his gun drawn, where does Tatiana say that she is heading with the jewels?

U MONACO
U BERLIN
U BUCHAREST
U VIENNA

35. 'Before I begin, I want to let you know I made a mistake.' Tommy summons the wider family to his drawing room. There, he has laid out cash from the robbery for distribution. He apologises to Arthur for doubting Linda. How much does he add to her share by way of apology?

U £2,000
U £3,000
U £4,000
U £6,000

36. Tommy turns to Esme and John, who must share the burden of taking innocent lives with his eldest brother. 'I hope the house you buy with this can become a place of _____,' he says, 'perhaps redemption.' Fill in the blank.

U ... FORGIVENESS
U ... ATONEMENT
U ... CONTEMPLATION
U ... PEACE

37. Lizzie rejects her cut, effectively paying for her company following Grace's death. Who else takes a stand about what the money represents?

U POLLY
U MICHAEL
U CURLY
U JOHNNY DOGS

SEASON THREE ▮ EPISODE SIX

38. Arthur rises to leave. He has a passage to America with Linda, but Tommy stops him in his tracks because the police have issued warrants for arrest. Who issued the warrants?

- ○ THE METROPOLITAN POLICE CHIEF
- ○ THE CHIEF CONSTABLE OF BIRMINGHAM
- ○ THE SUPERINTENDENT OF WARWICKSHIRE
- ○ SERGEANT MOSS

39. 'I've made a deal with people even more powerful than our enemies.' As the police arrest the family amid chaotic scenes, Tommy looks on impassively. Who spits on him as she is led away?

- ○ ESME
- ○ POLLY
- ○ LINDA
- ○ LIZZIE

KILLER QUESTIONS

40. In the formal family photograph taken on the steps outside the Shelby Institute, who is the only one smoking?

- ○ MICHAEL
- ○ TOMMY
- ○ ARTHUR
- ○ FINN

41. What is the name of the hymn that Polly invites the gathering to sing at the charity opening ceremony?

- ○ MY HOPE IS BUILT ON NOTHING LESS
- ○ FORTH IN THY NAME, O LORD
- ○ IMMORTAL, INVISIBLE
- ○ COME, YE THANKFUL PEOPLE, COME

42. When Sergeant Moss receives a telephone tip-off and circles the name of the individual who knows the whereabouts of Tommy's son, what is the name at the top of the list?

- ○ GILBERT PALMER
- ○ LORD TRISTAN ALDAR
- ○ GAVIN MONTGOMERY
- ○ STANLEY CHAPMAN

SEASON THREE ▮ EPISODE SIX

SEASON FOUR

1. In jail awaiting an appeal, Michael and Arthur are each awoken early by the ominous appearance of a guard and a priest. The noose awaits them. Desperately, Michael reminds them a hearing is scheduled but isn't due to begin until which month?

   ○ OCTOBER
   ○ JANUARY
   ○ JULY
   ○ MARCH

2. What is the name of the lawyer that Michael demands to see?

   ○ MR PATRICK
   ○ MR ABRAHAM
   ○ MR ELLIOTT
   ○ MR KEGLEY

3. How many police officers does it take to drag John from his cell?

   ○ NONE, HE LEAVES CALMLY
   ○ TWO
   ○ FOUR
   ○ SIX

4. When the officers come for Polly in her cell, what is she doing?

   ○ READING THE BIBLE
   ○ ROLLING A CIGARETTE
   ○ SLEEPING
   ○ PACING

5. As Polly, Michael, Arthur and John face hanging, a lawyer hurries through a grand corridor. Where is he?

   ○ THE HOUSES OF PARLIAMENT
   ○ 10 DOWNING STREET
   ○ WINDSOR CASTLE
   ○ BUCKINGHAM PALACE

6. A file in the lawyer's possession details the offences the Shelbys and the Grays have committed. What are they?

○ RACKETEERING
○ ARSON AND ROBBERY
○ FRAUD
○ MURDER AND SEDITION

7. The lawyer also has a letter from King George to Grand Duke Romanov, incriminating him in the conspiracy to break off relations with the Soviets using the armoured car robbery. How did the letter come into Tommy's possession?

○ HE STOLE IT FROM WILDERNESS HOUSE DURING THE ROBBERY
○ TATIANA PASSED IT TO HIM
○ THE PEAKY BLINDERS VETTED ALL POST ADDRESSED TO ROMANOV
○ ALFIE SOLOMONS STOLE IT DURING THE JEWELLERY VALUATION

8. Polly gasps as the noose is placed around her neck. In another execution room, and from left to right, in what order do the three men stand ready to be hanged?

○ ARTHUR, MICHAEL, JOHN
○ MICHAEL, JOHN, ARTHUR
○ JOHN, ARTHUR, MICHAEL
○ MICHAEL, ARTHUR, JOHN

9. Before the stay of execution comes for them all, which verse do Arthur and John begin to recite?

○ AND THEN THERE WAS SILENCE
○ IN THE BLEAK MIDWINTER
○ HOW GREAT THOU ART
○ I AM STRETCHED ON YOUR GRAVE

10. While Tommy successfully saves his loved ones from the noose, what else does he request in return for burning all evidence implicating the King in the conspiracy?

   ○ £5,000
   ○ IMMUNITY FROM FUTURE PROSECUTION
   ○ AN OBE
   ○ AN AUDIENCE WITH THE KING

11. With Arthur, John, Michael and Polly freed, the story moves forward to what date before Christmas in 1924?

   ○ 15TH DECEMBER
   ○ 19TH DECEMBER
   ○ 21ST DECEMBER
   ○ 23RD DECEMBER

12. Tommy enters a grand hotel. He's smartly dressed, carrying a briefcase and wearing a Homburg hat. What else is different about his appearance?

   ○ HE'S WEARING GLASSES
   ○ HE'S SMOKING A CIGAR
   ○ HE'S WEARING A WRISTWATCH
   ○ HE'S WEARING A BOW TIE

13. What is the name of the hotel?

   ○ THE GRAND HOTEL
   ○ MOOR HALL
   ○ MIDLAND HOTEL
   ○ THE ROYAL HOTEL

SEASON FOUR ▮ EPISODE ONE

14. 'I've wrapped all Charlie's presents and left them in the room.' Lizzy joins Tommy, who has to ask what he's giving his son for Christmas. As well as toy horses and cars, what else has Lizzie chosen on Tommy's behalf?

O DOMINOES
O TOY GUNS
O A TRAIN SET
O CRAYONS

15. In her role as company secretary, where does Lizzie remind Tommy that he needs to be the next day to address a union problem?

O THE SINGER FACTORY
O THE LANCHESTER CAR & VAN FACTORY
O THE BILLINGS MACHINE TOOLS FACTORY
O THE BILSTON FORGINGS & PRESSINGS FACTORY

16. In a bid to reunify the family, still fractured despite the pardon for their crimes, who has invited Tommy to a party to see in the New Year?

O POLLY
O MICHAEL
O JOHN
O ARTHUR

17. Lizzie says that Ada will be attending, having taken time off from her new overseas position in the company. Where has she been working?

O NEW YORK
O BOSTON
O PHILADELPHIA
O NEW JERSEY

18. Having taken solace in a world of 'sex, freedom and whiskey sours', Tommy is reluctant to bury the hatchet. Lizzie seeks to persuade him by mentioning the presence of what, that will help to make everything okay?

- ◯ ALCOHOL
- ◯ BABIES
- ◯ COCAINE
- ◯ A PIANO

19. The next day Tommy enters the factory boardroom. What is Michael doing as he enters?

- ◯ DRINKING WHISKEY
- ◯ SNORTING COCAINE
- ◯ CLOSING A TELEPHONE CALL
- ◯ COUNTING MONEY

20. Michael reports that the union leader, Jessie Eden, is demanding equal pay for the factory's wire-cutters. Michael is annoyed because he believes it could have been sorted with what?

- ◯ A POLITE THREAT
- ◯ A BRIBE AND A DRINK
- ◯ A REMINDER THAT SHE'S DEALING WITH PEAKY BLINDERS
- ◯ A QUIET WORD

21. Tommy is concerned that Michael's mother, Polly, has withdrawn since her brush with death. What observation does he make about the state of her house?

- ◯ WEEDS HAVE TAKEN OVER THE FLOWERBEDS
- ◯ HER CURTAINS ARE CLOSED THROUGHOUT THE DAY
- ◯ SHE DOESN'T ANSWER HER DOOR
- ◯ A DRAINPIPE IS HANGING LOOSE

SEASON FOUR ▮ EPISODE ONE

22. Polly is in a bad way. Since her escape from the noose she's been living in a twilight world and believes she's in touch with the spirit world. 'Inside the _____ loop,' she whispers while pouring herself a drink to wash down tablets. Fill in the blank.

   ○ ... INFERNAL
   ○ ... HEAVENLY
   ○ ... MERRY
   ○ ... WICKED

23. Polly receives a letter. What's the name of the town in her address on the envelope?

   ○ HALESOWEN
   ○ BROMSGROVE
   ○ HARBOURNE
   ○ BOURNVILLE

24. John has settled into his post-prison life as lord of the manor. He's shooting pheasant when Ada visits. What breed of dog accompanies him back to the house to meet her?

   ○ LABRADOR
   ○ SPANIEL
   ○ SETTER
   ○ RETRIEVER

25. Esme is less than happy to see Ada as she drops off presents. Ada's still on the payroll for Shelby Company Ltd and answering to Tommy, whom Esme holds responsible for putting John and the others through a horrific experience. What does she remark about her husband's time in the noose that makes him uncomfortable?

   ○ HE WEPT
   ○ HE SOILED HIMSELF
   ○ HE BEGGED FOR MERCY
   ○ HE PRAYED

26. Linda finds Arthur outside. He's collecting eggs with his son. What is their boy called?

O JOHNNY
O BILLY
O GEORGE
O HARRY

27. Jessie Eden meets Tommy at the factory. She's a formidable woman, who holds her own on workers' rights and has done her research on Tommy's business holdings. Where does she visit before entering the boardroom?

O THE PANEL BEATERS' FLOOR
O THE MEN'S TOILETS
O THE CANTEEN
O THE SWITCHBOARD

28. In negotiating with Tommy, and demanding pay parity, Jessie says that the men in which department are earning 10 shillings more than their female counterparts?

O BOOKKEEPING
O POST ROOM
O WIRE-CUTTING
O UPHOLSTERY

29. Jessie leaves the room threatening a strike. What term of address does Tommy deliberately use to provoke her?

O MY LOVE
O SWEETHEART
O SWEETIE
O HONEY

30. Back at Arrow Hall, Frances the housekeeper brings Tommy the post and enquires how many people will be present for Christmas dinner. Tommy tells her that he's invited Johnny Dogs and members of the Lee tribe. How many places does he request be set out?

- ◯ 6
- ◯ 12
- ◯ 18
- ◯ 27

31. Tommy has also received an envelope, by airmail. He opens it to find a Christmas card from Italian American New York mobster – and eldest son of Vicente – Luca Changretta. What is the ominous print on the card's facing page?

- ◯ A RED HAND
- ◯ A BLACK HAND
- ◯ A BLACK FLAG
- ◯ A BLACK GUN

32. Ada finds Arthur transformed. Living under Linda's rules, he spends his time tending to chickens and volunteering as a driver for those in need. What ambition does he have that his wife doesn't share?

- ◯ RUNNING A TAXI FIRM
- ◯ OPENING A GARAGE
- ◯ DELIVERING MILK
- ◯ LANDSCAPE GARDENING

33. Arthur takes a call from John, who has also received a card from Luca Changretta and urges Arthur to check his post. 'It's Mafia shit,' John tells him. 'The _____ fucking mafia.' Fill in the blank.

- ◯ ... SICILIAN
- ◯ ... ITALIAN
- ◯ ... CALABRIAN
- ◯ ... NEAPOLITAN

34. Once Arthur puts Ada in the picture about what they've just been served in the post, what does she pass him?

   ○ A BOTTLE OF WHISKEY
   ○ A GUN
   ○ HER TELEPHONE NUMBER
   ○ A KNIFE

35. Luca Changretta disembarks from his Atlantic crossing with two associates. The last of the trio to show his passport, what request does the customs officer make of him?

   ○ TAKE A STEP BACK
   ○ REMOVE HIS HAT
   ○ STATE HIS FULL NAME
   ○ CONFIRM HIS PLACE OF BIRTH

36. Ada visits Tommy late on Christmas Eve, and finds him jumpy. He knows that Luca Changretta will have Mafia foot soldiers in the country waiting for him. How many men does he expect the mobster to have at his disposal?

   ○ FIVE
   ○ EIGHT
   ○ TEN
   ○ TWELVE

37. Ada hands him a Christmas present. 'What is it?' he asks bleakly. '_____?' Complete the sentence.

   ○ ... A LOADED GUN
   ○ ... A TIME MACHINE
   ○ ... A SECRET HIDEOUT
   ○ ... AN ITALIAN PHRASE BOOK

SEASON FOUR ▮▮ EPISODE ONE

SEASON FOUR ◼ EPISODE ONE

38. 'Anyone who wants to see another Christmas needs to come where it's safe.' Tommy calls for a family meeting back in Small Heath on Boxing Day. Where?

- ○ THE GARRISON
- ○ THE BETTING SHOP
- ○ THE SHELBY FRONT PARLOUR
- ○ CHARLIE STRONG'S YARD

39. Polly is agitated and unhappy with Michael, who is trying to help bring her back to herself. What has he done with the tablets she's become so dependent on?

- ○ HIDDEN THEM
- ○ FLUSHED THEM AWAY
- ○ BINNED THEM
- ○ THROWN THEM ON THE FIRE

40. Tommy's chef continues to dispatch Frances the housekeeper to ask questions about the Christmas Day timetable, rousing his suspicions. When she reminds him that he's new to the staff, and has a sous-chef, Tommy heads for the kitchen. In what month were the pair hired?

- ○ MARCH
- ○ MAY
- ○ OCTOBER
- ○ DECEMBER

41. Tommy find the sous-chef, Antonio, peeling potatoes. The man's detached, laid-back manner immediately raises suspicions. Next Tommy seeks out the chef in the cold store. What is he in the process of butchering?

- ○ VENISON
- ○ PHEASANT
- ○ GOOSE
- ○ PORK

42. With his suspicions confirmed, Tommy demands that the chef summons Antonio. The sous-chef creeps in with a pistol in one hand. What weapon does Tommy reach for?

   ○ A HACKSAW
   ○ A FRYING PAN
   ○ A MEAT CLEAVER
   ○ A MEAT HOOK

43. Knowing that Luca Changretta plans to strike on Christmas Day, Michael races to persuade John to hide out in Small Heath as a family. What gets in his way on the lane — carrying hidden mobsters — that ultimately proves to be John's undoing?

   ○ AN AMBULANCE
   ○ A HAY CART
   ○ A GYPSY WAGON
   ○ A ROLLS-ROYCE

SEASON FOUR EPISODE ONE

KILLER QUESTIONS

44. What drink does Lizzie order for herself when she joins Tommy at the table in the hotel?

   ○ GIN AND TONIC
   ○ WHISKEY
   ○ VODKA AND TONIC
   ○ RUM

45. When Linda receives a phone call from Esme, warning her that Ada is on her way round, what is the location and number that she gives on picking up?

   ○ MAYPOLE 245
   ○ WYTHALL 135
   ○ MAYPOLE 346
   ○ WYTHALL 137

46. When Michael visits his mother on Christmas Eve, and finds the house in disarray, what does Polly use as an ashtray?

   ○ THE CARPET
   ○ THE SINK
   ○ HER POCKET
   ○ THE FIREPLACE

1. It's dawn on Boxing Day. Lost in thought, Tommy stands at the window in his bedroom at Watery Lane. What is he wearing?

   ○ A SUIT
   ○ UNDERWEAR
   ○ A BLANKET
   ○ NOTHING

2. The day before, as Michael is rushed into hospital, why does Polly reject the two Peaky Blinders that Tommy brings to guard the patient?

   ○ THEY'RE IN SHOCK AT WHAT THEY SEE
   ○ THEY'RE LACKING EXPERIENCE
   ○ POLLY WANTS NOTHING MORE TO DO WITH PEAKY BLINDERS
   ○ THEIR UNIFORM MAKES MICHAEL A TARGET

3. Tommy meets Arthur at the mortuary, where a policeman and mortician stand beside John's body. What does Tommy order the pair to do?

   ○ STAND ASIDE
   ○ GET OUT
   ○ FACE THE WALL
   ○ FETCH TWO CUPS OF TEA

4. John is laid out on a slab. His body is riddled with bullet wounds, but he's at peace. What does Tommy say to him that he then has to encourage Arthur to repeat?

   ○ 'I LOVE YOU.'
   ○ 'IN THE BLEAK MIDWINTER.'
   ○ 'I'M SORRY.'
   ○ 'I LET YOU DOWN.'

SEASON FOUR ▮ EPISODE TWO

5. When Esme joins them, in shock and grief-stricken, what is her first reaction?

○ SHE FALLS TO HER KNEES
○ SHE LUNGES AT TOMMY
○ SHE THROWS HERSELF OVER JOHN'S BODY
○ SHE ATTACKS ARTHUR

6. 'No _____ for either of you,' she snarls on asking Tommy and Arthur to leave her alone with her dead husband. 'Ever.' Fill in the blank.

○ ... FORGIVENESS
○ ... REST
○ ... PEACE
○ ... SLEEP

7. Esme removes John's jewellery and tells him she's taking the children away. Where is she planning on heading?

○ IRELAND
○ INTO THE HILLS
○ ON THE ROAD
○ FRANCE

8. Tommy addresses the Shelbys at a gathering in the parlour. What odds does he report that the doctors give in favour of Michael's survival?

○ ODDS ON
○ 60:40
○ 2:3
○ EVENS

9. 'These men will not leave our city until our whole family is dead,' says Tommy. What does he call Luca Changretta's objective?

U VENDETTA
U PAYBACK
U GRUDGE
U REVENGE

10. What has Arthur prepared for Luca?

U A BULLET WITH HIS NAME ON IT
U A LETTER GUARANTEEING HE WILL NOT LIVE TO SEE THE YEAR OUT
U A NOOSE
U A CROSS

11. Tommy outlines the dangers they face, insisting everyone stay on home turf. To help them take on Changretta, he has enrolled the help of a gypsy, Aberama Gold. Johnny Dogs is alarmed, calling him a savage. How many Lee men does he offer Tommy instead?

U 25
U 30
U 40
U 50

12. Despite having Moss in his pocket, why does Tommy feel they cannot rely on the police at this time?

U UNREST IN THE WORKPLACE IS BREWING
U THE POLICE ARE ON STRIKE
U THE POLICE HAVE BEEN DRAFTED OUT OF THE CITY AND POSTED ELSEWHERE
U THE FORCE HAS BEEN CLEANED UP FOLLOWING AN ANTI-CORRUPTION DRIVE

SEASON FOUR ▮ EPISODE TWO

THE OFFICIAL PEAKY BLINDERS QUIZ BOOK

SEASON FOUR ▮ EPISODE TWO

13. To end the 'war' between them, Tommy asks for peace from every family member. What does Polly offer instead?

○ ABSTENTION
○ TRUCE
○ CEASEFIRE
○ RETREAT

14. Locals aligned to the Peaky Blinders line up at Charlie Strong's yard to be issued with BSA guns and bullets. What question does Charlie ask one man to be sure he's not an infiltrator?

○ THE NAME OF THE CITY MAYOR
○ THE NAME OF THE GOALKEEPERS FOR TWO LOCAL FOOTBALL TEAMS
○ THE NAME OF THE BARMAN AT THE GARRISON
○ THE NAME OF CHARLIE'S RIGHT-HAND MAN, SITTING BESIDE HIM ISSUING BULLETS

15. The family hold a traditional gypsy funeral for John at Black Patch. What contains his body that is surrounded by firewood and about to be set alight?

○ A WOODEN CASKET
○ A GYPSY CARAVAN
○ A WICKER CASKET
○ A HORSE CART

16. 'We died together once before,' says Tommy of the war in his final words for his late brother. 'Arthur, me, Danny Whizz-Bang, Freddie Thorne, _____ and John.' Fill in the missing name.

○ SCUDBOAT
○ CURLY
○ JEREMIAH
○ JOHNNY DOGS

226

17. As Arthur sets light to the funeral pyre, two Italians prepare to fire on Tommy and the party from long range. Aberama Gold makes his first appearance, with deadly consequences. As well as a gun, what other weapon does he use?

   ○ A DAGGER
   ○ A GARROTTE
   ○ A RAZORBLADE
   ○ A BROKEN BOTTLE

18. 'They will take you hostage and the baby. They will use the baby.' Who persuades Linda not to break ranks from the family and retreat to her countryside cottage?

   ○ ARTHUR SHELBY
   ○ ADA THORNE
   ○ POLLY GRAY
   ○ LIZZIE STARK

19. 'The doctor said they've sewn you up like a _____.' Polly is relieved to see that Michael is conscious, and keen to share her plans for the pair to emigrate. Complete the sentence.

   ○ ... BUTTON
   ○ ... TORN SHIRT
   ○ ... RAG DOLL
   ○ ... FOOTBALL

20. Polly tells Michael that he was shot four times. One was ricochet, she says, and another was live. What was significant about the other two shots?

   ○ THEY PASSED CLEAN THROUGH HIS BODY
   ○ THEY WERE STILL LODGED INSIDE HIM
   ○ THEY HAD ALREADY PASSED THROUGH JOHN
   ○ THEY HAD ONLY GRAZED HIM

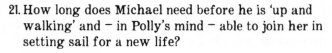

SEASON FOUR ▮ EPISODE TWO

21. How long does Michael need before he is 'up and walking' and – in Polly's mind – able to join her in setting sail for a new life?

   ○ FOUR WEEKS
   ○ FIVE WEEKS
   ○ SIX WEEKS
   ○ TWO MONTHS

22. Ahead of a belated Christmas dinner, Aberama Gold tours Charlie Strong's yard. He's interested in the place, even though Charlie nervously tells him it's not for sale. 'Fire for melting silver,' he observes to Tommy in highlighting the appeal. 'Canal to _____.'

   ○ ... GET IT AWAY
   ○ ... HIDE IT UNDER THE WATER
   ○ ... BRING IT IN
   ○ ... PROTECT AGAINST ATTACK

23. When Aberama presses for the yard, Tommy suggests tossing a penny coin for it. What does Tommy propose he wins if the coin lands in his favour?

   ○ A NIGHT WITH ABERAMA'S DAUGHTER
   ○ ALL OF ABERAMA'S MEN
   ○ A NIGHT WITH ABERAMA'S WIFE
   ○ ABERAMA'S LIFELONG ALLEGIANCE TO THE PEAKY BLINDERS

24. When the wager proves too much for Aberama, what does he pledge to do with the penny instead?

   ○ BUY A NAIL TO ETCH HIS NAME ON A BULLET
   ○ MATCH IT WITH ANOTHER PENNY FOR TOMMY'S EYES WHEN HE'S DEAD
   ○ BUY A FLOWER FOR TOMMY'S GRAVE
   ○ KEEP IT FOR ANOTHER COIN TOSS WITH TOMMY BUT WITH HIGHER STAKES

25. Despite the tension between them, Tommy joins Polly on a bench. He's concerned about her and Michael, and in the same way she's worried about Changretta's threat against him. Who does she nominate to vet the prostitutes he uses 'because they'll use any weakness'?

   ◌ ESME
   ◌ ADA
   ◌ JEREMIAH
   ◌ LIZZIE

26. Tommy tells Aberama that Polly senses he wants something more than just his fee in combatting the Changretta threat. 'My company treasurer,' Tommy says by way of explanation, 'is a certified accountant and also, apparently, _____.' Complete the sentence.

   ◌ ... DRIVEN BY SUSPICION
   ◌ ... A WITCH
   ◌ ... INTUITIVE
   ◌ ... DISTRUSTFUL OF YOU

27. Aberama responds by inviting his son, Bonnie, to take off his shirt. 'I want you to help my son achieve his ambition,' he tells Tommy, as Bonnie does what?

   ◌ GOES NOSE TO NOSE WITH TOMMY
   ◌ SHADOW-BOXES
   ◌ STARES AT TOMMY
   ◌ HOLDS HIS FISTS ALOFT

28. Late at night, Linda answers the door to find Sergeant Moss with a message for Tommy. He reveals that officers have been dispatched from London to investigate Ada. What do they believe is the true purpose of her return from the USA?

   ◌ MONEY LAUNDERING
   ◌ SHE INTENDS TO STIR A COMMUNIST UPRISING
   ◌ RECRUITING SPIES
   ◌ SHE'S SERVING AS A MESSENGER FOR THE MARXISTS

SEASON FOUR ▮ EPISODE TWO

29. Racehorse trainer May Carleton arrives at Charlie Strong's yard to collect Tommy's horse. Before spilling all about the Mafia threat, what polite request does Curly ask of her?

   ○ NOT TO USE A WHIP ON THE HORSE
   ○ TO USE A GENTLE BIT
   ○ NOT TO FEED HER CARROTS
   ○ TO RIDE HER OUT IN COMPANY

30. Tommy strides across the factory floor while Mr Devlin, his factory manager, provides a rundown of his schedule, including the news that the revolution is scheduled for midday. Tommy has Bonnie in tow. What does he request from the foreman?

   ○ SOMEONE WHO CAN MANAGE BETS FROM THE WORKERS
   ○ A BUCKET AND TWO FLANNELS
   ○ A ROPE AND A BELL
   ○ SOMEONE WHO CAN REFEREE A FIGHT

31. Tommy recruits a worker, Billy Mills, to fight Bonnie. Billy is a former regional boxing champion in what division?

   ○ FLYWEIGHT
   ○ FEATHERWEIGHT
   ○ WELTERWEIGHT
   ○ HEAVYWEIGHT

32. When Bonnie puts Billy on the floor, Arthur wants to know if he's got horseshoes in his gloves. 'No,' says Aberama. 'Just his dad's strength and his mother's _____.' Complete the sentence.

   ○ ... IRE
   ○ ... TEMPER
   ○ ... FIRE
   ○ ... FURY

33. Tommy is impressed by Bonnie's potential. He talks to Arthur about what they could do by taking him on and promoting him. After London, where does Tommy foresee he might fight?

   ○ PARIS
   ○ BERLIN
   ○ BOSTON
   ○ NEW YORK

34. In sealing the deal with the Golds, Arthur hands Aberama 'the lion's share' of the takings from the bet he just ran on the fight. What does Tommy give to Bonnie?

   ○ £500
   ○ A CAP
   ○ A RAZOR BLADE
   ○ A PAIR OF BOXING GLOVES

35. 'Cold winter in the east,' union representative Jessie Eden tells Tommy as they meet to discuss a pay dispute and the threat of strike action. 'People are not _____ any more.' Fill in the blank.

   ○ ... WEAK
   ○ ... AFRAID
   ○ ... POWERLESS
   ○ ... FOOLED

36. 'Mr Shelby, this is Monsieur Paz from Paris.' As soon as the man steps into the factory boardroom, Tommy suspects it's Luca Changretta. Under his assumed name, what purpose for his visit did Luca give to the manager, Mr Devlin?

   ○ HE WISHES TO AUDIT AN ORDER BOUND FOR LYONS
   ○ TO DISCUSS THE IMPORT OF CAR PARTS TO FRANCE
   ○ TO NEGOTIATE THE EXPORT OF CAR PARTS TO AMERICA
   ○ TO PLACE AN ORDER FOR A DOZEN VEHICLES

SEASON FOUR ▮ EPISODE TWO

37. As the pair size each other up, exchanging tense pleasantries, Tommy mentions that when he last left Paris he did so in what vehicle?

   ○ A TANK
   ○ AN ARMOURED CAR
   ○ A HORSE AND CART
   ○ A CATTLE TRUCK

38. Tommy pulls a gun on Luca Changretta, only to find the chamber is empty. When did Luca's undercover associate empty the weapon of bullets?

   ○ BEFORE THE BOXING MATCH
   ○ DURING THE TROUBLE ON THE FACTORY FLOOR
   ○ AT CHARLIE STRONG'S YARD
   ○ WHILE TOMMY WAS SLEEPING

39. Luca lines up all six bullets on the boardroom table, naming each one after a Shelby in his crosshairs. What does he do with the bullet reserved for John?

   ○ POCKETS IT
   ○ FLICKS IT ACROSS THE TABLE
   ○ TOSSES IT IN THE BIN
   ○ CURLS IT INTO HIS FIST

KILLER QUESTIONS

40. Aberama Gold tells Tommy that their grandfathers once camped together. In what pub did that friendship 'end badly'?

○ THE WENLOCK
○ THE WREN
○ THE LOCKSMITH
○ THE LARK

41. When Mr Devlin, the factory manager, tells Jessie that Tommy is on his way to meet her, what is the number visible on his clipboard?

○ 15
○ 22
○ 29
○ 46

42. Luca Changretta sits before Tommy in the factory boardroom, taunting him regarding the purpose of his visit. Tommy compliments him on his suit. What is the name of the tailor?

○ GIOLITTI
○ FUNACCI
○ ZORZI
○ CANDELA

SEASON FOUR █ EPISODE TWO

1. 'Hungry men will learn fast.' With the factory staff on strike, Tommy fills the factory with replacements. According to Bradley, the new foreman, what kind of workers are these men?

○ LABOURERS
○ FARMHANDS
○ FRUIT PICKERS
○ DITCH DIGGERS

2. Arthur gets into a fight within moments of opening the factory doors. Who is on the receiving end?

○ A NEW WORKER WHO DOESN'T HAVE A CONTRACT
○ A PROTESTER WHO HOLDS UP A PLACARD DENOUNCING TOMMY
○ A NEW WORKER WHO FAILS TO SHOW ARTHUR RESPECT
○ A PROTESTOR WHO SMASHES A BOTTLE OF FLAMING PETROL ON THE FACTORY FLOOR

3. Bradley asks about protection for his men against further strike action as well as the wages they can expect. Arthur informs him that they are now under the protection of the Peaky Blinders. What's in their pay packet?

○ 3 CROWNS
○ 10 BOB
○ 2 SHILLINGS AND SIXPENCE
○ 10 SHILLINGS

4. Michael's adoptive mother, Rosemary, visits him in hospital. She's read about the shooting in the newspaper. What does she bring him as a gift?

○ ORANGES
○ A BOOK
○ APPLES
○ A NEWSPAPER

5. Even though he asks her to leave, what news does she bring that reveals Michael still has an emotional tie to his adoptive family?

- ○ HIS STEPBROTHER HAS BEEN INVOLVED IN AN ACCIDENT
- ○ HIS STEPFATHER HAS PASSED AWAY
- ○ ROSEMARY IS TERMINALLY ILL
- ○ HIS STEPFAMILY ARE BEING EVICTED FROM THEIR COTTAGE

6. Polly is waiting for a car to take her to a family meeting. She's dressed smartly, but what does she add to her wardrobe as Ada collects her?

- ○ A SWITCHBLADE
- ○ A PISTOL
- ○ A RAZOR
- ○ DARK GLASSES

7. Who are escorting Polly and Ada to the meeting?

- ○ FINN AND ISAIAH
- ○ ISAIAH AND TWO LEE BOYS
- ○ JOHNNY DOGS AND ONE OF THE LEE BOYS
- ○ CHARLIE STRONG AND CURLY

8. En route to the meeting, where she is to be formally reinstated to the company, Polly bridles at Ada's well-intended request for her to behave herself. 'While working for this company,' she points out, 'I have killed a man, lost a man, found a son, nearly lost a son, nearly _____.' Complete the sentence.

- ○ ... LOST MY MIND
- ○ ... LOST MY OWN LIFE
- ○ ... LOST MY FAITH
- ○ ... LOST MYSELF

9. Linda pays a surprise visit to Arthur at the factory. He should be at the family meeting, but then his wife shrugs off her coat to reveal she's wearing little more than silk underwear. Where does she say it's from?

   ○ JAPAN
   ○ FRANCE
   ○ SPAIN
   ○ PRUSSIA

10. As the Shelby meeting takes place at the hospital, Arthur has his hands full with Linda. Mr Devlin, the factory manager, tries and fails to get his attention from the other side of the door. What's the urgent problem?

   ○ THE STRIKERS HAVE BARRICADED THE MAIN DOORS
   ○ STRIKERS HAVE BROKEN INTO THE PAINT SHOP
   ○ A STRIKER IS FIGHTING WITH A PANEL BEATER
   ○ STRIKERS ARE OCCUPYING THE CANTEEN

11. Linda tells Arthur that she's seduced him in the workplace to keep him from being led astray. 'It is my responsibility as your wife to help you resist those temptations,' she says, 'by placing myself between you and _____.' Complete the sentence.

   ○ ... OTHER WOMEN
   ○ ... FORBIDDEN FRUIT
   ○ ... ENDLESS SIN
   ○ ... THE DEVIL

12. Tommy's contacts have returned a photograph of Luca Changretta and several of his men. Tommy plans to circulate it around the neighbourhood so people can be vigilant, and offers a reward for information on his whereabouts. Where was the photograph taken?

   ○ A RESTAURANT
   ○ A WEDDING
   ○ A BIRTHDAY
   ○ A CHRISTENING

13. Why is there tension in the meeting when Tommy proposes sharing the photo of Luca with Aberama Gold?

- ⟲ ARTHUR HAS REQUESTED THAT HE SHOULD PULL THE TRIGGER
- ⟲ POLLY DOESN'T FEEL THAT ABERAMA HAS SUFFICIENTLY EARNED THEIR TRUST
- ⟲ MICHAEL WANTS TO WITNESS LUCA DIE WITH HIS OWN EYES
- ⟲ ADA IS CONCERNED THAT ABERAMA IS NO MATCH FOR LUCA

14. 'Art is it?' growls Arthur, on finding strikers throwing red paint around the factory. What has he armed himself with?

- ⟲ A GUN
- ⟲ A HAMMER
- ⟲ A CROWBAR
- ⟲ A LENGTH OF PIPE

15. As the striker scrambles for the exit, two Mafia hitmen emerge with Arthur in their sights. After shooting one, how does Arthur dispatch the other?

- ⟲ STAMPS ON HIM
- ⟲ ATTACKS HIM WITH A HAMMER
- ⟲ DROWNS HIM IN A VAT OF PAINT
- ⟲ HAMMERS HIS HEAD AGAINST AN ANVIL

16. How does Arthur dispose of the bodies?

- ⟲ LOCKS THEM IN A CUPBOARD
- ⟲ DROPS THEM IN THE CANAL
- ⟲ BURIES THEM IN A COAL HEAP
- ⟲ BURNS THEM IN A FACTORY FURNACE

17. What is the name of the hotel in Stratford-upon-Avon where Luca Changretta is staying?

- ⟲ DODWELL HOUSE
- ⟲ ALVESTON PARK
- ⟲ GOLDICOT
- ⟲ INKBERROW

18. In conversation with two of his men, lamenting the loss of the pair killed by Arthur, he asks if they could at least dress less like hoodlums. One of the men complains that his clothes don't fit him because British food is not to his taste. What dessert does he single out as 'disgusting'?

○ RHUBARB FLAN
○ RICE PUDDING
○ SPOTTED DICK
○ SUET PUDDING

19. 'People in this place hate forever, like Sicilians.' The two men tell Luca that they have found someone with a grudge against the Shelbys who is prepared to help set a trap. Who is it?

○ ALFIE SOLOMONS
○ THE MOTHER OF THE BOXER SLAIN BY ARTHUR IN THE RING
○ MR SABINI
○ THE MOTHER OF THE DIGBETH KID

20. Tommy catches up with Arthur at the factory office, who is upset that Aberama Gold is now hunting Luca Changretta. Who told Arthur about the family vote?

○ FINN SHELBY
○ ADA THORNE
○ POLLY GRAY
○ MICHAEL GRAY

21. 'I want to make it right.' Why does Arthur feel that his actions led to John's death, which fuels his pledge to be the one to kill Luca?

○ IT WAS ARTHUR WHO STARTED A FIRE AT ANGEL'S RESTAURANT, WHICH STARTED THE FEUD

○ ARTHUR WISHES HE HAD BEEN MORE FORCEFUL IN STOPPING THE GRUDGE ESCALATE BETWEEN JOHN AND ANGEL CHANGRETTA

○ IT WAS ARTHUR WHO SHOT VICENTE CHANGRETTA

○ ARTHUR REGRETS NOT PROTECTING JOHN AS SOON AS HE RECEIVED THE BLACK HAND

22. Arthur has worked out that Linda visited him at the factory to keep him away from the family meeting, and the vote to hire Aberama Gold for the contract killing of Luca Changretta. Who does he claim put her up to it?

○ TOMMY SHELBY

○ ADA THORNE

○ POLLY GRAY

○ ESME SHELBY

23. Mr Devlin, the factory manager, is brought before Tommy, who suspects he opened the back door of the factory so the two hitmen could enter with a view to killing Arthur. What does Tommy find in his pocket to incriminate him?

○ A ONE-WAY TICKET TO LEEDS

○ A ONE-WAY TICKET TO LONDON

○ A ONE-WAY TICKET TO LIVERPOOL

○ A ONE-WAY TICKET TO GLASGOW

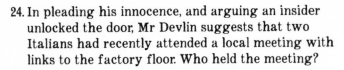
24. In pleading his innocence, and arguing an insider unlocked the door, Mr Devlin suggests that two Italians had recently attended a local meeting with links to the factory floor. Who held the meeting?

- ○ COMMUNIST PARTY MEMBERS
- ○ TRADE UNION LEADERS
- ○ ANARCHIST PARTY MEMBERS
- ○ WOMEN WORKERS

25. 'Before you, I was an ordinary working man.' Devlin swears he has done no wrong. He's already sent his family away, and intends to follow because it's just too dangerous working for the Peaky Blinders. Tommy insists that he stays. What precaution does he take to keep Devlin safe?

- ○ STATIONS THREE MEN WITH POLICE BADGES OUTSIDE DEVLIN'S HOUSE
- ○ INVITES DEVLIN TO STAY AT WATERY LANE
- ○ SUGGESTS DEVLIN SLEEP AT THE FACTORY AS IT'S GUARDED OVERNIGHT
- ○ ASKS MOSS TO STATION THREE COPPERS OUTSIDE HIS HOUSE

26. That same evening, Tommy visits Jesse Eden's house. She's in the parlour listening to what song on her gramophone?

- ○ AVALON
- ○ EVERYBODY LOVES MY BABY
- ○ BYE, BYE, BLACKBIRD
- ○ THE MAN I LOVE

27. Tommy shares his belief that 'outside agitators from overseas' have infiltrated meetings Jessie attended to foment trouble in the factories and a general strike. Ultimately, he wants to know if she can identify any of the Italians in the photograph. To persuade her, he produces a warrant card to prove he's authorised by the state. What is his title?

O SPECIAL OFFICER
O GOVERNMENT AGENT
O SPECIAL CONSTABLE
O AGENT OF THE CROWN

28. 'The sweet boy who left never came back.' Jessie tells Tommy that she's done her research on him. She knows that before the war he was in love with an Italian girl called Greta who died. What was the illness that killed her before Tommy signed up?

O CANCER
O CONSUMPTION
O TUBERCULOSIS
O FLU

29. Tommy counters that he has also looked into Jessie's background. What battle did her sweetheart fight in before returning home 'shell-shocked' and ultimately suicidal?

O VERDUN
O YPRES
O PASSCHENDAELE
O SOMME

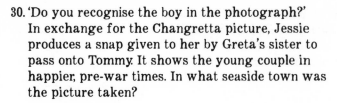
30. 'Do you recognise the boy in the photograph?' In exchange for the Changretta picture, Jessie produces a snap given to her by Greta's sister to pass onto Tommy. It shows the young couple in happier, pre-war times. In what seaside town was the picture taken?

- ○ SCARBOROUGH
- ○ MORECAMBE
- ○ BLACKPOOL
- ○ BANGOR

31. Once Tommy has left, what does Jessie do with the Changretta photograph?

- ○ BURNS IT IN THE FIRE
- ○ FILES IT
- ○ POCKETS IT
- ○ PROPS IT ON HER MANTELPIECE

32. Back in his room, Tommy studies the photograph of himself as a younger man with Greta. The handwritten inscription, dated 1913, reads, '_____ beside the seaside.' Fill in the blank.

- ○ ... YOUNG LOVERS
- ○ ... WILD ROVERS
- ○ ... TRUE SWEETHEARTS
- ○ ... BIRMINGHAM ROYALTY

33. 'It's the modern way.' Arthur has one bullet in the chamber of his gun, with Luca's name engraved on it. He's upset, but Linda is desperate for him to leave the killing to Aberama. Where does he fire the round?

- ○ INTO THE NIGHT SKY
- ○ INTO THE FIREPLACE
- ○ INTO THE FLOORBOARD
- ○ INTO THE YARD AT DAWN

34. 'It's not me that's doing the gambling,' says Linda, when she surprises Polly and Lizzie the next morning by volunteering at the betting shop to keep herself occupied. What work has she decided to do?

   ○ MAKE THE TEA
   ○ EMPTY THE ASHTRAYS
   ○ TAKE THE BETS
   ○ CHALK THE ODDS

35. Polly and Lizzie discover that Finn is a virgin, and organise a prostitute for him. 'Is she nice?' asks Tommy. What is Lizzie's response?

   ○ 'THEY'RE ALL NICE IN THEIR OWN WAY.'
   ○ 'DOES IT MATTER?'
   ○ 'NICE WOMEN DON'T DO THAT KIND OF THING.'
   ○ 'SHE'S KIND.'

36. 'Are you kissing her or me?' Tommy takes Lizzie to a meeting point where he used to wait for Greta. What does it overlook?

   ○ THE CITY
   ○ THE CANAL
   ○ THE RAILWAY LINE
   ○ THE COUNTRYSIDE

37. Afterwards, Tommy asks Lizzie to oversee the establishment of two more children's homes 'because I promised someone I'd change the world'. Where are the locations for the two homes?

   ○ MOSELEY AND SOUTHSIDE
   ○ BIRCHFIELD AND HAY MILLS
   ○ DIGBETH AND SALTLEY
   ○ SMALL HEATH AND ASTON

38. Tommy asks Finn about his day, knowing that Lizzie and Polly had arranged for him to sleep with a prostitute. Finn admits that he didn't enjoy the experience, and apologised to her because 'she looked so tired'. What is Tommy's advice?

    ♟ 'BE YOURSELF.'
    ♟ 'TELL NO ONE.'
    ♟ 'BE A MAN.'
    ♟ 'MOVE ON.'

39. 'You're an unlikely Cassius.' Polly secretly meets Luca Changretta, proposing a deal to spare Michael, Finn and Arthur. In what Shakespeare play does Cassius play a key role in the death of the protagonist?

    ♟ TITUS ANDRONICUS
    ♟ JULIUS CAESAR
    ♟ CORIOLANUS
    ♟ ANTHONY & CLEOPATRA

KILLER QUESTIONS

SEASON FOUR  EPISODE THREE

40. What model car takes Ada and Polly to the family meeting in Michael's hospital room?

   ○ CROSSLEY
   ○ BENTLEY
   ○ AUSTIN
   ○ MORRIS

41. What is Arthur's position in the factory, as seen on his office window when Linda visits and drops the blinds?

   ○ DEPUTY VICE PRESIDENT
   ○ MANAGING DIRECTOR
   ○ JOINT PRESIDENT
   ○ CO-DIRECTOR

42. When Luca Changretta studies the passports of the two men killed by Arthur, he goes on to ask his associates to inform their families. How many children does Luca say the second dead man has?

   ○ THREE
   ○ FOUR
   ○ FIVE
   ○ SIX

1. As part of Changretta's plan, Arthur receives an invitation to a commemorative tea party from Mrs Ross, the mother of the young boxer he killed by accident in the ring. What birthday does she say it would mark, had he lived?

   ○ 18TH
   ○ 20TH
   ○ 21ST
   ○ 24TH

2. Tommy suspects this is a trap set by Changretta. Where does he gather his men and hatch a plan to stage a counter-strike?

   ○ CHARLIE STRONG'S YARD
   ○ THE GARRISON
   ○ THE BETTING SHOP
   ○ THE OFFICE OF SHELBY COMPANY LTD

3. Tommy lays out a map and points to an address where Arthur is due to be at midday. What is the name of the road?

   ○ IMPERIAL STREET
   ○ ARTILLERY SQUARE
   ○ BATTALION STREET
   ○ RANGE ROAD

4. Tommy points out two ways to access the address. One is via Navigation Street. What is the other?

   ○ BEHIND THE STABLES
   ○ THE WASTE GROUND
   ○ THE STEPS
   ○ THE TOWPATH

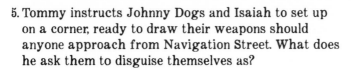

5. Tommy instructs Johnny Dogs and Isaiah to set up on a corner, ready to draw their weapons should anyone approach from Navigation Street. What does he ask them to disguise themselves as?

○ HAWKERS SELLING PORK
○ CAT MEAT MEN
○ KNIFE GRINDERS
○ STREET SWEEPERS

6. When Arthur arrives at Mrs Ross's house, what courtesy does she request before inviting him in?

○ HAT OFF
○ NO BLADES
○ SHOES OFF
○ NO FIREARMS

7. As Arthur settles at the table, Mrs Ross sends a young girl away. She runs into the street and signals to a driver who has stopped on Navigation Street. What does she wave with one hand to attract his attention?

○ A GREEN BLANKET
○ A RED SHAWL
○ A BLACK BONNET
○ A WHITE HANDKERCHIEF

8. Tommy is stationed at a window with a rifle overlooking Navigation Street. As the driver attempts a desperate three-point turn, with bullets ricocheting from his vehicle, what dawns on him?

○ THE ASSASSINATION ATTEMPT ON ARTHUR HAS FAILED
○ MRS ROSS HAS CONFESSED TO ARTHUR THAT HE'S IN DANGER
○ ARTHUR HAS REVEALED TO MRS ROSS THAT HE KNOWS SHE'S SET HIM UP
○ THE TEA PARTY IS IN FACT A DECOY

SEASON FOUR ▮ EPISODE FOUR

9. Michael is at the table in his hospital room. A nurse enters, drawing his attention from his paperwork. What does she do that arouses his suspicion, moments before Luca Changretta makes his presence known by killing the Peaky guard at the door?

- ROLLS MICHAEL'S WHEELCHAIR AWAY FROM HIS REACH
- PULLS AWAY HIS TABLE SO LUCA HAS A CLEAR SHOT
- PUSHES THE TABLE AGAINST MICHAEL TO JAM HIM AGAINST THE BED
- CLOSES THE CURTAIN AGAINST THE SUNLIGHT SO THAT LUCA IS NOT DAZZLED

10. What does Arthur threaten to do to a terrified Mrs Ross unless she leaves within the hour?

- SHOOT HER
- SLIT HER THROAT
- TAR AND FEATHER HER
- TAKE AWAY HER CHILDREN

11. Facing Luca Changretta, Michael scrambles to defend himself despite his injuries. Changretta calmly locks the door and then gestures at Michael's hat on the bed. What does he say it represents in his culture?

- GOOD FORTUNE
- PROTECTION
- BAD LUCK
- WEAKNESS

12. Luca presses the muzzle of his gun to Michael's head and pulls the trigger. The chamber is empty, however. 'Tell your mother, _____.' he says on leaving. Complete the sentence.

- ... SHE OWES ME
- ... WE HAVE A DEAL
- ... I'LL MEAN BUSINESS NEXT TIME
- ... TO COME AND FIND ME

13. Michael covers for his mother when Tommy and his men rush in. What reason does he give for the fact that Luca hadn't killed him?

  ○ MICHAEL PUSHED HIM OVER AND HE RAN
  ○ A POLICEMAN'S WHISTLE FROM THE STREET OUTSIDE SPOOKED THEM
  ○ THE GUN MISFIRED
  ○ A DOCTOR DISTURBED THEM

14. Tommy makes a call to head off the Italians as they drive out of Birmingham. What kind of car does he advise to look out for?

  ○ VAUXHALL
  ○ WOLSELEY
  ○ ROLLS-ROYCE
  ○ MORRIS

15. Luca and his men find the bridge blocked by an overturned cart. A police officer is in attendance. Stepping out of the car for a moment, what makes Luca suspect it's a trap?

  ○ THE OFFICER'S UNIFORM IS BADLY FITTED
  ○ THE OFFICER REMARKS THAT THE CART BELONGS TO GYPSIES
  ○ THE OFFICER HAS A ROMANY ACCENT
  ○ A CRATE THAT HAS FALLEN FROM THE CART IS STAMPED SHELBY COMPANY LTD

16. Moments before Aberama and his men open fire, what confirms Luca's fears?

  ○ HIS DRIVER HAS BEEN STRANGLED
  ○ THE CAR TYRES HAVE BEEN SLASHED
  ○ HIS DRIVER'S THROAT HAS BEEN SLASHED
  ○ HIS DRIVER IS MISSING

SEASON FOUR ▮ EPISODE FOUR

17. As Luca makes a desperate getaway, the policeman appeals for his attackers to put their guns down. Aberama takes careful aim at the officer and fires. Where does he hit him?

- ○ HEAD
- ○ LEG
- ○ ARM
- ○ HAND

18. Polly admits to Michael that she struck a deal with Changretta to spare him and Arthur. 'If it wasn't for me,' she tells him, 'you'd be _____.' Complete Polly's sentence.

- ○ ... ON THE SLAB LIKE JOHN
- ○ ... LYING DEAD ON THE FLOOR
- ○ ... SMOKE BLOWING OUT OF A MORTUARY CHIMNEY
- ○ ... SIX FEET UNDERGROUND

19. Tommy meets Aberama Gold and his son to pay them for the ambush. Why does Aberama ask for double?

- ○ A POLICEMAN WAS SHOT
- ○ THEY TOOK OUT NOT ONE ITALIAN BUT TWO
- ○ ABERAMA AND BONNIE ARE NOW KNOWN TO LUCA CHANGRETTA
- ○ LUCA AND HIS MEN ARE ARMED WITH MACHINE GUNS

20. On Tommy's advice, with security in mind, how does May Carleton travel from the station to meet him?

- ○ BARGE
- ○ BY FOOT ALONG THE TOWPATH
- ○ POLICE ESCORT
- ○ UNDER COVER IN A CART

21. May has been training a racehorse for Tommy. What name has she decided on that was 'stolen' from a horse that won the Epsom Derby in 1833?

   ○ TREACHEROUS
   ○ DANGEROUS
   ○ RECKLESS
   ○ JEOPARDOUS

22. 'You've lost your wife, and now your brother, too,' says May on the true nature of her visit. 'I thought it would make you _____.' Fill in the blank.

   ○ ... KINDER
   ○ ... CALMER
   ○ ... VULNERABLE
   ○ ... DIFFERENT

23. Lizzie interrupts and makes a loaded comment about Tommy's weakness for all things 'glamorous and expensive'. May responds by writing out a blank cheque for the Grace Shelby Foundation. How does she put Lizzie in her place?

   ○ SHE ASKS LIZZIE TO FILL IN A SUITABLE AMOUNT
   ○ MAY ASKS IF SHE HAS A PEN THAT SHE CAN USE
   ○ MAY REQUESTS THAT SHE LEAVES THE ROOM WHILE THEY DISCUSS THE AMOUNT
   ○ SHE ASKS LIZZIE TO PAY IT IN AT THE BANK FOR HER

24. Tommy suggests that May should stay overnight in Birmingham. What reason does he give?

   ○ TRAIN STRIKE
   ○ BAD WEATHER
   ○ RAIL MAINTENANCE WORK
   ○ CONCERNS FOR HER SAFETY

SEASON FOUR ▮▮▮ EPISODE FOUR

25. Tommy invites her to sample his home-made gin, brewed to his father's recipe and 'distilled for the eradication of seemingly incurable _____.' Fill in the blank.

- ○ ... SORROW
- ○ ... HEARTACHE
- ○ ... SADNESS
- ○ ... MELANCHOLY

26. Luca Changretta telephones Polly to remind her that he will kill her son unless she delivers on her promise. Where does he call her from?

- ○ THE HOTEL
- ○ A TELEPHONE BOOTH IN THE COUNTRYSIDE
- ○ A BAR
- ○ A TELEPHONE BOOTH IN THE CITY

27. Searching for Tommy, Polly learns from Lizzie that he's with May Carleton. Lizzie is still disgruntled that May has drawn his attention, and so she's filled in her blank cheque for the charity. How much has she made it out for?

- ○ £2,000
- ○ £5,000
- ○ £10,000
- ○ £15,000

28. 'I'll read your tea leaves if you go and get Tommy's diary.' What does Polly foresee?

- ○ LIZZIE IS PREGNANT
- ○ LIZZIE WILL BE MARRIED WITHIN THE YEAR
- ○ LIZZIE WILL BE SAVED FROM A DROWNING
- ○ LIZZIE WILL BE PROMOTED

29. In return, Lizzie finds Tommy's diary. Polly finds a free day and marks it with what?

   ○ A BLACK CIRCLE
   ○ A BLACK STAR
   ○ A RED CIRCLE
   ○ A RED STAR

30. Tommy and Aberama Gold watch Bonnie in the ring. According to his trainer, Bonnie is ready for his first fight. What's the name of the Alfie-backed boxer he'll be facing in Camden?

   ○ CAIN
   ○ HARAN
   ○ GOLIATH
   ○ LEVI

31. In conversation with Charlie at his yard, May Carleton learns that Tommy is making his own gin to kill time until it's safe to go home. 'He's going mad cooped up here, is what he is,' says Charlie. 'Like a wasp _____.' Complete the sentence.

   ○ ... TRAPPED BY A WINDOW
   ○ ... IN A BEER GLASS
   ○ ... HELL BENT ON FREEDOM
   ○ ... WITH NO CHOICE BUT TO STING

32. Factory manager Mr Devlin updates Tommy on the growing unrest across the city. He's concerned that if the communists spark a revolution they could be considered class traitors and what?

   ○ PUT ON A LIST
   ○ SHOT
   ○ IMPRISONED
   ○ DRIVEN OUT OF BIRMINGHAM

33. 'In this modern age, American women drink as much booze as the men.' Tommy shows May around his home distillery. 'And women, apparently, prefer gin.' What is May's opinion of his efforts?

U A TOUCH DRY
U A LITTLE SWEET
U SLIGHTLY BITTER
U TOO SHARP

34. Finn is in pensive mood after his role in the operation in Artillery Square, admitting to Arthur that he's not as comfortable with a gun as his brothers are. Arthur assures him that the decision to pull the trigger is out of his hands. In his view, whose responsibility is it?

U TOMMY
U GOD
U FATE
U INSTINCT

35. Ada catches the last moments of a rousing speech by Jessie Eden in front of members of the local Communist Party. She promises that they will stand shoulder to shoulder with the dock workers, railwaymen and who else?

U CAR WORKERS
U BOOTMAKERS
U STEELWORKERS
U COAL MINERS

36. Ada invites Jessie for a drink, where she puts forward a settlement proposal that Tommy is 'too arrogant and proud to offer in person'. What is Tommy requesting in return for equal pay across his workforce?

U AN INSTRUCTION FOR JESSIE TO STAND DOWN AS UNION REPRESENTATIVE
U DINNER WITH JESSIE
U A POST FOR JESSIE AT SHELBY COMPANY LTD
U AN ORDER FOR JESSIE TO LEAVE THE CITY

37. Alfie arrives by car in Watery Lane with his boxer in tow. He finds the street empty. What does he ask his minder to do to make their presence known?

   ○ BLOW A WHISTLE
   ○ LEAN ON THE CAR HORN
   ○ FIRE A GUN INTO THE AIR
   ○ SMASH A MILK BOTTLE AGAINST A WALL

38. On a tour of Tommy's distillery, before getting down to business about the boxing match, Alfie opines that gin leads to melancholy. Aware that Tommy has Mafia trouble, why does he suggest rum would be more appropriate?

   ○ RUM MAKES MEN STRONGER
   ○ IT BUILDS MUSCLE
   ○ IT BRINGS OUT THE DEVIL
   ○ IT INCITES VIOLENCE

39. Having visited Michael to sign some paperwork, Tommy drives away from the hospital to be followed by Changretta's men in the back of a bread van. Who witnesses them setting off?

   ○ MICHAEL GRAY
   ○ ADA THORNE
   ○ POLLY GRAY
   ○ FINN SHELBY

SEASON FOUR ▨ EPISODE FOUR

KILLER QUESTIONS

40. When Tommy picks up the phone to call Charlie Strong from the betting shop, what Small Heath number does he request from the operator?

   ○ 365
   ○ 333
   ○ 344
   ○ 371

41. In the betting shop, just before Luca Changretta calls Polly, a man calling bets offers 3:1 on what horse?

   ○ RED MOON
   ○ RAGING ROBBERS
   ○ MOON CIRCLE
   ○ CLUSKEYS CLOUD

42. What is the date in Lizzie's diary that Polly has marked to honour her agreement with Luca Changretta?

   ○ 5TH FEBRUARY
   ○ 12TH FEBRUARY
   ○ 19TH FEBRUARY
   ○ 26TH FEBRUARY

1. Tommy is aware that he's being followed, and is also prepared for this eventuality. Having driven back to Artillery Square in Small Heath, what does he uncover from a tenement balcony?

   ○ A SNIPER
   ○ A MACHINE GUN
   ○ A SHOTGUN
   ○ GRENADES

2. Tommy makes a break for the upper balconies. What provides cover for him as a chase ensues?

   ○ BICYCLES
   ○ DUSTBINS
   ○ WOODEN CRATES
   ○ WASHING LINES

3. Each time Luca comes across a fallen Mafia soldier, shot dead by Tommy, what does he do as a sign of respect?

   ○ STRAIGHTENS THEIR TIE
   ○ POCKETS THEIR WEDDING RING
   ○ PLACES THEIR HAT OVER THEIR FACE
   ○ REMOVES THE CRUCIFIX FROM AROUND THEIR NECK

4. Tommy and Luca Changretta find themselves in a face-off in the street. 'Dear Lord,' growls Luca, as the police rush to the scene before another shot is fired, '_____ is yours.' Fill in the blank.

   ○ … JUSTICE
   ○ … VENGEANCE
   ○ … RETRIBUTION
   ○ … REVENGE

SEASON FOUR ▉ EPISODE FIVE

257

5. While Changretta escapes, Sergeant Moss is on hand to break up the scuffle between Tommy and the coppers and prevent his arrest. Tommy hands him a fistful of banknotes. How does Moss react?

- ○ HE TAKES THE MONEY AND POCKETS IT
- ○ HE REFUSES THE MONEY, NO LONGER WILLING TO WORK FOR THE PEAKY BLINDERS
- ○ HE TELLS TOMMY TO GIVE THE MONEY TO THE PEOPLE
- ○ HE DEMANDS THAT TOMMY DOUBLE IT FOR THE TROUBLE HE'S CAUSED

6. 'Today I killed three men.' Polly and Tommy address the family at Watery Lane, explaining that the pair had hatched a plan to prepare for the Changretta attack. Tommy's son, Charlie, overhears the conversation. What does Tommy tell him that he got to cover for the truth?

- ○ THREE CANDLES BUT ONLY TWO MATCHES IN THE BOX
- ○ THREE SHILLINGS FOR A TWO SHILLING HORSE
- ○ THREE TOY CARS FOR THE PRICE OF TWO
- ○ THREE CARTS BUT ONLY TWO HORSES

7. 'I don't drink whiskey or gin any more.' Lizzie tells Tommy that she's expecting his baby. What does he ask her to do?

- ○ TELL NOBODY UNTIL SHE SHOWS
- ○ ADVERTISE FOR SOMEONE TO FILL HER POSITION IN THE COMPANY
- ○ WORK HALF-DAYS ONLY
- ○ TAKE TIME OFF TO REST

8. Arthur is last in the office. It's dark, he's drunk, and depositing wads of cash in the safe. What does he put onto the table and share with his imaginary dead brother?

- ○ A BOTTLE OF ALFIE'S RUM
- ○ VIALS OF COCAINE
- ○ CAKE FROM THE FUNERAL
- ○ A BOTTLE OF TOMMY'S GIN

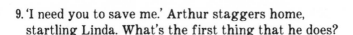

9. 'I need you to save me.' Arthur staggers home, startling Linda. What's the first thing that he does?

  ○ LIES ON THE BED
  ○ LOSES HIS BALANCE
  ○ CRUMPLES INTO THE CORNER OF THE ROOM
  ○ FLOPS INTO AN ARMCHAIR

10. To calm him, what special place does Linda promise Arthur that they'll soon return to?

  ○ THE SEASIDE
  ○ THEIR GARDEN
  ○ THEIR COTTAGE
  ○ THE COUNTRYSIDE

11. Polly brings Michael to Aberama Gold's gypsy camp. Despite her son's reluctance, she wants him to stay for protection. 'Have you ever eaten _____, Michael?' Aberama asks him with glee. Fill in the blank.

  ○ SWAN
  ○ BADGER
  ○ HEDGEHOG
  ○ SHREW

12. Aberama drives Polly back to Small Heath, stopping with her beside a brook to talk and roast what over a fire?

  ○ RABBIT
  ○ PIGEON
  ○ PIKE
  ○ SQUIRREL

SEASON FOUR ▮ EPISODE FIVE

13. Polly is in her element. She reminisces about her time as a girl on the road with her father. Why did he often escape into the countryside?

- ○ THE MONEYLENDERS WERE AFTER HIM
- ○ HE'D HAD AN ARGUMENT WITH POLLY'S MOTHER
- ○ THE POLICE WERE AFTER HIM
- ○ HE FOUND IT SUFFOCATING IN THE CITY

14. In order to gut their catch, Polly asks Aberama if he has a sharp knife. Where does he keep one sheathed?

- ○ AT HIS ANKLE
- ○ IN HIS WAISTBAND
- ○ UNDER HIS ARM
- ○ BY HIS THIGH

15. 'It's like putting your head through the window and seeing the whole world.' In conversation around their campfire, Polly tells Aberama about her ability to commune with the dead. According to Polly, what episode in her life sparked a resurgence in this gift?

- ○ WHEN SHE LEARNED THAT HER DAUGHTER WAS DEAD
- ○ WHEN MICHAEL CAME BACK INTO HER LIFE
- ○ WHEN SHE FEARED MICHAEL MIGHT NOT SURVIVE THE CHANGRETTA ASSASSINATION ATTEMPT
- ○ WHEN HER HEAD WAS IN THE NOOSE

16. Aberama hands Polly the blade, only for her to drop it and pull him close to her. Why does she break off from their kiss and press the blade to the gypsy's throat?

- ○ TO MAKE HIM PROMISE NEVER TO BREATHE A WORD ABOUT THIS ENCOUNTER
- ○ FOR PRESUMING SHE WOULD WANT TO KISS HIM
- ○ TO ASSERT THAT SHE'LL HOLD HIM RESPONSIBLE IF ANY HARM COMES TO HER SON
- ○ TO MAKE IT CLEAR TO ABERAMA THAT HE SHOULD NEVER TAKE HER FOR GRANTED

17. Alfie Solomons meets Changretta's men with his eyes closed. He explains that he does so as an exercise in empathy as he 'donates a considerable amount of money to a charity that gives dogs with eyes to blind Jews'. Which member of Alfie's family does he tell them lives without sight?

   ⟳ HIS BROTHER
   ⟳ HIS AUNT
   ⟳ HIS COUSIN
   ⟳ HIS GRANDFATHER

18. 'I already know what you want,' Alfie tells Changretta. 'I just want to hear you say it out loud, so I can check how _____.' Complete the sentence.

   ⟳ ... BADLY YOU WANT MY HELP
   ⟳ ... RIDICULOUS IT IS
   ⟳ ... EXPENSIVE IT'S GOING TO BE
   ⟳ ... FOOLISH YOU ARE TO THINK I'D AGREE

19. How many barrels of rum does Alfie expect them to distribute in America for him each month in exchange for giving up Tommy Shelby?

   ⟳ 100
   ⟳ 150
   ⟳ 175
   ⟳ 200

20. Alfie reads out a list of additional costs, finishing with a demand for £500. What is it for?

   ⟳ TIME AND EFFORT
   ⟳ BECAUSE TOMMY IS A GOOD FRIEND
   ⟳ EMOTIONAL DISTRESS
   ⟳ BECAUSE DEALING WITH GANGSTERS SHOULD COME AT A PREMIUM

SEASON FOUR ▮ EPISODE FIVE

21. 'You will bring my men to Birmingham,' says Luca, rapidly losing patience with Alfie's provocative manner. What condition does Alfie set down before he can agree?

- ○ THEY MUST LEARN THE SHEMA PRAYER
- ○ THEY MUST WEAR TRADITIONAL JEWISH ATTIRE
- ○ THEY MUST BE CIRCUMCISED
- ○ THEY MUST SING KADDISH

22. When Luca agrees to handling 200 barrels of rum in return for Tommy Shelby, Alfie points out that he did so without negotiating. Acknowledging that Tommy was right about the Mafia man, what does he mutter to himself in Yiddish?

- ○ 'THE ENEMY OF MY ENEMY IS MY FRIEND.'
- ○ 'YOU PLAN TO KILL US ALL.'
- ○ 'HOLD YOUR FRIENDS CLOSE.'
- ○ 'I SEE YOU FOR WHAT YOU ARE.'

23. Ada opens her front door to members of the British Army. Having been detained, what has happened to her in the time before Colonel Ben Younger arrives to begin questioning?

- ○ SHE'S BEEN STRIP-SEARCHED
- ○ SHE'S BEEN INSULTED
- ○ SHE'S HAD HER JEWELLERY REMOVED
- ○ SHE'S BEEN REFUSED FOOD AND DRINK

24. 'I'm sorry this has got off to a bad start.' While Colonel Younger has a dossier on each member of the Shelby family, he's brought Ada in because she was observed having a drink with Jessie Eden after the Communist Party meeting. What detail does Younger share that tells Ada he's not bluffing?

- ○ THE NAME OF THE PUB THEY WENT TO
- ○ WHAT DRINKS THEY ORDERED
- ○ WHAT TABLE THEY SAT AT
- ○ WHAT TIME THEY LEFT

25. Ada announces that she's leaving. Having informed him that her Communist Party involvement is in the past, what does she suggest that Colonel Younger do with her dossier?

O BIN IT
O TEAR IT UP
O BURN IT
O GIVE IT TO HER

26. Colonel Younger persists. 'Most of the more active subversives shed their allegiance to _____,' he says. Fill in the blank.

O ... OPERATE INVISIBLY
O ... AVOID DETECTION
O ... CONTINUE SOWING DISCORD
O ... SHAKE US OFF

27. While Colonel Younger considers Ada to be potentially useful 'with a foot in both camps', what does he hint before she leaves?

O TOMMY SHOULD BOLSTER HER PROTECTION
O TOMMY IS SET TO BE ARRESTED
O TOMMY IS AWARE THAT ADA WOULD BE MEETING HIM
O TOMMY IS NEXT TO BE QUESTIONED

28. Tommy observes Bonnie sparring in the gym. His trainer urges him to put some effort into it. How many days are left before his first fight?

O TWO
O THREE
O FOUR
O FIVE

29. 'Talk to me about Ben Younger.' Heading back to the office, Tommy finds Ada in the chair behind his desk. What is the connection between the two men?

   ○ THEY WERE BOTH IN THE WARWICKSHIRE YEOMANRY IN FRANCE
   ○ TOMMY TAUGHT BEN TO RIDE A HORSE
   ○ THEY WENT TO SCHOOL TOGETHER
   ○ BEN WAS BEST FRIENDS WITH JOHN

30. In Tommy's view, Ada's public detention by the army will dampen down the flames of revolution. What is the one thing he's sorry about?

   ○ ADA'S HUMILIATION IN FRONT OF THE NEIGHBOURS
   ○ HER STRIP-SEARCH ORDEAL
   ○ THE LENGTH OF TIME SHE WAS HELD
   ○ THE CONDITIONS IN WHICH SHE WAS HELD

31. According to Tommy, what area has Colonel Younger been assigned as part of a state operation to counter armed revolution?

   ○ SMALL HEATH
   ○ BIRMINGHAM
   ○ THE MIDLANDS
   ○ ENGLAND

32. 'Tommy Shelby is going to stop the revolution with his cock.' In putting Ada in the picture, what does Tommy say he hopes to gain from taking Jessie to dinner?

   ○ THE CHANCE TO CHALLENGE HER VALUES
   ○ THE NAMES OF HER CONTACTS WHO ARE GUNNING FOR REVOLUTION
   ○ AN OPPORTUNITY TO EXTRACT PERSONAL INFORMATION FOR POSSIBLE BLACKMAIL
   ○ A BID TO BRIBE HER INTO RETURNING HER WORKFORCE TO THE FACTORIES

33. Ada is incredulous. Why would the British military turn to a man like Tommy for assistance? Tommy details the contracts he will be awarded on completion of a successful mission for the supply of forces vehicles. How much are the contracts worth?

   ○ £250,000
   ○ £500,000
   ○ £1 MILLION
   ○ £2 MILLION

34. When Tommy has finished explaining his role in the attempt to stop an armed uprising, Ada says she'll put his initial response to the military's offer on his grave. What is it?

   ○ 'WHEN I'M READY.'
   ○ 'WHY NOT?'
   ○ 'WHAT'S IT WORTH?'
   ○ 'I HAVE NO CHOICE.'

35. Where does Tommy host dinner for Jessie?

   ○ HIS HOUSE IN WATERY LANE
   ○ THE FACTORY FLOOR
   ○ CHARLIE STRONG'S YARD
   ○ THE BACK ROOM AT THE GARRISON

36. 'I'm approaching the current political crisis in this country in the way I would a horse race.' As they settle in over candlelight, Tommy tells Jessie that he's undecided about whether to back the communists or the establishment. With his offer of pay parity on the table, what does he ask for in return?

   ○ EVERYTHING JESSIE KNOWS ABOUT SOCIALISM
   ○ JESSIE'S VISION FOR THE FUTURE
   ○ EVERYTHING JESSIE KNOWS ABOUT CAPITALISM
   ○ DETAILS OF FURTHER PLANNED STRIKE ACTION AND PROTESTS

SEASON FOUR ▮ EPISODE FIVE

37. With the drink flowing, Tommy tells an entertaining story in a way that brings out the best in Jessie. As she laughs, prior to a dance and a request from him 'to arrange a meeting with the appropriate people', what does his punchline involve?

   O A PLUM AND A TOOTHBRUSH
   O A TOP HAT AND A COCONUT
   O A COMPASS AND A PARROT
   O A TROMBONE AND A TEACUP

38. It's fight night, the boxing ring is lit but empty, and the crowds are jostling to gain entry to the hall. What is barred, by order of the Peaky Blinders?

   O SWEARING
   O DRINK
   O DRUGS
   O WEAPONS

39. In the dressing room, Aberama tells Bonnie that Tommy will reward him if he puts down his opponent in the fourth round. What percentage cut does the young boxer stand to make if he's successful?

   O 5%
   O 10%
   O 20%
   O 25%

KILLER QUESTIONS

40. When Tommy and Polly talk in the parlour at Watery Lane, shortly after his narrow escape from Luca and his men, we see a framed picture of a verse from the Bible hanging on the wall. What does it say?

    O BE STRONG AND COURAGEOUS
    O CERTAINLY I WILL BE WITH THEE
    O LET LOVE BE GENUINE
    O OUR FAITH CAN MOVE MOUNTAINS

41. 'They follow the patrin and the crows,' Polly tells Michael when convincing him to hide out from Changretta and his men by staying with Aberama Gold. What does the Romany gypsy term 'patrin' mean?

    O SCORCH MARKS IN THE GRASS THAT SERVE AS SIGNPOSTS FOR OTHER GYPSIES
    O MARKERS MADE OF GRASS, TWIGS OR LEAVES TO SHOW FELLOW TRAVELLERS THE WAY
    O A MEANS OF READING CLOUD FORMATION FOR DIRECTIONS
    O PATHWAYS FORMED BY DEER THAT ALWAYS LEAD TO CLEARINGS

42. When Michael climbs into the back of a gypsy wagon, preparing to go to ground, Polly tells him that he'll be welcomed on account of her grandmother, Birdy Boswell. Who was she?

    O A GYPSY BRIDE
    O A GYPSY SEER
    O A GYPSY PRINCESS
    O A NURSE WHO HELPED SICK GYPSY CHILDREN

1. With the boxers in the ring, preparing for the bell, Tommy sits alone in the dressing room. He's joined by Alfie Solomons, who suggests they share the same reason for not watching a fight. What is it?

   ○ THEY EACH HAVE AN EMOTIONAL CONNECTION TO THEIR FIGHTERS
   ○ THE FIGHT HAS RULES
   ○ THERE'S MONEY RIDING ON IT
   ○ THE BEST DEALS ARE DONE BEHIND THE SCENES

2. 'Imagine spending your life in the dark. Born blind.' Alone together, Alfie paints a picture for Tommy. 'Then, one day, you see the world you've only ever touched and smelled. A _____. I've had one.' Fill in the blank.

   ○ ... DISCOVERY
   ○ ... VISION
   ○ ... REALISATION
   ○ ... REVELATION

3. Alfie reveals that he plans to sell up and move to Margate. What does he hope to buy there?

   ○ PEACE
   ○ SECURITY
   ○ TIME
   ○ PLEASURE

4. 4. He tells Tommy that he's seen a house with white Greek columns and what kind of tree?

   ○ YEW
   ○ CYPRUS
   ○ SPRUCE
   ○ MONKEY PUZZLE

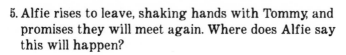

5. Alfie rises to leave, shaking hands with Tommy, and promises they will meet again. Where does Alfie say this will happen?

   ○ ON THE PROMENADE
   ○ BY THE PIER
   ○ AT THE DOCK
   ○ BEHIND THE JETTY

6. Ringside, Arthur is suspicious of the men in the corner with Alfie's boxer as they 'don't know fighters'. According to Tommy, what security procedure did Alfie's men undergo on entering the building?

   ○ PAT DOWN
   ○ STRIP-SEARCH
   ○ IDENTITY PAPER CHECK
   ○ WEAPONS CONFISCATED

7. Polly finds Lizzie at the mirror in the ladies' toilet. She asks how Tommy reacted when she told him she was pregnant. What does Lizzie tell her that prompts Polly to observe sarcastically how romantic her nephew can be?

   ○ TOMMY OFFERED HER A WEEKLY ALLOWANCE
   ○ HE SUGGESTED SHE CUT HER HOURS AS COMPANY SECRETARY
   ○ HE QUESTIONED IF IT WAS HIS BABY
   ○ HER OFFERED HER A ONE-TIME PAYMENT

8. 'Have a swig. You're going to need it.' Polly invites Lizzie to tell Ada her news when she joins them in the toilets. What does Ada ask her aunt to foretell?

   ○ THE DUE DATE OF THE BABY
   ○ THE GENDER OF THE BABY
   ○ THE COLOUR OF THE BABY'S EYES
   ○ THE BABY'S DESTINY

SEASON FOUR ▮▮▮ EPISODE SIX

9. Linda joins the women, complaining that she has spit on her back. What advice does Polly give to her?

○ TELL ARTHUR
○ RESPOND WITH A SLAP TO THE FACE
○ SPIT BACK
○ RESPOND WITH A PUNCH ON THE NOSE

10. The bell goes for round three. Arthur is still troubled by the men in the corner with Alfie's fighter, while the women rejoin their seats in high spirits and swig from a bottle of Tommy's gin. What is Arthur's opinion of this new batch?

○ TOO SWEET
○ TOO DRY
○ TOO STRONG
○ TOO DRINKABLE

11. Arthur heads into the corridors, following one of the men from Alfie's corner. The man is in the changing room, collecting a garrotte. He has smuggled it into the building inside what?

○ A KIT BAG
○ A BOXING GLOVE
○ A MEDICAL BOX
○ A SHOE

12. Arthur is drunk and wired on pills, but draws his gun on entering the fighters' bath house. A moment later, the man reveals himself to be one of Luca's Mafia assassins. What alerts Tommy to the attack?

○ A CRY
○ A GUNSHOT
○ A BOTTLE SMASHING ON THE FLOOR
○ A SCREAM

13. Tommy takes out the assassin, but finds Arthur motionless on the floor. Out in the corridor, whom does he prevent from entering?

   ○ ADA
   ○ LINDA
   ○ POLLY
   ○ LIZZIE

14. Dazed but determined, Tommy rallies his men. In the ring, at the same time, Bonnie delivers the knockout blow. As what is he crowned?

   ○ MIDLANDS LIGHTWEIGHT CHAMPION
   ○ WELTERWEIGHT CHAMPION OF MIDLANDS SOUTH
   ○ CENTRAL WELTERWEIGHT CHAMPION
   ○ NORTHERN FEATHERWEIGHT CHAMPION

15. When Polly tells Linda about Arthur, what is her first reaction?

   ○ SHE DROPS INTO A CHAIR
   ○ SHE COLLAPSES
   ○ SHE WAILS
   ○ SHE FALLS TO THE FLOOR

16. Finn and Isaiah capture the second mobster in the corridor. What does Tommy instruct his youngest brother to do 'for Arthur'?

   ○ KILL HIM
   ○ CUT HIS THROAT
   ○ TAKE HIS EYES
   ○ SHOOT HIM

SEASON FOUR EPISODE SIX

17. 'My brother is dead! You hear me?' Tommy addresses the audience from the ring, having fired his gun into the air to command their attention. Who attempts to console him?

   ○ BONNIE
   ○ ABERAMA GOLD
   ○ CHARLIE STRONG
   ○ JOHNNY DOGS

18. With funeral preparations underway, Polly takes a call from Michael. She tells him that they won't be sailing to Australia after all, and he no longer needs to remain in hiding. Who has she arranged to collect him?

   ○ BONNIE GOLD
   ○ TOMMY
   ○ ABERAMA GOLD
   ○ CURLY

19. When Michael arrives, Polly is waiting for him with Tommy and Ada. There, he learns that Tommy is dispatching him to New York to handle company business. Tommy also tells him he's aware Michael chose not to warn him of the Changretta ambush. What is Michael's response?

   ○ 'I CHOSE MY MUM.'
   ○ 'I HAD NO CHOICE.'
   ○ 'I'M SORRY.'
   ○ 'YOU WOULD HAVE DONE THE SAME.'

20. Tommy informs him that the ship sails the next day. What is the name of the vessel?

   ○ SS DORIC
   ○ SS ALBERTIC
   ○ SS MONROE
   ○ SS DEVONIAN

21. The Peaky Blinders gather at Black Patch for the funeral, only for proceedings to halt when Mrs Changretta approaches with a white flag. What does Tommy ask her?

   - ○ TO JOIN THEM AS A MARK OF RESPECT FOR ALL WHO HAVE DIED
   - ○ TO LEAVE AND HE WILL FIND HER LATER
   - ○ TO STAND WITH HIM FOR HER OWN PROTECTION
   - ○ TO WAIT UNTIL THE FUNERAL HAS FINISHED

22. 'The vendetta is won.' What does Mrs Changretta demand in return for an end to the killing?

   - ○ THE BETTING SHOP AND RACE TRACKS
   - ○ ALL THE SHELBY BUSINESSES
   - ○ TOMMY MUST LEAVE BIRMINGHAM FOREVER
   - ○ TOMMY AND FINN MUST SWEAR ALLEGIANCE TO THE MAFIA

23. Luca Changretta pays a visit to Alfie Solomon's bakery. He's there to buy his business. How does he discover that Alfie 'has already left town'?

   - ○ THE BAKERY WORKERS TELL HIM ALFIE HAS GONE
   - ○ ALFIE HAS LEFT A PROVOCATIVE NOTE FOR LUCA PINNED TO THE DOOR
   - ○ ALFIE HAS BOOBY-TRAPPED THE OFFICE DOOR
   - ○ THE OFFICE HAS BEEN CLEARED OUT

24. Lizzie bursts in on Tommy and Polly, who are busy preparing for Luca Changretta's arrival in Birmingham the next day. Why is she upset with him?

   - ○ HE NEVER VISITS HER
   - ○ HE HASN'T ASKED ABOUT THE BABY
   - ○ SHE KNOWS ABOUT HIS EVENING WITH JESSIE EDEN
   - ○ SHE WANTS JOHN TO STAY IN ENGLAND

SEASON FOUR ▮ EPISODE SIX

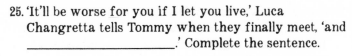

25. 'It'll be worse for you if I let you live,' Luca Changretta tells Tommy when they finally meet, 'and _____.' Complete the sentence.

   ○ ... LEAVE YOU WITH NOTHING BUT REGRET FOR STARTING THIS WAR
   ○ ... TAKE AWAY EVERYTHING THAT YOU HAVE
   ○ ... CARRY THE RESPONSIBILITY FOR YOUR OWN DOWNFALL
   ○ ... EVERY DAY YOU'LL WISH I HAD PUT YOU OUT OF YOUR MISERY

26. Where does Changretta demand that Tommy sign the documents that will complete his downfall?

   ○ AT THE TABLE
   ○ ON HIS KNEES
   ○ ON THE BENCH
   ○ BEFORE WHAT'S LEFT OF HIS FAMILY

27. When Tommy responds, he calmly reveals that he's been in touch with several contacts who plan to make a move on the Changretta family's New York business should Luca fail to return home. What is the name of his contact in Chicago?

   ○ BUGS MORAN
   ○ DEAN O'BANION
   ○ ALPHONSE CAPONE
   ○ VINCENT DRUCCI

28. To complete his counterstrike, Tommy informs Luca that the men standing behind him have been bought out by the Peaky Blinders. Luca turns to find their guns trained on him, including that of his right-hand man. What is his name?

   ○ FREDERICO
   ○ MATTEO
   ○ LORENZO
   ○ ROCCO

29. Enraged, Luca draws his gun to shoot Tommy. Before a fight breaks out between the two men, what does Tommy use to knock the weapon from his grasp?

- ○ A SPANNER
- ○ A GIN BOTTLE
- ○ A TABLE LEG
- ○ A CHAIR

30. Bloodied and beaten, Luca is forced to face Arthur as he returns from the dead. Who else knew about Tommy's plan to hide his brother and convince everyone he'd been killed?

- ○ LIZZIE AND ESME
- ○ POLLY AND LINDA
- ○ ADA AND FINN
- ○ CHARLIE STRONG AND CURLY

31. With a bullet in Luca's head, engraved with his name, Tommy addresses the Mafia men. He orders them to go home and tell their bosses that the Shelby Company Ltd will be importing gin into New York. How many barrels a month do they plan to ship?

- ○ 300
- ○ 350
- ○ 400
- ○ 450

32. 'Last time we were all here, it ended badly.' Tommy gathers friends and family back at his manor house, but it's Arthur who takes over from him to say a few words. What does he say they have found for the first time since he, Tommy and John enlisted with the Warwickshire Yeomanry?

- ○ CALM
- ○ HARMONY
- ○ PEACE
- ○ SILENCE

SEASON FOUR EPISODE SIX

33. With no more enemies to face, what does Arthur suggest Tommy consider?

○ RETIREMENT
○ A QUIETER LIFE
○ A HOLIDAY
○ A GYPSY LIFE

34. The next time Tommy faces Alfie Solomons, they're on a beach in Margate. Who else is present as they discuss the past, present and future?

○ ALFIE'S DOG, CYRIL
○ ALFIE'S RIGHT-HAND MAN, OLLIE
○ FINN SHELBY
○ CURLY

35. 'I once told you,' says Tommy, 'that for business reasons or _____, I would kill you.' Complete the sentence.

○ ... THE SAFETY OF MY FAMILY
○ ... IN BAD BLOOD
○ ... SETTLING SCORES
○ ... ACTS OF TREACHERY

36. As Tommy levels his gun, Alfie reveals that he has cancer. Where does the doctor say he might have 'picked it up'?

○ AT THE BAKERY FROM THE FUMES
○ IN FRANCE FROM THE GAS
○ IN LONDON FROM THE SMOKE
○ FROM HIS MOTHER'S SIDE

SEASON FOUR ▮ EPISODE SIX

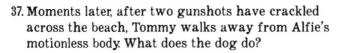

37. Moments later, after two gunshots have crackled across the beach, Tommy walks away from Alfie's motionless body. What does the dog do?

   ○ SNARLS AT TOMMY IN HIS WAKE
   ○ LICKS THE BLOOD FROM ALFIE'S FACE
   ○ RUNS AWAY
   ○ LIES BESIDE HIS FALLEN MASTER

38. 'It's just myself talking to myself about myself.' Three months later, Tommy is struggling with the quiet life. He's plagued by wartime memories and finally accepts there can be no rest. Returning to work, he asks Mr Devlin to deliver a note to Jessie Eden before what?

   ○ PROMOTING HIM TO RUN THE MOTOR COMPANY
   ○ GIVING HIM A MONTH OFF WITH PAY TO SPEND TIME WITH HIS FAMILY
   ○ INVITING HIM TO MANAGE THE BETTING SHOP
   ○ RELEASING HIM FROM THE PEAKY BLINDERS TO JOIN HIS FAMILY IN GLASGOW

39. Amid a general strike, Tommy seduces Jessie and convinces her that he's joined her cause. With his position as an insider secured, he forges a deal with establishment figures to stand in the next general election. What seat does Tommy win?

   ○ LABOUR MP FOR BIRMINGHAM SOUTH
   ○ CONSERVATIVE MP FOR BIRMINGHAM SOUTH
   ○ LIBERAL MP FOR BIRMINGHAM LADYWOOD
   ○ INDEPENDENT MP FOR BIRMINGHAM LADYWOOD

SEASON FOUR ▮ EPISODE SIX

KILLER QUESTIONS

40. What is the central flag that hangs behind the boxing ring when Bonnie faces Alfie's fighter?

   ○ UNION JACK
   ○ FLAG OF ENGLAND
   ○ FLAG OF ISRAEL
   ○ FLAG OF THE ROMANY PEOPLE

41. At the boxing match, when Arthur acts on his suspicions and follows one of the men from the ringside, he walks past a poster promoting the fight. What is the date?

   ○ FEBRUARY 09
   ○ FEBRUARY 10
   ○ FEBRUARY 11
   ○ FEBRUARY 12

42. Preparing for his showdown with Luca Changretta, Tommy inspects a bottle in his gin distillery. The number in the corner of the label denotes a limited edition. What is it?

   ○ 2/500
   ○ 18/300
   ○ 5/200
   ○ 25/400

SEASON FIVE

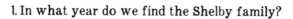

1. In what year do we find the Shelby family?

   ○ 1926
   ○ 1927
   ○ 1928
   ○ 1929

2. Tommy approaches a red phone box on horseback. It's a cold, blustery day in October. The phone is ringing. Where is he?

   ○ SMALL HEATH, BIRMINGHAM
   ○ MALVERN HILLS, WORCESTERSHIRE
   ○ MAYFAIR, LONDON
   ○ THE LICKEY HILLS, WARWICKSHIRE

3. 'We cannot give you the assurance that you are asking for. We expect payment in full ... we are not afraid of your threats.' Down the line, Arthur reads out a letter to Tommy. Who is it signed by?

   ○ THE ANGELS OF DEATH
   ○ THE ANGELS OF RETRIBUTION
   ○ THE ANGELS FROM HELL
   ○ THE ANGELS OF JUSTICE

4. 'They say they haven't even heard of us.' Who does Tommy call, ordering Aberama Gold and Isaiah to pay a visit to the man responsible and make sure he never forgets?

   ○ CHARLIE STRONG
   ○ FINN
   ○ JEREMIAH JESUS
   ○ BONNIE GOLD

SEASON FIVE ▮ EPISODE ONE

5. At the Shelby Company office in America, Michael Gray is out cold amid empty bottles, cocaine vials, overflowing ashtrays and a beautiful woman called Gina asleep on the floor. Where is the office?

   ○ BOSTON
   ○ NEW YORK
   ○ DETROIT
   ○ CHICAGO

6. Michael is roused by a telephone call, and it appears to be bad news. What does he scramble to check to confirm his worst fears?

   ○ A TELEGRAM
   ○ THE TICKER TAPE MACHINE
   ○ THE NEWSPAPER
   ○ THE RADIO

7. 'Now will you please fly me, and my winnings, back to England.' Polly, meanwhile, is enjoying the attentions of a handsome young pilot called Peter. Where is she?

   ○ PARIS
   ○ MONTE CARLO
   ○ MALTA
   ○ PRAGUE

8. Tommy rides back to the riverside gypsy camp where Lizzie and their daughter, Ruby, await him. He takes a swig from a little bottle of medicine. Young Ruby is pretending to pour tea. How many spoonfuls of sugar does Lizzie request?

   ○ ONE
   ○ TWO
   ○ FIVE
   ○ TEN

9. 'This morning in New York at 6am, the Wall Street
Stock Exchange crashed like a steam train,' says
Arthur, relaying the news from Michael to Polly.
What does he add to finish?

   ○ 'AND WE WERE RIDING IN THE FIRST CARRIAGE.'
   ○ 'AND WE'RE CASUALTIES IN THE WRECKAGE.'
   ○ 'AND WE WERE MOST DEFINITELY ON BOARD.'
   ○ 'AND THERE ARE VERY FEW SURVIVORS.'

10. Michael scrambles to board the first passage back to
England. What reason does Gina give for insisting on
accompanying him?

   ○ SHE'S WORRIED MICHAEL MIGHT NEVER COME BACK
   ○ HE SUPPLIES HER COCAINE
   ○ SHE WANTS TO MEET HIS FAMILY
   ○ IT'S AN OPPORTUNITY TO SEE THE SIGHTS

11. Finn and Isaiah have cornered their quarry. He's
backed up in a darkened room, firing wildly at the
pair in the corridor. When Finn takes a bullet to the
arm, how does Aberama make his entrance and take
the man down?

   ○ SWINGING THROUGH THE WINDOW
   ○ DROPPING DOWN FROM AN ATTIC
   ○ RUSHING UP THE STAIRS
   ○ SMASHING THROUGH THE PARTITION WALL

12. 'Peaky boy, give me your blade.' Aberama tends to
Finn's wound, prising out the bullet and washing it
down with alcohol. Where does this take place?

   ○ AN ALLEYWAY
   ○ THE BACK OF ABERAMA'S CAR
   ○ ADA'S TOWNHOUSE
   ○ ON THE FLOOR BESIDE THE DEAD MAN

SEASON FIVE ▮ EPISODE ONE

13. In reassuring Finn, Aberama tells him that he once removed a bullet from a horse that was an inch away from its heart. What does he say happened to the horse?

○ IT WON EVERY RACE THE FOLLOWING SEASON
○ IT DIED
○ IT WENT ON TO SIRE A DERBY WINNER
○ IT SOLD AT AUCTION FOR 500 GUINEAS

14. Tommy rides into camp, where Johnny Dogs and his men have finished digging a grave to bury a horse. His son, Charles, is refusing to come out of one of the wagons. Why?

○ HE'D WITNESSED HIS FATHER SHOOT THE HORSE BECAUSE IT WAS SICK
○ HE'D OVERHEARD JOHNNY SAYING IN ROMANY THAT TOMMY HAD PUT THE HORSE DOWN
○ HE WASN'T ALLOWED TO HELP DIG THE GRAVE
○ THE HORSE BELONGED TO HIM

15. Taking Ruby by the hand, Tommy pays his last respects to 'Dangerous, my beautiful horse.' He falters before finishing, and reminds himself of the moment he pulled the trigger. In his reverie, what does he do with the gun immediately afterwards?

○ THROWS IT AWAY
○ FIRES IT IN THE AIR
○ PRESSES THE MUZZLE TO HIS OWN HEAD
○ HANDS IT TO JOHNNY DOGS

16. Arthur drives out to break the news to Tommy about the stock market crash. What day does Tommy say he warned his cousin this would happen, so that he could protect the company investments?

○ TUESDAY
○ WEDNESDAY
○ THURSDAY
○ FRIDAY

17. According to Arthur, why did Michael leave the company money invested in the market as prices dropped just prior to the crash?

   ○ THE BROKER ADVISED HIM THAT PRICES WOULD REBOUND
   ○ MICHAEL FORGOT TO PUT THE CALL IN TO SELL
   ○ MICHAEL CALLED THE BROKER TO SELL BUT HE WOULDN'T RETURN HIS CALL
   ○ MICHAEL HAD PLANNED TO SELL THAT MORNING BUT OVERSLEPT

18. In shock and frustrated that people aren't listening to him, Tommy sends Arthur and Lizzie away so he can consider their next move alone. Before leaving, he asks his brother to give young Charles some advice following the loss of Dangerous. 'Sometimes, death is _____,' he says. Fill in the blank.

   ○ ... THE ONLY PATH IN LIFE
   ○ ... A KINDNESS
   ○ ... FOR THE BEST
   ○ ... ALL THAT STANDS IN THE WAY OF PEACE

19. 'What am I? Your genie?' Grace appears to Tommy across the campfire. What does she suggest is fuelling these comforting visions of his dead wife?

   ○ MEDICINE
   ○ ALCOHOL
   ○ GRIEF
   ○ ANGER

20. 'You must listen to the voices you hear. Do what they are telling you to do.' Apart from the children, what else does Tommy say is stopping him from joining Grace in the next life?

   ○ HE CAN'T BRING HIMSELF TO DO IT
   ○ HE HAS LIZZIE NOW
   ○ HE HAS TOO MUCH TO DO
   ○ ARTHUR AND FINN CAN'T AFFORD TO LOSE ANOTHER BROTHER

SEASON FIVE ▮ EPISODE ONE

21. Arthur finds Linda in the office at Shelby Company Ltd, just after she's secretly fuelled her growing cocaine habit. He is Chairman now, but what reason does he give for this promotion?

   O TOMMY BELIEVES THE RESPONSIBILITY WOULD KEEP HIS BROTHER FROM DRINK AND DRUGS
   O SO THAT TOMMY CAN STAY CLEAN FROM ANY CRIMINAL ENTERPRISE IN HIS ROLE AS MP
   O TO HELP ARTHUR IN HIS STRUGGLE TO MOVE ON FROM THE HORRORS OF WAR
   O TOMMY HAS LOST INTEREST IN THE COMPANY

22. Linda voices her resentment of Tommy, believing he has put his own interests first by spending time on parliamentary business in London. Who does she compare him to?

   O GLADSTONE
   O THE SHERRIFF OF NOTTINGHAM
   O ROOSEVELT
   O ROBIN HOOD

23. Arthur chairs the board meeting, but struggles without Tommy. As they wait for his arrival, new member Mr Greene expresses his pleasure at being in a boardroom with so many females. How does he describe them?

   O FORMIDABLE AND ATTRACTIVE
   O SHARP-WITTED AND DECORATIVE
   O SMART AND PRETTY
   O IMPRESSIVE AND ALLURING

24. Tommy arrives, and outlines the gravity of the situation. The company had invested heavily in the New York Stock Exchange, he tells them, and stocks are effectively worthless. When Tommy adds that there is hope, Polly scoffs and suggests he's about to produce what from his briefcase?

○ £1 MILLION
○ A ROYAL DECREE
○ A TIME MACHINE
○ A MAGIC WAND

25. With the meeting concluded, Tommy leads the Peaky Blinders to the Garrison. There, he's given a hero's welcome for his political services to the community. One man pumps his hand, thanks Tommy for stepping in to stop his landlord from evicting him. What is the outcome of Tommy's intervention?

○ THE TENANT NOW LIVES RENT-FREE
○ HE'S HAD HIS RENT HALVED
○ THE LANDLORD RETIRED
○ THE TENANCY HAS BEEN EXTENDED BY FIVE YEARS

26. Addressing the throng, Tommy invites his constituents to move to the saloon bar and enjoy a free pint of what?

○ PICKWICK
○ STINGO
○ GUINNESS
○ ARROW

SEASON FIVE ▓ EPISODE ONE

27. With the main bar emptied, Tommy, Ada, Lizzie, Arthur and Polly sit down for the real meeting. Ada wants to know why Tommy dispatched Finn as part of a hit squad to kill a man in Chinatown. What is Tommy's explanation?

○ THE MAN WAS THREATENING TO KIDNAP KARL
○ THE MAN WAS PIMPING CHILDREN AND BRIBING A SENIOR JUDGE
○ THE MAN WAS THREATENING TO KIDNAP CHARLIE AND RUBY
○ THE MAN WAS TRAFFICKING DRUGS AND BRIBING A SENIOR POLICEMAN

28. Tommy explains that the assassination was carried out with the blessing of the police. What assistance did they provide?

○ ALERTING THE PEAKY BLINDERS TO THE TARGET'S LOCATION
○ CLEARING THE STREETS
○ CLEANING THE SCENE OF THE CRIME
○ ENSURING THAT FINN, ISAIAH AND ABERAMA MADE A SAFE GETAWAY

29. 'The corridors of _____ are very dimly lit,' Tommy tells Lizzie. Fill in the blank.

○ ... PARLIAMENT
○ ... POWER
○ ... WESTMINSTER
○ ... THE HOUSE OF COMMONS

30. Ada is equally upset with Tommy, who believes he is going back on his promise to put the business on a legitimate footing. What is Tommy's argument for pursuing this line of work in light of the stock market crash?

○ CASH IS KING
○ NO OTHER WORK IS AVAILABLE
○ IT'S THE ONLY WAY TO COVER WAGES
○ SHELBY COMPANY LTD FACES RUIN WITHOUT IT

31. After Ada leaves the pub, Polly asks Tommy to go easy on her. Tommy has already worked out that Ada is pregnant, but what else does Polly know?

    ○ THE GENDER OF THE BABY
    ○ THE IDENTITY OF THE FATHER
    ○ THE DUE DATE
    ○ ADA IS STRUGGLING WITH MORNING SICKNESS

32. Tommy asks Arthur to inspect the bullet that shot Finn. What 'funny writing' does Arthur notice inscribed on it?

    ○ GERMAN
    ○ CHINESE
    ○ POLISH
    ○ RUSSIAN

33. Tommy travels to Westminster, where he makes a rousing speech defending the working man from the 'establishment' in recovering from the crash. Afterwards, he is congratulated by Oswald Mosley. What connection does Mosley make between then?

    ○ THEY SHARE THE SAME TAILOR
    ○ THEY EACH LIVE IN MANORS DESIGNED BY THE SAME ARCHITECT
    ○ THEIR CONSTITUENCIES BORDER ONE ANOTHER
    ○ THEY DRIVE THE SAME MODEL CAR

34. 'I'm afraid my wife and I have had some misfortune on the London Stock Exchange.' Tommy visits the parliamentary office of Lord Suckerby, who owes him money. Having set a deadline for Suckerby to pay, what else does Tommy do before leaving?

    ○ TIPS A BOTTLE OF WINE ACROSS THE PAPERS ON SUCKERBY'S DESK
    ○ TIPS THE ASHTRAY ONTO HIS PAPERWORK
    ○ TIPS A GLASS OF WHISKEY ACROSS THE BLOTTER ON HIS DESK
    ○ DROPS HIS CIGARETTE INTO SUCKERBY'S GLASS OF WHISKEY

SEASON FIVE ▮ EPISODE ONE

35. Colonel Ben Younger visits Ada. She has an envelope for him containing intelligence gathered from Tommy on anti-establishment activities. What does Younger say he will receive for his efforts?

- ⭘ TWO MORE MILITARY CONTACTS
- ⭘ A CASH PAYMENT
- ⭘ AN EXPORT PERMIT FOR NORTH AFRICA
- ⭘ A RECOMMENDATION FOR THE NEW YEAR'S HONOURS LIST

36. Tommy is visited in his parliamentary offices by Mr Levitt, a former Birmingham journalist now working for The Times. Levitt begins to ask uncomfortable questions about Tommy's past. In particular, he's interested in the death of which individual?

- ⭘ BILLY KIMBER
- ⭘ VICENTE CHANGRETTA
- ⭘ MAJOR CAMPBELL
- ⭘ GRACE SHELBY

37. How does Tommy respond to Levitt's line of questioning?

- ⭘ BY REFUSING TO ANSWER ANY FURTHER QUESTIONS AND ASKING HIM TO LEAVE
- ⭘ BY THREATENING TO CALL HIS EDITOR IN THE MORNING
- ⭘ BY REVEALING THAT HE'S UNDERTAKEN HIS OWN RESEARCH, INTO THE JOURNALIST'S PERSONAL AFFAIRS
- ⭘ BY PROMISING TO END HIS CAREER IF HE EVER PUBLISHES A STORY ABOUT HIM

38. 'We're flying above the rules now.' Polly is expecting
    Ada when she visits that evening. Ada has some
    reservations about keeping the baby, but her aunt
    reminds her that they live in a modern world and
    the family are in a fortunate position. What do they
    drink as they talk?

    O PALE ALE
    O CHAMPAGNE
    O TEA
    O PORT

39. Mr Levitt, the journalist, returns to his apartment
    building only to meet a brutal, bloody end in a hail
    of gunfire from two men in flat caps and overcoats.
    Where does he die?

    O THE LOBBY
    O THE STAIRS
    O THE LIFT
    O THE CORRIDOR

SEASON FIVE ▓ EPISODE ONE

KILLER QUESTIONS

40. In Limehouse, as Aberama, Finn and Isaiah hunt down the lone Angel, they pass through a door into a shop. What does the sign read on the panelling?

   ○ TAILOR SHOP
   ○ HARDWARE
   ○ CHINESE MEDICINE
   ○ HERBALIST

41. What is the name of the newspaper that Arthur hands Tommy to break the news to him about the Wall Street Crash?

   ○ THE TIMES
   ○ THE NEW YORK TIMES
   ○ DAILY ECHO
   ○ THE DAILY MAIL

42. What is the name of the American bank where Shelby Company Ltd invested their cash?

   ○ CALDWELL
   ○ NOLAN BANK
   ○ BANK OF ITALY
   ○ AMERICAN UNION BANK

1. From his master bedroom, Tommy spots an effigy. It's strapped to a cross in a ploughed field, complete with Peaky cap and overcoat, that has appeared overnight. What does he arm himself with on heading out to investigate?

   ○ A PISTOL
   ○ A MACHINE GUN
   ○ A SHOTGUN
   ○ A RIFLE

2. 'Look down on earth,' reads the note addressed to Tommy, '_____ .' Complete the sentence.

   ○ ... AND REMEMBER THIS MOMENT
   ○ ... AND REPENT OF YOUR SINS
   ○ ... AND SEE THE SEEDS YOU HAVE SOWN
   ○ ... AND THERE YOU WILL FIND HUMILITY

3. What does Tommy do with the note on registering the landmines planted all around?

   ○ FOLDS IT INTO A SQUARE
   ○ SCREWS IT UP IN HIS FIST
   ○ SLIPS IT INSIDE HIS POCKET
   ○ LETS THE WIND CARRY IT AWAY

4. A pocket watch is ticking, strapped around the effigy's neck. Slowly, Tommy retraces his steps. What causes him to run from the effigy?

   ○ THE TIMER STOPS TICKING
   ○ CHARLIE RUNS TOWARDS HIM FROM THE HOUSE
   ○ HE DISTURBS A LANDMINE
   ○ A MINE DETONATES BEHIND HIM

SEASON FIVE ▮ EPISODE TWO

5. How does Tommy deal with the landmines?

- ○ HE DIFFUSES THEM IN TURN
- ○ CALLS THE ROYAL ORDINANCE CORPS
- ○ DETONATES THEM IN A HAIL OF BULLETS
- ○ LOBS GRENADES FROM BEHIND THE GATE

6. Tommy missed a call from Belfast while dealing with the landmines. When he rings back, Michael answers. Very quickly, Tommy learns that he's been captured by nationalist Captain Swing and her men. Which region does Swing say she's from?

- ○ THE NORTH OF IRELAND
- ○ THE OCCUPIED TERRITORIES
- ○ THE OCCUPIED SIX COUNTIES
- ○ THE OCCUPIED ZONE

7. Despite Michael's denials, what does Swing allege that Michael had been caught doing when his home-bound ship docked at Belfast?

- ○ PLOTTING A BREAKAWAY BUSINESS VENTURE THAT UNDERMINES SHELBY COMPANY LTD
- ○ COLLABORATING WITH LOYALISTS TO BRING DOWN THE IRA
- ○ OFFERING TO SELL INFORMATION ON TOMMY'S COVERT GOVERNMENT OPERATIONS
- ○ MAKING DEALS WITH MEN TO TAKE DOWN TOMMY AND DIVIDE UP THE RACETRACKS

8. Captain Swing offers to put a bullet in Michael's head or return him home. Tommy takes the latter option, but why is Swing prepared to help him?

- ○ CAPTAIN SWING KNOWS THE SHELBYS WERE RESPONSIBLE FOR THE DEATH OF UNIONIST POLICE OFFICER – AND IRA ENEMY – MAJOR CAMPBELL
- ○ SWING IS PLANNING TO BLACKMAIL TOMMY
- ○ TOMMY'S POLITICAL ACTIVITIES AND POSITION IN A SOCIALIST PARTY COULD BE USEFUL TO HER
- ○ SHE INTENDS TO USE MICHAEL TO SPY ON TOMMY

SEASON FIVE ▬ EPISODE TWO

9. Frances the housekeeper asks Tommy to account for the loud explosions that have been heard across the manor. What does he tell her was responsible?

- ○ A CAR BACKFIRING
- ○ FIREWORKS
- ○ A PHEASANT SHOOT
- ○ THUNDER

10. Tommy joins Arthur as they head for the Garrison. Inside, with sunlight pushing through the windows, they find the remnants of a wild party. A girl lies passed out in her underwear. What does Arthur do when she wakes with a start?

- ○ THROWS HER A COAT
- ○ HANDS HER A WHISKEY
- ○ TURNS HIS BACK ON HER TO SPARE HER FROM EMBARRASSMENT
- ○ TURNS AROUND AND WALKS BACK OUTSIDE

11. Finn is out cold on a nearby seat. How does Arthur wake him?

- ○ ROLLS HIM ONTO THE FLOOR
- ○ SHOUTS IN HIS EAR
- ○ POURS A DRINK OVER HIS FACE
- ○ SHOOT A ROUND INTO THE CEILING

12. Tommy is upset with Finn because he's 'running round the streets' with a gun. Arthur chimes in that they have 'privates, corporals, captains' to take care of that side of the business. What does Tommy say this makes Finn?

- ○ A FOOL
- ○ A GENERAL
- ○ A LONE WOLF
- ○ A TARGET

SEASON FIVE ▮ EPISODE TWO

13. 'When I do sleep, I dream,' Tommy tells Arthur. 'And in my dream, someone wants my crown. I think it might be Michael.' With their cousin due back that day, Tommy asks Arthur to arm himself before heading for the station. Where is Michael's train coming from?

- ○ LONDON
- ○ PORTSMOUTH
- ○ LIVERPOOL
- ○ CHESTER

14. As Tommy leaves the Garrison, what plans does Finn have for the bullet that Aberama dug out of his arm?

- ○ TO HANG IT FROM A NECKLACE
- ○ TO MOUNT AND DISPLAY IT ON THE MANTELPIECE
- ○ TO STORE IT IN A TREASURE BOX
- ○ TO ASK POLLY IF SHE CAN SEE HIS FUTURE FROM IT

15. A police officer visits Tommy at his parliamentary office. How does he know that the journalist, Mr Levitt, visited Tommy on the night before his murder?

- ○ LEVITT HAD LEFT DETAILS OF THE APPOINTMENT ON NOTEPAPER BY HIS TELEPHONE
- ○ LEVITT TOLD HIS EDITOR ABOUT THE MEETING
- ○ LEVITT HAD A COMMONS PASS AND TOMMY'S NAME WAS IN HIS DIARY
- ○ LEVITT TOLD HIS LOVER ABOUT THE MEETING

16. Tommy resists further questioning on the matter by mentioning the fact that he knows the officer's superior, Chief Constable Wyatt. 'He likes persistence, as do I, and thoroughness,' Tommy tells him. 'But not _____.' Complete the sentence.

- ○ … FRIVOLITY
- ○ … FOOLISHNESS
- ○ … FISHING
- ○ … FRIPPERY

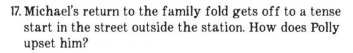

17. Michael's return to the family fold gets off to a tense start in the street outside the station. How does Polly upset him?

- ○ SHE'S LATE
- ○ SHE DEMANDS TO KNOW IF HE'S TELLING THE TRUTH ABOUT THE INCIDENT ON THE SHIP AT BELFAST
- ○ SHE REFUSES TO BELIEVE HE'S GOT MARRIED ON THE CROSSING
- ○ SHE SUGGESTS THAT GINA LOOKS LIKE TROUBLE

18. Michael's mood sours further when Arthur tells him he'll be staying at a nearby hotel. Why has Tommy made a reservation for him there?

- ○ IT'S NOT THE BEST HOTEL IN TOWN, AND MICHAEL PERCEIVES THAT AS A SLIGHT
- ○ TOMMY HAS CONTACTS IN THE HOTEL WHO CAN KEEP AN EYE ON MICHAEL
- ○ THERE IS NO PENTHOUSE SUITE, WHICH MICHAEL REGARDS AS AN INSULT
- ○ IT'S LOCATED NEAR A BUSY ROAD, MEANING THEIR STAY WILL NOT BE PEACEFUL

19. Oswald Mosley invites Tommy for a drink in the House of Commons bar. Ada accompanies him. What bird does Mosley compare her to as he charms her into a seat?

- ○ A BLACKBIRD
- ○ A FINCH
- ○ A ROBIN
- ○ A WREN

20. Mosley has some background information on Tommy, and admits they have a mutual acquaintance. Who is it?

- ○ RUBEN OLIVER
- ○ MAY CARLETON
- ○ TATIANA PETROVNA
- ○ COLONEL BEN YOUNGER

SEASON FIVE ▐ EPISODE TWO

21. 'We are the people and we have had enough.' Mosley quotes a line from Tommy's speech in the Commons, which appeals, out of context, to his political leaning in what direction?

   ○ LIBERTARIANISM
   ○ CONSERVATISM
   ○ FASCISM
   ○ ANARCHISM

22. 'We are looking for someone to begin a dialogue with certain elements in Belfast.' Mosley sounds out Tommy for the role, offering him a junior ministerial role to whom?

   ○ THE FIRST SECRETARY OF STATE
   ○ THE CHANCELLOR OF THE DUCHY OF LANCASTER
   ○ THE LORD CHANCELLOR
   ○ THE FIRST LORD OF THE TREASURY

23. Tommy declines the role, reminding Mosley that his priority is with his constituency members, and leaves with Ada. 'Ireland _____,' he says. Complete the sentence.

   ○ ... FAILS TO ENGAGE ME
   ○ ... BORES ME
   ○ ... IS BEYOND ME
   ○ ... WOULD OUTWIT A MAN LIKE ME

24. In the corridors of Parliament after dark, Tommy confides in Ada about his fear that his seat at the head of the Shelby empire is under threat. As well as Michael, Aberama Gold and Linda with her aspirations for Arthur, who else concerns him?

   ○ PEOPLE IN THE NORTH
   ○ THE ITALIANS
   ○ THE RUSSIANS
   ○ PEOPLE SOUTH OF LONDON

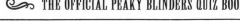
25. Back at the Garrison, before Michael arrives, what does Polly ask Arthur and Tommy to do?

   ○ SIT DOWN
   ○ POUR THEMSELVES A DRINK
   ○ REFRAIN FROM SWEARING
   ○ LAY DOWN THEIR WEAPONS

26. As a car pulls up outside, Tommy mentions that he's had a dream about a black cat, and that it suggests a traitor is close by. What else does Polly say it can symbolise?

   ○ TOMMY IS HURTING OR BETRAYING HIMSELF
   ○ TOMMY IS VULNERABLE TO MISFORTUNE
   ○ TOMMY IS MELANCHOLY OR DEPRESSED
   ○ TOMMY MUST FACE UP TO HIS DEEPEST FEARS

27. Michael introduces his new wife, Gina, to Tommy, before asking to address him, Arthur and Polly. 'I betrayed you,' he says, '_____.' Complete the sentence.

   ○ ... BUT WITH NO DAMAGE DONE
   ○ ... BUT I MADE AMENDS
   ○ ... BUT ONLY IN MY HEART
   ○ ... BUT NOT AS YOU MIGHT IMAGINE

28. What does Michael say stopped him from stealing company money, moving to California and 'investing in pictures'.

   ○ HIS CONSCIENCE
   ○ MEETING GINA
   ○ LIVING IN FEAR OF RETRIBUTION
   ○ HAVING TO FACE HIS MOTHER

SEASON FIVE ▮ EPISODE TWO

29. Michael accounts for what happened before the IRA seized him. He claims that whiskey smugglers had come on board to discuss business, only to reveal themselves as members of the protestant Glaswegian razor gang, Billy Boys. According to Michael, how did they describe Tommy?

○ A WEAK KING
○ A SPENT FORCE
○ A POWERLESS POLITICIAN
○ A DEAD MAN

30. 'They also dabble in politics,' says Arthur. Where have the Billy Boys earned a reputation in this field?

○ POLLING STATION INTIMIDATION
○ PROTECTION AT FASCIST RALLIES
○ ANTI-LEFT-WING PROTESTS
○ BODYGUARDS FOR HARD-RIGHT-WING MPS

31. Having sworn he's telling the truth, Michael also reveals that Gina is pregnant. Tommy offers his congratulations, but what then causes Michael to erupt in fury?

○ TOMMY QUESTIONS IF HE'S THE FATHER
○ TOMMY SUGGESTS THAT THERE COULD BE CONSEQUENCES FOR MICHAEL'S UNBORN BABY IF HE'S LYING
○ HE TELLS MICHAEL THAT THE UNBORN BABY NEEDS A BETTER ROLE MODEL AS A FATHER
○ TOMMY SUGGESTS THAT GINA IS UNFIT TO BE A MOTHER

32. In addition, what does Tommy demand from Michael?

○ RECOGNITION THAT DISLOYALTY COULD HAVE FATAL CONSEQUENCES
○ PAYBACK FOR THE MONEY HE LOST IN THE CRASH
○ A GUARANTEE THAT HE WON'T FLEE BACK TO AMERICA
○ PAYBACK FOR THE MONEY TOMMY KNOWS HE'S SPENT ON DRUGS

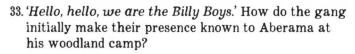

33. *'Hello, hello, we are the Billy Boys.'* How do the gang initially make their presence known to Aberama at his woodland camp?

- O THEY CAPTURE HIM WITH A KNIFE TO HIS THROAT
- O THEY SHOOT HIM IN THE THIGH
- O THEY DROP HIM WITH A BULLET TO THE SHOULDER
- O THEY SET A ROPE SNARE FOR HIM WALK INTO

34. How does Billy Boy leader Jimmy introduce himself to Bonnie Gold?

- O KNEECAPPING HIM
- O SLASHING HIS FACE
- O SHOOTING HIM IN THE FOOT
- O BREAKING HIS JAW

35. Bonnie is subject to a horrifying crucifixion at the hands of Jimmy and his gang. Before leaving Aberama distraught on the woodland floor, what do they tell him they want from Tommy?

- O HIS EXPORT LICENCES
- O HIS PRIMARY HORSE-RACING TRACKS
- O HIS ALCOHOL-SMUGGLING BUSINESS
- O HIS CAR-MANUFACTURING FACTORIES

36. Arthur, Finn and Isaiah approach pub singer Billy Grade, giving him little option but to work on a match-fixing venture. What is his former profession?

- O REFEREE
- O FOOTBALLER
- O COACH
- O CLUB TREASURER

37. Arthur sinks into the sofa after another long day, but peace is hard to find when Linda says she's written him an ultimatum about their future. She adds that Lizzie has also written one to Tommy because he won't have long to live unless he changes. How much time does Lizzie give him?

○ SIX MONTHS
○ A YEAR
○ EIGHTEEN MONTHS
○ TWO YEARS

38. At Arrow House, Lizzie learns that Tommy burned her letter after reading it. When he refuses to engage in a discussion, what does she have to remind him about regarding the significance of the day?

○ IT'S THEIR WEDDING ANNIVERSARY
○ IT'S CHARLES'S BIRTHDAY
○ IT'S RUBY'S BIRTHDAY
○ IT'S THE ANNIVERSARY OF HIS FATHER'S DEATH

39. With his shoulder shattered, Aberama disturbs the peace in the driveway at Arrow House. Who does he kick out of the car outside the main entrance, beaten and bleeding, convinced he told the Billy Boys where he and his son could be found?

○ JOHNNY DOGS
○ JEREMIAH JESUS
○ CHARLIE STRONG
○ ISAIAH JESUS

KILLER QUESTIONS

40. As Tommy dresses for the day in the opening scene, what play by William Shakespeare lies open on the table beside him?

- ⟡ HENRY V
- ⟡ RICHARD II
- ⟡ EDWARD III
- ⟡ HENRY VIII

41. What is the name of the station where Polly meets Michael and his new wife?

- ⟡ YARDLEY WOOD
- ⟡ SNOW HILL
- ⟡ NEW STREET
- ⟡ SMALL HEATH & SPARKBROOK

42. During a debate in the House of Commons, what is the name of the bill that Tommy supports, raising the school-leaving age to 15?

- ⟡ TURNISS EDUCATION BILL
- ⟡ TROWTON EDUCATION BILL
- ⟡ TREVELYAN EDUCATION BILL
- ⟡ TREMAIN EDUCATION BILL

SEASON FIVE ▮▮▮ EPISODE TWO

1. Tommy and Polly visit a convent where the children in care are funded by the Grace Shelby Foundation. What is their issue with the Mother Superior?

   U SHE HAS BEEN SYPHONING FUNDS FOR HER OWN USE
   U THE CHILDREN IN HER CARE HAVE BEEN ABUSED
   U SHE HAS BEEN SENDING THE CHILDREN OUT TO WORK
   U THE CHILDREN IN HER CARE ARE GOING HUNGRY

2. 'We are much, much closer at hand than God.' Tommy seizes the glasses from Mother Superior's face. What does he do with them?

   U SNAPS THEM IN TWO
   U POCKETS THEM
   U SMASHES THE LENSES
   U FLINGS THEM AT THE CROSS ON THE WALL

3. What sanction does Tommy impose on Mother Superior before declaring that the children will be rehomed?

   U HE WITHDRAWS ALL FUNDING
   U HE IMPOSES A FINE
   U HE DEMANDS THAT SHE STEP DOWN WITH IMMEDIATE EFFECT
   U HE SUGGESTS SHE ANSWERS TO GOD

4. 'Happy birthday, Pol.' The Peaky Blinders are waiting for Tommy and her aunt when they pull up at Charlie Strong's yard. What gift does Finn give her?

   U A NECKLACE
   U A BOTTLE OF CHAMPAGNE
   U THE KEY TO A NEW CAR
   U A BUNCH OF RED ROSES

5. How old is Polly on this day?

   U 40
   U 42
   U 45
   U 48

6. Tommy tells his men that they'll be travelling to London as part of a plan to avenge the death of Aberama's son. What reason does Michael give for staying in Birmingham, before relenting at Tommy's insistence?

   ○ HE'D ARRANGED TO SHOW GINA AROUND THE CITY
   ○ HE'S EXPECTING A BUSINESS CALL FROM AMERICA
   ○ GINA HAS A MATERNITY APPOINTMENT AT HOSPITAL
   ○ GINA IS FEELING UNWELL

7. Tommy asks Polly to visit Aberama Gold in hospital to promise him that his son, Bonnie, has not died in vain. Polly asks why she should be the one to see him. What is Tommy's response?

   ○ SHE HAS A GIFT FOR CONSOLING THE BEREAVED
   ○ ABERAMA IS IN LOVE WITH HER
   ○ ABERAMA STILL BLAMES TOMMY FOR BONNIE'S DEATH
   ○ BONNIE WAS FOND OF POLLY

8. 'Curly,' Tommy says, 'organise a wagon to take Bonnie Gold's soul to heaven.' What does he ask Isaiah to fetch to burn with his body?

   ○ HIS CHAMPIONSHIP BELT
   ○ HIS BOXING GLOVES
   ○ HIS NECKERCHIEF
   ○ A PHOTOGRAPH OF HIS MOTHER

9. When Tommy asks Michael to turn the Bentley around, what does Charlie Strong lob at him?

   ○ THE STARTING HANDLE
   ○ A PAIR OF DRIVING GLOVES
   ○ AN OILY RAG
   ○ MICHAEL'S HAT

SEASON FIVE EPISODE THREE

10. In the corridors of Westminster, approaching their meeting with Oswald Mosley, Michael asks Tommy what the strategy is. He tells Michael to smile. What are his instructions for Arthur?

ひ DON'T SMILE
ひ DON'T SPEAK
ひ DON'T BLINK
ひ DON'T LOSE YOUR COOL

11. 'The man we're about to meet is _____,' Tommy warns them just moments before Oswald Mosley joins them. Complete the sentence.

ひ ... SATAN HIMSELF
ひ ... THE BEAST
ひ ... A MONSTER
ひ ... THE DEVIL

12. While Tommy wants to know his connection to Jimmy McCavern, Mosley reveals that he has done his research on the Shelby family. What is the name of the Chicago nightclub that Mosley says Michael frequented?

ひ THE EMPIRE ROOM
ひ THE GLADIATOR
ひ THE BOULEVARD ROOM
ひ THE PANTHER

13. In provocative mood, what does he allege about Linda that tests Arthur's self-control?

ひ SHE BELITTLES ARTHUR WHEN HIS BACK IS TURNED
ひ SHE'S SEEING ANOTHER MAN
ひ SHE'S PLANNING ON LEAVING HIM
ひ ARTHUR IS NOT THE FATHER OF THEIR SON

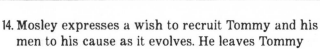

14. Mosley expresses a wish to recruit Tommy and his men to his cause as it evolves. He leaves Tommy with an envelope, and suggests he should accept the invitation inside as he's made a recent problem 'go away'. What is he referring to?

○ THE IRA'S INTEREST IN HIS ILLEGAL ALCOHOL-SMUGGLING BUSINESS
○ MOVES TO REOPEN THE INVESTIGATION INTO THE DEATH OF MAJOR CAMPBELL
○ THE MURDER OF THE JOURNALIST, MR LEVITT
○ A FREEZE ON SHELBY COMPANY LTD EXPORTS TO INDIA

15. After Mosley makes his exit, leaving Arthur to topple furniture in fury, Tommy opens the letter. What position has Mosley invited him to take in a new political party he's forming?

○ DEPUTY LEADER
○ TREASURER
○ LEADER
○ CHAIRMAN

16. Linda visits Lizzie to tell her she's been consulting with 'the friends' about the future of her marriage. Who is she referring to?

○ HER OLD SCHOOL FRIENDS
○ THE QUAKERS
○ THE PARISH VICAR AND HIS WIFE
○ WESLEYAN METHODISTS

17. Linda has also decided to talk to a solicitor, but Lizzie advises her to appoint one from London. Why?

○ LINDA CAN AFFORD THE BEST
○ NO BIRMINGHAM SOLICITOR WOULD DARE OVERSEE THE DIVORCE OF A SHELBY MAN
○ LOCAL SOLICITORS WILL NOTIFY ARTHUR BEFORE SHE IS READY
○ A LONDON SOLICITOR CANNOT BE BOUGHT OFF BY THE PEAKY BLINDERS

SEASON FIVE ▣ EPISODE THREE

18. 'I chose this life, it didn't choose me.' Lizzie reveals she has already contacted a solicitor to end her marriage with Tommy. What does she say happened next?

   ○ SHE RECEIVED A DRAFT OF THE DIVORCE PAPERS BUT BURNED THEM
   ○ SHE CAN'T DECIDE WHETHER TO SIGN THE PAPERS
   ○ SHE PUT THE PHONE DOWN
   ○ SHE MADE AN APPOINTMENT WITH THE SOLICITOR BUT DIDN'T KEEP IT

19. When Linda confesses that she's drawn to another man, Lizzie is clear that he will 'die without his eyes' should anything happen between them. Linda protests that he's just a friend who listens. What fate does she say befell his wife?

   ○ SHE WAS TRAMPLED TO DEATH BY A HORSE
   ○ SHE LEFT HIM AND DISAPPEARED
   ○ SHE DIED FROM SPANISH FLU
   ○ SHE'S BEEN COMMITTED TO AN ASYLUM

20. Ada meets Gina at the hotel steps, but she's insistent on attending her hospital appointment alone. What does Ada say the taxi drivers are likely to do if they hear her accent?

   ○ CRITICISE AMERICA'S LATE ENTRY INTO THE WAR
   ○ CHARGE HER TREBLE
   ○ FIND OUT WHERE SHE'S STAYING AND BURGLE HER ROOM
   ○ TAKE HER ON A LONGER JOURNEY THAN NECESSARY

21. While playing chess with Ada's son, Karl, Ben Younger learns that the young lad holds some troubling views about race. 'Karl, these days there are some very stupid people _____,' he says. Complete the sentence.

   ○ ... AND YOU ARE SMARTER THAN THEM
   ○ ... SAYING SOME VERY STUPID THINGS
   ○ ... WHO ARE SHOUTING THE LOUDEST
   ○ ... WITH DANGEROUS BELIEFS

22. Polly drives Aberama to a gypsy camp. He's
    discharged himself from hospital, and is notably
    quiet when she insists that Tommy avenge the death
    of his son. What family member is here to help him
    recuperate?

    ○ HIS AUNT
    ○ HIS SISTER
    ○ HIS WIFE
    ○ HIS COUSIN

23. 'I need my hunting rifle, fifty bullets. I'm going to
    Scotland tonight.' Aberama reveals his intentions
    before Polly has even rejoined the road. What gypsy
    family does he wish to recruit to help him hunt down
    his son's killers?

    ○ THE COOPER FAMILY
    ○ THE FURY FAMILY
    ○ THE BOSWELL FAMILY
    ○ THE CODONA FAMILY

24. Tommy visits Ben Younger at Ada's townhouse.
    He wishes to talk business, sending Michael away
    because 'the man doesn't trust you'. Michael is on
    his feet at this, squaring up to Tommy. 'By the
    time that baby draws his first breath,' he growls,
    '_____.' Complete the sentence.

    ○ ... WE WILL BE HOME IN AMERICA
    ○ ... I WILL BE KING
    ○ ... YOU AND I WILL BE DONE
    ○ ... YOU WILL BE IN MY DEBT

25. Before Tommy hands over the Mosley letter, Ben
    points out that they're still not alone. What does
    Tommy have to say about Arthur?

    ○ 'I TRUST MY BROTHER WITH MY LIFE.'
    ○ 'WHAT I HEAR, ARTHUR HEARS.'
    ○ 'I TRUST MY BROTHER MORE THAN I TRUST YOU.'
    ○ 'MY BROTHER AND I ARE THE SAME PERSON.'

SEASON FIVE ▬ EPISODE THREE

26. Why does Colonel Younger say that Mosley's plan to create a fascist party is beyond his intelligence-gathering remit, which means he cannot provide assistance?

    ○ YOUNGER HAS BEEN REMOVED FROM THE OPERATION
    ○ HIS FOCUS IS ON COMMUNIST ACTIVITY
    ○ THE OPERATION HAS BEEN CLOSED
    ○ MOSLEY IS UNTOUCHABLE

27. Tommy persists until Younger reconsiders his position. He tells the Colonel he will fight Mosley alone if necessary, unwilling to see fascism creep into the nation, or undermine him on behalf of whom?

    ○ THE PEOPLE
    ○ THE KING
    ○ THE PRIME MINISTER
    ○ ALL THOSE WHO CONSIDER THEMSELVES TO BE A MINORITY

28. 'Don't worry, Sandra. The only way to get fired from this household is through burned toast or talking to the police.' Returning home after dark, Tommy catches one of his staff in flagrante with whom?'

    ○ FINN SHELBY
    ○ JOHNNY DOGS
    ○ CHARLIE STRONG
    ○ ISAIAH JESUS

29. Gina visits Polly with a birthday gift. What is it?

    ○ A BRONZE CAST OF NEW YORK'S TALLEST SKYSCRAPER OF THE ERA, THE WOOLWORTH BUILDING
    ○ A MINIATURE STATUE OF LIBERTY
    ○ A BRONZE CAST OF ABRAHAM LINCOLN
    ○ A MINIATURE STARS AND STRIPES FLAG

30. Gina asks Polly if she'd like to move to New York with her and Michael, where she intends the baby to be born. Where does Gina propose that they would live?

○ BROOKLYN
○ QUEENS
○ LONG ISLAND
○ NEWARK

31. 'So, how is life as a socialist?' Jessie Eden finds Tommy drinking alone late at night in the Garrison. What drink does Tommy use to illustrate how all the bubbles have an equal chance to rise to the top, which leaves Jessie questioning his commitment to her cause?

○ PALE ALE
○ TONIC WATER
○ CHAMPAGNE
○ BEER

32. Lizzie is waiting in bed for Tommy when he finally returns home. She tells him that she has decided to stay, with conditions. One is that he must agree not to sleep with another woman a day on either side of what?

○ MAKING LOVE TO LIZZIE
○ HOLDING THEIR DAUGHTER'S HAND
○ DINING AS A FAMILY TOGETHER
○ TELLING LIZZIE THAT HE LOVES HER

33. Arthur is awoken by a late-night phone call from Tommy, who wants him to travel north to take care of business. Arthur refuses until he reveals where Linda is staying. What does Tommy tell him?

○ STIRCHLEY
○ COTTERIDGE
○ BOURNVILLE
○ KING'S HEATH

SEASON FIVE ▮ EPISODE THREE

34. Tommy provides details of the man Linda has been confiding in, but stresses that his religious beliefs mean he can be trusted with her. 'They're not like us,' says Tommy. '_____ .' Fill in the blank.

    ○ ... THEY TALK
    ○ ... THEY DON'T TAKE CHANCES
    ○ ... TREAT HIM WITH RESPECT
    ○ ... DO NOT HARM HIM

35. Arthur visits the widower in whom Linda has been confiding, but gives him little chance to talk. What is the slogan on a banner that Arthur reads aloud before losing his cool?

    ○ STAND STILL IN THE LIGHT
    ○ A PLACE TO MEET
    ○ PEACE IS THE WAY
    ○ SEARCH FOR THE TRUTH WITHIN

36. Later, reeling from what happened in his search for Linda, Arthur prepares for the journey to Scotland. 'It's so far up north they run out of the bloody stuff,' he tells Charlie Strong. What is he referring to?

    ○ MOTOR OIL
    ○ PETROL
    ○ TARMAC
    ○ TEA

37. In the hills outside Glasgow, Aberama and his gypsy kin masquerade as a road gang fixing potholes. When a truck approaches carrying the Billy Boys, a brutal ambush takes place. With the Glaswegians grievously wounded, Aberama sends them back with a message. How does he vow to finish the leader, Jimmy McCavern?

    ○ BURNING HIM ALIVE
    ○ NAILING HIM TO A CROSS
    ○ CUTTING HIS HEART OUT
    ○ KILLING EVERY MEMBER OF HIS FAMILY IN FRONT OF HIM

38. 'The 1930s, Mr Shelby, will belong to us.' In conversation during a pheasant shoot, what date does Mosley tell Tommy he plans to launch his new party?

   ○ DECEMBER 1ST 1929
   ○ DECEMBER 30TH 1929
   ○ NEW YEAR'S EVE 1929
   ○ JANUARY 1ST 1930

39. Aberama Gold is awoken in his gypsy wagon by Arthur, and with not a moment to spare before the Billy Boys overrun the camp in search of him. What does Arthur leave in the wagon as a declaration of war?

   ○ A SHELBY COMPANY LTD BUSINESS CARD
   ○ A PRIMED GRENADE
   ○ THE BODY OF A BILLY BOY WITH HIS THROAT CUT
   ○ A MOLOTOV COCKTAIL WITH THE RAG AFLAME

SEASON FIVE █ EPISODE THREE

KILLER QUESTIONS

40. When Tommy, Arthur and Michael arrive at Ada's townhouse, they are met by Colonel Ben Younger. Arthur asks after Karl. Where does Ben say that he has gone?

   ○ TO BUY A PINT OF MILK
   ○ TO BUY AN ICE CREAM
   ○ TO FLY A KITE IN THE PARK
   ○ TO BUY A NEWSPAPER FOR HIM

41. In his study at home, Tommy learns that Aberama Gold has travelled to Scotland to hunt down Jimmy McCavern. He is told that a cousin of Aberama's has 'galloped' to join him, but from where?

   ○ MILLISONS WOOD
   ○ MERIDEN
   ○ CHAPEL GREEN
   ○ BRADNOCKS MARSH

42. During his phone conversation with Arthur, in which he persuades his older brother to head to Scotland once he's addressed his issues with Linda, what does Tommy toy with in his hand?

   ○ A CIGARETTE
   ○ A LIGHTER
   ○ A BULLET
   ○ A COIN

1. Tommy is still haunted by visions of his late wife, Grace. In the opening scene, what does she say to him?

   ○ 'IS IT TIME?'
   ○ 'WHEN WILL YOU JOIN ME?'
   ○ 'HAPPY OR SAD, TOMMY?'
   ○ 'THIS IS NO LIFE, MY LOVE.'

2. 'Mr Shelby, my bullets ache to get inside your tinker head.' Jimmy McCavern travels to Birmingham for a meeting with Tommy. By what transport does he arrive?

   ○ HORSEBACK
   ○ BARGE
   ○ TAXI
   ○ TRAIN

3. Both men display a white flag of truce. What does Tommy propose sealing it with?

   ○ A HANDSHAKE
   ○ WHISKEY
   ○ BUSINESS
   ○ A CIGARETTE

4. Tommy refuses to take the bait when Jimmy goads him about his status as a politician while standing in a yard full of stolen goods. 'Nothing here is stolen, Mr McCavern,' he replies. '_____.' Fill in the blank.

   ○ ... NOT TO MY KNOWLEDGE
   ○ ... CHARLIE IS IN THE REDISTRIBUTION BUSINESS
   ○ ... IT'S JUST A QUESTION OF CREATIVE PAPERWORK
   ○ ... CHARLIE SIMPLY FINDS THINGS BEFORE THEY'RE LOST

5. Tommy hands Jimmy an envelope containing the terms of a proposal. It also contains a cheque for £500 should he break the truce. What is this for?

   O JIMMY'S FUNERAL COSTS
   O THE FIRST PAYMENT TO HIS WIFE AS A WIDOW
   O COSTS FOR JIMMY TO DISAPPEAR
   O THE COST OF THE NURSE HE'LL BE NEEDING FOR ROUND-THE-CLOCK CARE

6. Who does Tommy leave watching over Jimmy from a distance?

   O FINN
   O ISAIAH
   O JEREMIAH
   O SCUDBOAT

7. Under duress, pub singer turned Peaky Blinder Billy Grade reports to Finn and Arthur on his progress recruiting football players to fix matches. What teams has Billy had success with this week?

   O CARDIFF AND LEEDS
   O BURNLEY AND BLACKBURN
   O YORK AND LINCOLN CITY
   O BURY AND SUNDERLAND

8. Arthur tells Billy that they'll soon have telephone numbers for all the referees in the First Division. 'We can offer them _____,' he tells the quivering new recruit to the business. Complete the sentence.

   O ... REWARDS THAT BUY US WHAT WE NEED
   O ... IRRESISTIBLE THINGS THAT MEAN WE OWN THEM
   O ... ALL THE LOVELY THINGS THAT PEOPLE LIKE
   O ... WHATEVER IT TAKES TO SECURE THEIR SERVICES

9. Where does Tommy hold his MP's surgery?

   ○ THE PARLOUR AT WATERY LANE
   ○ THE SNUG AT THE GARRISON
   ○ POLLY'S OFFICE AT THE BETTING SHOP
   ○ HIS OFFICE AT SHELBY COMPANY LTD

10. Mrs Connors, a constituent, sits before Tommy and describes how her drunk husband strangled three household members to silence their noise. Arthur sits in a corner, aghast when she adds that she's brought the corpses with her. What are they?

   ○ KITTENS
   ○ BABIES
   ○ SONGBIRDS
   ○ HOMING PIGEONS

11. Once Mrs Connors has departed with a promise from Tommy to resolve the issue with her husband, Arthur presents him with 'our list of _____' from the match-fixing operation. Fill in the blank.

   ○ … WINNERS
   ○ … LOSERS
   ○ … VICTIMS
   ○ … MONEY MAKERS

12. Tommy and Arthur are on full alert when infamous opium dealer, Brilliant Chang, enters the MP's surgery. 'The moment is now pure,' he says, after Arthur takes a phone call from Finn and immediately draws his gun. What has his younger brother just reported?

   ○ RUBY HAS BEEN KIDNAPPED
   ○ HE IS BEING HELD AT GUNPOINT
   ○ THE OFFICE HAS BEEN BOOBY-TRAPPED
   ○ CHANG'S MEN ARE OUTSIDE TOMMY'S MANOR

13. 'If you die here today,' Tommy warns Chang, who stands down the threat reported by Finn, 'we'll bury you face down _____. You'll go straight to hell.' Complete the sentence.

   ○ ... WITH NO HANDS
   ○ ... WITH NO ARMS
   ○ ... WITH NO EYES
   ○ ... WITH NO FINGERS

14. With their attention focused, Chang presents a sample of the 'the purest opium that has ever arrived in Europe'. Tommy is already aware of the seven-ton shipment, and the subsequent theft by lantern-light. Chang assures him it's free from salt, flour and what?

   ○ CHALK
   ○ LIES
   ○ POWDERED MILK
   ○ TROUBLE

15. Finn bursts into the meeting, furious at what he's just been subjected to. What does he fire his gun into as Tommy and Arthur restrain him?

   ○ THE FLOOR
   ○ THE CEILING
   ○ CHANG'S CHAIR
   ○ THE WINDOW

16. With the meeting concluded, and a plan in the making, Chang invites Tommy to keep the drug sample. What does Tommy say he'll do with it?

   ○ GIVE IT TO ARTHUR TO ASSESS THE QUALITY
   ○ THROW IT IN THE CANAL
   ○ GIVE IT TO FINN TO MAKE AMENDS
   ○ THROW IT ON THE FIRE

17. Polly attends a family meeting called by Tommy at Charlie Strong's yard. Why does she arrive barefoot?

   ○ SHE'S BROKEN A HEEL ON THE COBBLESTONES
   ○ SHE'S STEPPED IN HORSE MANURE AND REMOVED HER HEELS
   ○ SHE'S RUSHED THERE FROM THE BEDROOM OF A YOUNG LOVER
   ○ SHE'S JUST BRANDISHED A HEEL AS A WEAPON TO SCARE OFF A DOG

18. Tommy is on board with Chang's operation to smuggle opium by barge from London to Birmingham. In selling the plan to Arthur and Polly, why does he say the Chinese can't do it themselves by truck?

   ○ THE RISK OF ROADSIDE AMBUSH IS TOO GREAT
   ○ CHANG DOESN'T TRUST THE DRIVERS
   ○ THEY'LL GET STOPPED BY THE POLICE
   ○ THE WEIGHT IS TOO GREAT FOR THE VEHICLES

19. What cargo will the opium be hidden underneath?

   ○ TARPAULINS
   ○ COAL
   ○ POTATOES
   ○ SCRAP METAL

20. The plan is for the Peaky Blinders to store the consignment for a week, before transporting it to a ship setting sail from Liverpool to where?

   ○ BOSTON
   ○ SAN FRANCISCO
   ○ NEW YORK
   ○ PORTLAND

21. How much does Tommy say they stand to make for their part in the operation?

- ⃝ HALF THE LOSS INCURRED IN THE STOCK MARKET CRASH
- ⃝ ALL THE MONEY FROM THE TANKED SHARES
- ⃝ ENOUGH TO BUY THEIR OWN SHIP
- ⃝ MORE THAN THEY COULD EVER MAKE FROM MATCH-FIXING

22. 'It is time to give up on Linda,' Polly advises Arthur, having told him she's dealt with the aftermath of his visit to find her. 'Find someone else who might be able to _____.' Complete the sentence.

- ⃝ ... DEAL WITH YOUR DEMONS
- ⃝ ... PUT OUT YOUR FIRES
- ⃝ ... BRING OUT THE BEST IN YOU
- ⃝ ... MANAGE YOUR TEMPER

23. Tommy tells Aberama Gold that he needs Jimmy McCavern alive as part of his wider operation to tackle Oswald Mosley. Still hell-bent on avenging his son's murder, Aberama tells him that he already has 'a time and place for the killing'. Where does he plan to shoot McCavern, using a bullet with his name on?

- ⃝ A PUB
- ⃝ A DOCK
- ⃝ A SHIPYARD
- ⃝ A FACTORY

24. Who has Aberama recruited to help deliver Jimmy into his hands?

- ⃝ A MAN CALLED DOUGLAS WHO LIVES IN FEAR OF THE BILLY BOYS
- ⃝ A GIRL CALLED KAREN WHO HATES HIM
- ⃝ A COPPER CALLED CONNER WHO WANTS JIMMY DEALT WITH
- ⃝ A WIDOW CALLED AMY WHO HOLDS HIM RESPONSIBLE FOR THE DEATH OF HER HUSBAND

25. What does Tommy offer Aberama to postpone the killing until his business with the Billy Boys is complete?

   ○ £500
   ○ POLLY'S HAND IN MARRIAGE
   ○ THE GARRISON PUB
   ○ A LIFELONG CAMP PITCH IN THE GROUNDS OF TOMMY'S MANOR HOUSE

26. Following a controversial speech in the Commons, in which Tommy signals a move towards national socialism, he is visited in his office by Mosley. He's been invited to a ballet Tommy is hosting at his manor. Whose birthday is it?

   ○ CHARLES SHELBY
   ○ RUBY SHELBY
   ○ LIZZIE SHELBY
   ○ TOMMY SHELBY

27. 'Two men for whom forbidding is forbidden,' says Mosley, having revealed he's aware of Lizzie's past as a prostitute. What else does Mosley share that prompts Tommy to counter that he also has compromising material on his guest?

   ○ HE'S PREPARED TO GO PUBLIC ABOUT HER PAST AS LEVERAGE TO KEEP TOMMY ON SIDE
   ○ HE CLAIMS TO HAVE DISCOVERED SHE HAS A CRIMINAL RECORD FOR PICKING CLIENTS' POCKETS
   ○ HE BELIEVES THAT AS A YOUNGER MAN HE MAY HAVE SLEPT WITH LIZZIE
   ○ HE ASSERTS THAT TOMMY TOOK A PERCENTAGE OF HER EARNINGS

SEASON FIVE ▬ EPISODE FOUR

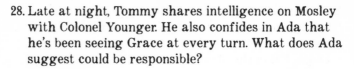

28. Late at night, Tommy shares intelligence on Mosley with Colonel Younger. He also confides in Ada that he's been seeing Grace at every turn. What does Ada suggest could be responsible?

   ○ GRIEF
   ○ LAUDANUM
   ○ WHISKEY
   ○ LACK OF SLEEP

29. 'There is more money in this,' says Polly on introducing Michael to the opium-trafficking plan, 'than there is in all the other parts of our business put together.' What role does Tommy wish Michael to take in the Shelby haulage company overseeing the shipment?

   ○ OPERATIONS MANAGER
   ○ MANAGING DIRECTOR
   ○ JUNIOR PARTNER
   ○ LOGISTICS MANAGER

30. As part of his grand plan, Tommy skims ten bags of opium and invites Jimmy McCavern and his men to 'test the market' in return for £10,000. Jimmy offers to write him a cheque. What condition does Tommy put on this?

   ○ JIMMY MUST WRITE A CHEQUE FOR HALF THE AMOUNT BEFORE LEAVING
   ○ THE CHEQUE MUST BE UNDERWRITTEN BY MOSLEY
   ○ THE PRICE INCREASES TO £12,000
   ○ JIMMY MUST LEAVE HIM WITH A POST-DATED CHEQUE

31. 'An evening with a tribe of gypsies.' Oswald Mosley arrives for the ballet performance at Tommy's manor. He is kept waiting by Tommy, who asks Polly to make his apologies and keep Mosley entertained. What does she offer him?

   ○ OPIUM, COCAINE AND BRANDY
   ○ COCAINE, SALMON AND CAVIAR
   ○ OPIUM, CHAMPAGNE AND OLIVES
   ○ CHAMPAGNE, COCAINE AND CIGARS

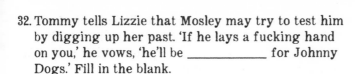
32. Tommy tells Lizzie that Mosley may try to test him by digging up her past. 'If he lays a fucking hand on you,' he vows, 'he'll be _____ for Johnny Dogs.' Fill in the blank.

- ○ ... GROUND UP
- ○ ... MEAT
- ○ ... PIG FEED
- ○ ... DISMEMBERED

33. Mosley is scathing of Tommy's efforts as a host, and mocks him for admitting he's now doing business with McCavern, but still agrees to underwrite the cheque. In doing so, he admits what he considers to be a weakness. What is it?

- ○ GENEROSITY
- ○ A TENDENCY TO TRUST PEOPLE
- ○ A DESIRE FOR THE PEAKY BLINDERS TO UNITE WITH THE BILLY BOYS IN SERVING HIM
- ○ A NEED TO BE VALUED

34. Lizzie recognises Mosley at once. How does she react to his provocative comment that their first encounter was 'a bottle of champagne and an evening well spent'.

- ○ SHE MARCHES FROM THE ROOM
- ○ SHE TOSSES HIM A COIN FOR THE DRINK HE BOUGHT HER
- ○ SHE THROWS HER DRINK AT HIM
- ○ SHE DENIES THEY EVER MET

35. The performance of Swan Lake begins on a raised platform in a grand tent. Before the climax, who is snoring in the audience?

- ○ CHARLIE STRONG
- ○ ARTHUR
- ○ JOHNNY DOGS
- ○ FINN

SEASON FIVE ▬ EPISODE FOUR

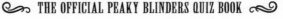

36. How does Aberama Gold draw Polly from the ballet to a moment with him under the stars?

- ○ HE TOSSES A ROSE INTO HER LAP
- ○ HE TAPS HIS CHAMPAGNE FLUTE
- ○ HE TOSSES A PEBBLE INTO HER LAP
- ○ HE WHISTLES SOFTLY

37. 'Polly Gray, gypsy queen,' says Aberama as he drops to one knee with a ring in hand, 'will you marry me, a _____ who loves you?' Fill in the blank.

- ○ ... POOR COMMONER
- ○ ... HUMBLE MAN
- ○ ... SIMPLE TRAVELLER
- ○ ... ROMANY WANDERER

38. With the white swan set to die on stage, Linda sweeps up the driveway in her car. Arthur steps out into the headlights to meet her, and the pair come face to face. Hiding a gun in one hand, Linda is in anguish at the suffering her husband has caused her friend. What is his name?

- ○ JAMES
- ○ FREDERICK
- ○ JOSEPH
- ○ PETER

39. 'May you Peaky Blinders rot in fucking hell!' As the swan hits the floor to great applause, gunshot fills the night air outside. Who steps out from the shadows with a pistol in hand?

- ○ ABERAMA GOLD
- ○ POLLY GRAY
- ○ GINA GRAY
- ○ FINN SHELBY

KILLER QUESTIONS

40. When Jimmy McCavern sets eyes on Tommy for the truce talk, he raises his gun to the sky. How many rounds does he fire?

- ○ ONE
- ○ TWO
- ○ THREE
- ○ FOUR

41. When the barman at the Garrison informs Tommy and Arthur that a Chinese man is waiting in the saloon to see them, what does Tommy hand his brother before letting him in?

- ○ A REVOLVER
- ○ A RAZOR
- ○ A LETTER OPENER
- ○ A DAGGER

42. What is the date for the ballet performance at Arrow House, as seen on the invitation left on Tommy's desk by Aberama Gold?

- ○ 16TH NOVEMBER
- ○ 20TH NOVEMBER
- ○ 22ND NOVEMBER
- ○ 28TH NOVEMBER

SEASON FIVE EPISODE FOUR

1. 'Linda, I'd have taken your bullet,' Arthur beseeches his gravely injured wife, as Polly, Lizzie and Tommy rush her inside to save her. What do they lay her down on?

   ○ A BED
   ○ A BANQUETING TABLE
   ○ THE FLOOR
   ○ A SOFA

2. As Tommy prepares to dig the bullet from her upper arm, what small handgun does Polly say she fired?

   ○ DERRINGER
   ○ SMITH & WESSON
   ○ BROWNING
   ○ COLT

3. As Arthur draws his gun on Oswald Mosley and orders him to return to the party, what does Tommy order Lizzie to fetch from the kitchen?

   ○ WHISKEY
   ○ IODINE
   ○ LEMON JUICE
   ○ HOT WATER

4. With the bullet removed from Linda's arm, what does Tommy use to sedate her?

   ○ BRANDY
   ○ LAUDANUM
   ○ OPIUM
   ○ MORPHINE

5. Arthur struggles with guilt and remorse at the shooting, prompting Tommy to remind his brother how much they need him. What does Polly add to help Arthur focus on the future?

   ○ HE'LL ALWAYS BE THE OLDER BROTHER TO TOMMY, FINN AND ADA
   ○ ABERAMA WANTS HIM TO BE BEST MAN AT HIS WEDDING TO POLLY
   ○ HIS SON, BILLY, LOOKS UP TO HIM
   ○ ABERAMA HAS COME TO CONSIDER HIM AS A BROTHER

6. 'I have known that change is coming.' In addressing the guests in Tommy's absence, Mosley turns from giving thanks to an insidious political speech. 'He is a man,' he says of Tommy, introducing him as his lieutenant in the new party, 'well suited to _____ that England is now in.' Fill in the blank.

   ○ ... HARNESSING THE SPIRIT
   ○ ... THE MIGHTY MOOD
   ○ ... THE NOBLE BEARING
   ○ ... GALVANISING THE DISCONTENT

7. Aberama Gold listens to the speech, in which Mosley conjures up ethnic scapegoats for the crash, and melts away into the shadows of the night. How does he express his distaste first?

   ○ HE TIPS HIS CHAMPAGNE AWAY
   ○ HE SHAKES HIS HEAD
   ○ HE SPITS ON THE GROUND
   ○ HE MUTTERS A ROMANY CURSE

8. 'England lives tonight,' declares Mosley, closing his speech to a standing ovation, '_____' Complete the sentence.

   ○ ... AND HER ENEMIES WILL SOON BOW BEFORE HER!
   ○ ... AND WILL BE UNSHACKLED TOMORROW!
   ○ ... AND MARCHES ON!
   ○ ... IN PURITY AND PRIDE!

9. What is the name of Mosley's new political party?

   ○ THE FASCIST PARTY OF GREAT BRITAIN
   ○ THE BRITISH UNION OF FASCISTS
   ○ THE UNITED FRONT
   ○ FIRST FOR BRITAIN

10. 'What the fuck are you doing dealing with a man like that, Tommy?' Lizzie does not like what she's just witnessed. What does Tommy ask her to do?

    ○ TRUST HIM
    ○ IGNORE IT
    ○ KEEP OUT OF MOSLEY'S WAY
    ○ DON'T TAKE IT SERIOUSLY

11. Mosley takes Tommy aside. He tells him to cease bringing family dramas – like Linda's stand-off with Arthur – into the public sphere. What is his reasoning?

    ○ IT'S BAD FOR PRESS
    ○ IT'S LOWER CLASS
    ○ IT'S GYPSY BEHAVIOUR
    ○ IT'S NOT BEFITTING OF A POLITICAL FIGUREHEAD

12. 'I looked into the audience,' Mosley tells Tommy, 'and I saw medals, and Savile Row suits, and _____. They are my people,' he says to finish. What is the missing word?

    ○ RESENTMENT
    ○ HATRED
    ○ RESTLESSNESS
    ○ BITTERNESS

13. Mosley outlines his strategy for the new party. He expects the Peaky Blinders and the Billy Boys to control rallies and break up demonstrations, but what does he ask Tommy to hand over to Jimmy McCavern to keep him on side?

○ ABERAMA GOLD
○ ALL SHELBY COMPANY LTD RESIDENTIAL PROPERTIES NORTH OF WINCANTON
○ CONTROL OF THE RACECOURSES IN THE NORTH
○ 20% OF ALL SHELBY EXPORTS LEAVING LIVERPOOL AND GLASGOW DOCKS

14. 'When we succeed,' Mosley assures Tommy, 'even _____ will not be above us.' Fill in the blank.

○ ... THE PRIME MINISTER
○ ... THE LORD GOD
○ ... THE BANKERS
○ ... THE KING

15. What is Mosley's final piece of advice, before he leaves with instructions for the ballerina who played the swan to join him in his room?

○ DRINK LESS
○ STOP FIGHTING
○ FOLD AWAY YOUR RAZOR FOR GOOD
○ HANG UP YOUR GUN

16. As Lizzie heads for bed, she is met on the landing by Mosley. What suggestion does he have for her, which she declines?

○ AN INVITATION TO VISIT HIS OFFICE ALONE ONE DAY
○ TO JOIN HIM WITH THE BALLERINA IN HIS BEDROOM
○ TO WEAR SOMETHING LESS REVEALING SO AS NOT TO OFFEND HER GUESTS
○ TO JOIN HIM ALONE IN AN EMPTY GUEST ROOM

SEASON FIVE ▮ EPISODE FIVE

17. As Linda comes round, Arthur is at her side with a plan. Where does he suggest they drive to in order to begin a new life?

   ○ THE HILLS
   ○ THE RAILWAY STATION
   ○ THE NORTH
   ○ THE DOCKS

18. Linda rejects his invitation, suggesting instead that Arthur stay behind with his demons. Before she leaves, what reason does she give for being glad she didn't kill him?

   ○ SHE COULDN'T LIVE WITH MORE GUILT
   ○ IT WOULD'VE BEEN A KINDNESS, AND SHE WANTS HIM TO LIVE WITH WHAT HE'S DONE
   ○ SHE WOULD'VE BEEN HANGED FOR MURDER AND THEIR SON ORPHANED
   ○ ARTHUR DESERVES A CHANCE FOR REDEMPTION, BUT WITHOUT HER

19. Colonel Ben Younger pays a visit to Tommy to collect intelligence he's gathered on Mosley. A group of children are playing football outside the building where he parks. What does he do before going inside?

   ○ KICKS THE BALL BACK
   ○ HEADS THE BALL
   ○ FLICKS THE BALL FROM HIS FOOT TO HIS KNEE AND THEN BACK
   ○ KICKS THE BALL AGAINST THE BUILDING SO IT BOUNCES BACK TO THE CHILDREN

20. As Tommy details the information he has gathered, including the underwritten cheque linking Mosley to gang leader, McCavern, Ben Younger expresses reservations. What's the issue?

   ⚬ ADA HAS EXPRESSED CONCERN ABOUT TOMMY'S STATE OF MIND, AND SO YOUNGER FEELS IT'S UNETHICAL TO CONTINUE USING HIM
   ⚬ YOUNGER HAS EXPERIENCED RESISTANCE FROM HIS SUPERIORS
   ⚬ MOSLEY HAS MADE CONTACT AND IS INTIMIDATING HIM
   ⚬ HE'S LEAVING THE ARMY

21. 'Please don't listen to my sister's opinions of me,' says Tommy, after Younger shares Ada's theory that her brother has ceased providing intelligence on Jessie Eden because he's begun to believe in a cause. 'They are always hopeful,' he adds. 'Therefore they are always_____.' Complete the sentence.

   ⚬ ... IGNORANT
   ⚬ ... DOOMED
   ⚬ ... WRONG
   ⚬ ... OFF

22. When the car bomb detonates, killing Ben Younger, Tommy rushes out to attend to the children caught up in the explosion. He urges a woman from his office to call for an ambulance. Who else does he ask her to contact?

   ⚬ ARTHUR SHELBY
   ⚬ SERGEANT MOSS
   ⚬ POLLY GRAY
   ⚬ ADA SHELBY

SEASON FIVE ▮ EPISODE FIVE

23. Ada is numbed by news of Younger's death. She tells Tommy that he didn't know she was pregnant. What else does she admit?

○ SHE DIDN'T LOVE HIM
○ SHE WANTED HIM TO PROPOSE
○ SHE WANTED HIM TO MOVE OUT
○ SHE PLANNED TO MOVE AWAY WITH HIM AND KARL

24. Despite his conviction that the establishment were involved, how does Tommy say the killing will be recorded?

○ AN IRA ASSASSINATION OF A BRITISH MILITARY OFFICER
○ A CASE OF MISTAKEN IDENTITY
○ AN ACT OF TERRORISM BY FOREIGN AGENTS
○ A GANGLAND DISPUTE

25. 'If I'd have stuck to what I do, he'd still be kicking a ball in the street.' How old was the boy who died in the explosion?

○ EIGHT
○ NINE
○ TEN
○ ELEVEN

26. 'Push the button,' Grace urges Tommy from the back seat of his car as his finger hovers over the starter. 'Unlock the door and _____.' How does she finish before Tommy starts the car without incident and she vanishes?

○ ... LET THE LIGHT IN
○ ... COME HOME TO ME
○ ... THIS ALL ENDS NOW
○ ... THE JOURNEY IS OVER

27. 'Chinese lanterns! Brass on deck!' Charlie Strong navigates the barge at night towards the warehouse hiding the opium consignment. Aberama Gold and Isaiah emerge from below quarters, followed by Arthur clutching what?

- ○ A PISTOL
- ○ A BOTTLE OF WHISKEY
- ○ A RIFLE
- ○ A KEROSENE LAMP

28. Reaching the wharf, the Peaky Blinders pick their way cautiously under the lanterns. Sensing something is not right, they rush for cover as gunfire breaks out. In the shadows, behind crates, Arthur finds Brilliant Chang, beaten but conscious. Who does he claim is responsible for the ambush?

- ○ IRISH
- ○ ITALIANS
- ○ RUSSIANS
- ○ SCOTS

29. Arthur figures out the attackers, disguised as policemen, are from a notorious band of former soldiers from Poplar known as what?

- ○ THE STEAMER GANG
- ○ THE TITANIC GANG
- ○ THE EMPIRE GANG
- ○ THE ATLANTIC GANG

30. What weapon does he instruct Curly and Charlie to assemble from the bag of munitions they're carrying with them?

- ○ AN ANTI-TANK GUN
- ○ AN ANTI-AIRCRAFT GUN
- ○ A SNIPER
- ○ A MACHINE GUN

31. With the wharf back under his control, Arthur and his men instruct Chang to show them where the opium is hidden. How does Arthur present a sample to the Chinese smuggler to ensure it's the pure-grade consignment?

   ○ ON HIS FINGERTIP
   ○ ON A TEASPOON
   ○ ON THE EDGE OF HIS KNIFE
   ○ ON THE MUZZLE OF HIS GUN

32. Isaiah asks if he should drop one of the dead gang members in the cut, but Arthur demands that he dispose of the body like a proper Peaky Blinder. 'Burn it to the bone,' he growls, 'and if anybody speaks to you on that, you offer them the chance to _____ .' Complete the sentence.

   ○ ... BURN IN THAT FURNACE WITH HIM
   ○ ... THINK AGAIN OR LOSE THEIR EYES
   ○ ... RUN BEFORE YOU SHOOT THEM
   ○ ... ARGUE WITH YOUR RAZOR

33. Tommy pays his respects as the funeral procession for the boy killed in the car explosion passes by. What was the boy's name, as spelled out by the floral tribute adoring his coffin?

   ○ STANLEY
   ○ THOMAS
   ○ PETER
   ○ ROBERT

34. 'For your own safety, I need to search you for items that could potentially be used against you.' Tommy has come to visit an old friend at the asylum for the insane. He spreads his arms as a male nurse pats him down. What item does the nurse compliment him on?

- ○ HIS WALLET
- ○ HIS POCKET WATCH
- ○ HIS GLASSES
- ○ HIS CUFFLINKS

35. Tommy visits Barney, straight-jacketed in his cell. He's a former brother-in-arms from the war, and Tommy updates him on those who fought alongside him that have died. Initially, how does Barney address him?

- ○ SERGEANT MAJOR
- ○ SIR
- ○ MR SHELBY
- ○ CAPTAIN

36. Tommy produces a capsule of cyanide and opium, offering it to Barney to end the torture of his existence. How did he smuggle it in?

- ○ IN HIS SOCK
- ○ IN HIS MOUTH
- ○ UNDER HIS SHIRT COLLAR
- ○ INSIDE A CUFFLINK

37. 'You're in here, Barney. You have no hands. There is no daylight. And you don't want to die.' Why does Barney decline the capsule?

- ○ HE BELIEVES THAT TOMMY IS THE DEVIL IN DISGUISE
- ○ HE HOPES HIS SITUATION MIGHT CHANGE
- ○ HE'S TOO SCARED TO TAKE HIS OWN LIFE
- ○ HE'S FRIGHTENED THERE WILL BE AN AFTERLIFE

SEASON FIVE ■ EPISODE FIVE

38. Keen to harness Barney's skill as 'the best sniper in the company', Tommy offers to break him out of the asylum. When can Barney expect 'a big fucking bang'?

- O AFTER THE CHURCH BELLS ON SUNDAY
- O BEFORE DAYBREAK ON TUESDAY
- O AFTER MIDNIGHT ON WEDNESDAY
- O WHEN THE LARK SINGS ON FRIDAY

39. Jimmy McCavern waits with Tommy for the boat to arrive carrying the opium shipment. When it arrives, Arthur squares up to Jimmy. He tells him Aberama is ready to cut his throat, which is why he'd disembarked earlier. Where?

- O OLTON
- O HAY MILLS
- O SOLIHULL
- O ULVERLEY GREEN

336

KILLER QUESTIONS

40. When Ben Younger pays his last visit to Tommy, he parks his car in front of a building with what number beside the door?

   - ◡ THREE
   - ◡ FIVE
   - ◡ SEVEN
   - ◡ NINE

41. What is the registration plate of the car that explodes when Colonel Ben Younger turns the ignition?

   - ◡ MN 1535
   - ◡ WS 4377
   - ◡ BM 1394
   - ◡ HY 2056

42. What is the name of the bank on the cheque that Jimmy McCavern gives to Tommy for his share of the opium shipment?

   - ◡ LLOYDS
   - ◡ NATIONAL PROVINCIAL
   - ◡ THE WESTERN ISLES BANK
   - ◡ MIDLAND

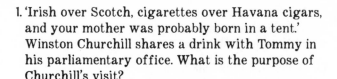

1. 'Irish over Scotch, cigarettes over Havana cigars, and your mother was probably born in a tent.' Winston Churchill shares a drink with Tommy in his parliamentary office. What is the purpose of Churchill's visit?

    ○ HE IS IMPRESSED BY TOMMY'S ORATORY IN THE COMMONS AND WANTS HIM TO CONSIDER DEFECTING TO THE CONSERVATIVES
    ○ HE IS TROUBLED BY A GROWING FAR-RIGHT MOVEMENT IN ITALY
    ○ HE HAS LEARNED THAT TOMMY'S ALLIANCE WITH MOSLEY IS A COVER TO SPY ON HIM
    ○ HE'S CONCERNED BY TOMMY'S APPARENT FASCIST LEANINGS

2. Tommy corrects Churchill about his mother. Where does he say she was born?

    ○ IN THE BACKROOM OF A PUB
    ○ IN A STABLE YARD
    ○ ON A NARROWBOAT
    ○ IN A WAGON

3. Tommy admits that sometimes he struggles to understand his own motives, comparing himself to three members of his staff 'with no ambition, who are happier than I will ever be.' What is their profession?

    ○ COOKS
    ○ GARDENERS
    ○ DRIVERS
    ○ STABLE LADS

4. Tommy says he doesn't wish to burden Churchill with his next move. What does Churchill deduce from this?

    ○ TOMMY HAS NO STRATEGY
    ○ HE INTENDS TO BREAK THE LAW
    ○ TOMMY DOESN'T TRUST CHURCHILL
    ○ HIS PLAN IS A WORK IN PROGRESS

5. On leaving, Churchill asks if Tommy was responsible for the death of Major Campbell. Tommy admits it was his aunt. How does Churchill react?

○ HE ASSURES TOMMY HIS SECRET HIS SAFE
○ HE EXPRESSES AN INTEREST IN SPENDING AN EVENING WITH THE SHELBY FAMILY
○ HE TELLS HIM HE NEVER TRUSTED CAMPBELL
○ HE JOKES THAT A CHAPERONE WOULD BE REQUIRED SHOULD HE EVER DINE WITH POLLY

6. Finn and Billy Grade are enjoying the fruits of their success at match-fixing. They are sharing cocaine and whiskey while working through a list of footballing names who have agreed to be paid off. Why does Billy say one referee, Tom, requires a man to be beaten up as part of the deal?

○ THE MAN OWES HIM MONEY
○ THE MAN HAS GOT TOM'S DAUGHTER PREGNANT
○ THE MAN IS SLEEPING WITH HIS WIFE
○ TOM HAS BEEN IN A BAR FIGHT WITH THE MAN

7. When Arthur walks in, noting their high spirits, what does he learn about Billy's success at match-fixing?

○ IT'S BECOME MORE PROFITABLE THAN FIXING THE RACES
○ HE HAS COMPLETELY SHAPED THE LEAGUE
○ EVERY TEAM HAS AT LEAST FOUR PLAYERS AT HIS BIDDING
○ IT'S CLOSE TO RIVALLING THE RACES IN TERMS OF WEEKLY PROFIT

8. 'You could sing like a bird in a cage,' Arthur tells Billy with an air of menace. 'We opened that cage and _____.' Complete the sentence.

○ ... NOW YOU'RE SINGING FREELY
○ ... SET THAT BIRD FREE
○ ... THE REAL MAN FLEW OUT
○ ... A GOLDEN EAGLE SOARED OUT

SEASON FIVE EPISODE SIX

9. Arthur becomes increasingly threatening, warning Finn there will be consequences if he discusses family business with Billy. What does Billy insist they only ever talk about?

- ⚬ FOOTBALL AND WOMEN
- ⚬ SPORT AND PROSTITUTES
- ⚬ WHISKEY AND FOOTBALL
- ⚬ WOMEN AND COCAINE

10. Coming to terms with the collapse of his marriage, Arthur remains in a tense, provocative mood when he escorts Finn to a family meeting at the Garrison. What does Arthur call the shot of whiskey he slugs down?

- ⚬ A SLUG OF HAPPINESS
- ⚬ MEDICINE TO FORGET
- ⚬ MELANCHOLY WATER
- ⚬ A GLASS OF 'SO WHAT?'

11. Tommy arrives with Charlie Strong, who is limping. He says that Barney kicked him in the shin when he woke up. Where have they left the former asylum inmate while they attend the meeting?

- ⚬ CHAINED BY A LEG IRON IN CHARLIE'S YARD
- ⚬ LOCKED IN A CELLAR
- ⚬ TIED TO A LAMP POST
- ⚬ SHUT IN A STABLE

12. Tommy commences the meeting with an apology for Lizzie's absence. Where is she?

- ⚬ OVERSEEING THE PLANTING OF AN ORCHARD
- ⚬ WITH CHARLES AT HIS VIOLIN LESSON
- ⚬ SICK IN BED
- ⚬ WITH RUBY AT A SHOE FITTING

13. Tommy welcomes Aberama Gold, who will be marrying Polly in how many weeks' time?

- ○ TWO
- ○ THREE
- ○ FOUR
- ○ SIX

14. 'Here is my proposal.' Michael interrupts proceedings. He takes the floor to estimate that expanding the drug-trafficking business into America will increase revenue by millions. Gina hands him a file, which he presents to Tommy. How does Michael sum up his plan here?

- ○ DISSOLVING SHELBY COMPANY LTD AND CREATING AN AMERICAN CORPORATION
- ○ A FULL RESTRUCTURING OF THE COMPANY
- ○ CLOSING DOWN LESS PROFITABLE SHELBY BUSINESS VENTURES TO FOCUS ON THE DRUG MARKET
- ○ INSTALLING GINA AS THE NEW MANAGING DIRECTOR OF THE EXPORT BUSINESS

15. As part of the pitch, Michael requests that Tommy stand down as Managing Director, and become a non-executive chairman under an assumed name to protect his reputation. What is the name of the dead man whose identity Michael has already arranged for Tommy to use?

- ○ MR MORRIS
- ○ MR NELSON
- ○ MR PETERS
- ○ MR JONES

16. What does Tommy do with the file containing the proposal?

- ○ THROWS IT ON THE FIRE
- ○ TAKES IT TO THE BAR TO READ
- ○ SCATTERS IT ACROSS THE FLOOR
- ○ HANDS IT TO POLLY TO READ

SEASON FIVE ▮ EPISODE SIX

17. What is the last thing that Michael has to say on the matter before the meeting is interrupted because Barney is on the loose?

   ○ THE AMERICANS DON'T WISH TO BE ASSOCIATED WITH THE MAN WHO BROUGHT DOWN THE CHANGRETTAS
   ○ GINA'S FAMILY RUN THE SUPPLY LINES ACROSS AMERICA, AND THEY WANT MICHAEL TO RUN IT
   ○ THE AMERICANS DON'T WISH TO DEAL WITH A STREET GANG
   ○ TOMMY'S BUSINESS DEALINGS IN AMERICA ARE SET TO BE UNDER IRS INVESTIGATION

18. 'See this for what it is,' says Michael as Tommy squares up to him. 'A natural succession that someday must happen.' What does Polly leave her son with as she follows Tommy from the bar?

   ○ A KISS TO THE FOREHEAD
   ○ A GUN FOR HIS OWN PROTECTION
   ○ A SLAP AROUND THE CHEEK
   ○ MONEY TO GET OUT OF TOWN

19. In the street outside, Tommy finds Barney cornered by the Peaky Blinders. What has he armed himself with?

   ○ AN IRON BAR
   ○ A REVOLVER AND A DUSTBIN LID
   ○ A BRICK AND A KNIFE
   ○ A BROKEN GLASS BOTTLE

20. With Barney under control, and Michael and Gina departed from the bar, Tommy reconvenes the meeting. There, he sets out his plan for Barney to assassinate Mosley, citing his experience as a sniper and his insanity as a motive. According to Tommy, what will happen if he's caught?

   ○ BARNEY WILL AVOID THE ROPE BUT GO TO PRISON FOR LIFE
   ○ HE'LL BE MEDICATED AND FREED FROM HIS DEMONS
   ○ HE'LL BE SENT BACK TO THE ASYLUM
   ○ HE'LL BE PUT OUT OF HIS TORMENT BY HANGING

SEASON FIVE ▮ EPISODE SIX

21. Tommy explains that the assassination is due to take place at a fascist rally where Mosley is speaking. Where is the rally due to take place?

- ○ BINGLEY HALL
- ○ BIRMINGHAM PUBLIC LIBRARY
- ○ THE GREAT HALL
- ○ BIRMINGHAM TOWN HALL

22. Aberama is aghast at Tommy's ambition when he lays out his plan to take over the party following Mosley's death. When Tommy tells him that McCavern is running security for the rally, Aberama realises he has an opportunity of his own. Where does Tommy say that his enemy is likely to be?

- ○ AT THE EXIT
- ○ BY THE MAIN DOORS
- ○ IN THE WINGS
- ○ BACKSTAGE

23. What is Charlie Strong's role while the police in the city are occupied with the assassination?

- ○ TO GUARD THE BOAT IN CASE THE LONDON GANG ATTEMPT TO STEAL IT
- ○ TO GET THE BOAT LOADED WITH OPIUM TO TOMMY'S CHINESE CONTACTS
- ○ TO PREPARE FOR TOMMY'S CHINESE CONTACTS TO COLLECT THE OPIUM THEMSELVES
- ○ TO GUARD THE BOAT IN CASE MICHAEL ATTEMPTS TO COMMANDEER IT

24. Tommy and Arthur have one more item of business, and wait alone in the Garrison for Mickey the barman. Who has provided proof that Mickey's tip-offs were behind both Younger's death and the ambush at the opium pickup?

   ○ MICKEY'S WIFE
   ○ BRILLIANT CHANG
   ○ THE GIRLS AT THE TELEPHONE EXCHANGE
   ○ THE GIRLS WHO DRINK AT THE BAR

25. 'You've been working behind the bar,' says Arthur, before Tommy issues swift, bloody justice, 'seeing what goes on, listening, taking notes, and _____.' Complete the sentence.

   ○ ... SELLING OUT THE VERY PEOPLE WHO WELCOMED YOU INTO THEIR FAMILY
   ○ ... SELLING YOUR STORIES TO THE HIGHEST BIDDER
   ○ ... SINGING TO ANYONE WHO OFFERS YOU MONEY
   ○ ... BETRAYING YOUR OWN

26. 'Life is so much easier to deal with when you are dead.' Alfie welcomes Tommy to his Margate apartment. How did Tommy learn that Alfie had survived the shooting on the beach?

   ○ ALFIE WROTE TO TOMMY VOWING TO SEE HIM IN HELL
   ○ ALFIE WROTE HIM A LETTER ASKING AFTER HIS DOG
   ○ ALFIE SENT HIM A TELEGRAM REQUESTING AN AUDIENCE
   ○ ALFIE'S RIGHT-HAND MAN, OLLIE, TIPPED HIM OFF

27. Tommy has come to commission Alfie to send his soldiers to the Mosley rally. He plans to use the inevitable clash with the Billy Boys to create a distraction for the assassination to take place. Why does Alfie increase the price per soldier by £5?

   ○ FASCISTS HAVE A REPUTATION FOR FIGHTING UGLY
   ○ THE RALLY IS IN BIRMINGHAM
   ○ THE BILLY BOYS ARE KNOWN FOR BEING RUTHLESS
   ○ THE RALLY IS ON THE SABBATH

28. 'Soon you'll have a stage to stand on. Millions of people listening to you. And you will run this country like you run this family.' Polly is waiting with an envelope for Tommy when he returns to his office. What's in it?

○ A LETTER OF APOLOGY FROM MICHAEL
○ HER RESIGNATION FROM THE COMPANY
○ A ONE-WAY PASSAGE TO AUSTRALIA, SO HE CAN GET OUT BEFORE IT'S TOO LATE
○ A LETTER FROM POLLY EXPLAINING WHY SHE HAS TO GO AWAY

29. In a long, searching night, Tommy visits Charlie at his yard to ask about his mother's death. What does Charlie tell him?

○ SHE WAS MURDERED
○ IT WAS AN ACCIDENT
○ SHE COMMITTED SUICIDE
○ SHE VANISHED WITHOUT TRACE

30. On the day of the Mosley rally, as the Billy Boys martial the crowds outside the hall, where does Arthur hand out coshes to Alfie's Jewish gang?

○ CHARLIE STRONG'S YARD
○ THE GARRISON
○ THE BSA FACTORY
○ ARTILLERY SQUARE

31. 'We can do more damage from the inside.' Tommy rescues Jessie from the police as the crowd becomes rowdy outside the rally. What station does he say she could've been taken to and potentially mistreated in a cell?

○ STECHFORD
○ DIGBETH
○ SMETHWICK
○ SALTHOUSE LANE

32. As the auditorium fills, Arthur settles Barney into position in the upper reaches. What signal will Tommy give from the stage for the ex-army sniper to count to ten and then fire?

   O LOOSEN HIS SHIRT COLLAR
   O RUB HIS SHOE ON THE BACK OF HIS TROUSER HEM
   O COUGH INTO HIS FIST
   O CHECK HIS POCKET WATCH

33. 'Whenever I do a good thing, innocent people get hurt.' Tommy is reluctant to tell Jessie his plan. What does he ask her to do once the rally gets underway?

   O STAND AT THE BACK
   O STICK WITH ARTHUR
   O GO HOME
   O STICK WITH JOHNNY DOGS

34. 'Our enemies deal in bricks and stones and _____,' declares Mosley as he begins his speech from the stage. Fill in the blank.

   O ... KNIVES
   O ... BULLETS
   O ... VIOLENCE
   O ... BOTTLES

35. As the protestors breach the theatre doors, and scuffles break out, Tommy gives the signal. As the countdown from ten begins, what is the last thing to leave Barney's lips?

   O 'FIVE EGG CUSTARD.'
   O 'FOUR SPONGE CAKE.'
   O 'THREE PLUM PUDDING.'
   O 'TWO APPLE CRUMBLE.'

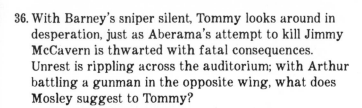

36. With Barney's sniper silent, Tommy looks around in desperation, just as Aberama's attempt to kill Jimmy McCavern is thwarted with fatal consequences. Unrest is rippling across the auditorium; with Arthur battling a gunman in the opposite wing, what does Mosley suggest to Tommy?

   O LEAVING THE STAGE UNTIL ORDER IS RESTORED
   O SUMMONING POLICE PROTECTION
   O LEAVING THE HALL AND ABANDONING THE RALLY
   O STOKING THE VIOLENCE AND BLAMING THE JEWS

37. 'The Chinese? The Italians? Branch? _____? McCavern? Mosley?' Taking refuge in a dressing room with Arthur, unaware that Billy Grade is in the frame for making a call, Tommy screams in frustration now his plan has come apart. Fill in the missing name on his list of suspects.

   O MICKEY THE BARMAN
   O INTELLIGENCE
   O ALFIE
   O MICHAEL

38. In the mist early next morning, Tommy and Arthur are standing before Arrow House. Tommy is wondering if he's facing an enemy he cannot defeat. Arthur suggests they go inside, but Tommy needs time to himself. Where does he head to?

   O HIS STUDY
   O THE FIELDS
   O THE STABLE
   O THE KITCHEN

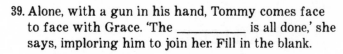

39. Alone, with a gun in his hand, Tommy comes face
    to face with Grace. 'The _____ is all done,' she
    says, imploring him to join her. Fill in the blank.

    ○ ... BLOODSHED
    ○ ... GRIEF
    ○ ... KILLING
    ○ ... WORK

KILLER QUESTIONS

40. At Alfie's Margate apartment, Tommy steps across floor tiles from the balcony that bear the word LETHE. In Greek mythology, what does this represent?

   ○ SORROW
   ○ FORGIVENESS
   ○ OBLIVION
   ○ REPENTANCE

41. According to the posters outside the hall, what time is the rally scheduled to take place?

   ○ 6.30PM
   ○ 7.00PM
   ○ 7.30PM
   ○ 8.00PM

42. Before Mosley takes to the stage, what music is played as the Union Jack is unfurled as a backdrop?

   ○ THE NATIONAL ANTHEM
   ○ JERUSALEM
   ○ GIOVINEZZA
   ○ LAND OF HOPE AND GLORY

SEASON FIVE ◼ EPISODE SIX

ANSWERS

SEASON ONE

EPISODE ONE

1. A razor blade
2. Monaghan Boy
3. Red
4. Kempton Park
5. 1919
6. Red Right Hand
7. Small Heath
8. Garrison Lane
9. Think
10. 6 Watery Lane
11. 179th Tunnelling Company
12. A racecourse boss
13. Communist
14. Of national significance
15. He's shell-shocked from his war experience
16. The pistol belongs to John and his younger brother, Finn, had been found playing with it
17. Protestant Irishmen
18. The church
19. Four motorbikes
20. Tramline
21. Ada Shelby
22. Employment as a barmaid
23. The IRA
24. Lead Pack Dog
25. 35 years
26. The Blues
27. Rum
28. Winston Churchill
29. His sister, Ada
30. The Boy I Love is Up in the Gallery
31. Little Italy
32. Beaver
33. He will only make the journey when there's no moon in the night sky
34. The old tobacco wharf
35. The museum
36. Her father was murdered by the IRA
37. To be buried on a hill, but not in mud
38. London
39. To build the horse's winning reputation then fix a race so that it loses
40. Harts Hill Iron Co Ltd
41. mansion
42. Arthur Shelby

EPISODE TWO

1. The fair
2. Two Up
3. A king
4. A didicoi whore
5. On horseback
6. Every gun and bullet
7. A prescription in her name
8. The Chain
9. He didn't fight in France
10. The tea room

11. Made sure the brothers were out of town before the raid took place
12. Handing out cash to the raided pubs
13. 3:1
14. The proposed meeting with Chief Inspector Campbell
15. King George V
16. Birmingham Evening Dispatch
17. ... want to see that happening
18. A bear and a boat
19. The Lee family
20. A bookmaker
21. Rudolph Valentino
22. Two
23. Distribute it to the locals
24. Burns it
25. Cardiff
26. Visit the castle

27. The return of the stolen crate from the British Small Arms Company
28. A pistol
29. Tosca
30. A bad seed in the hoof
31. She's a girl from a good family who fell pregnant
32. A sad song
33. He proposes to her, but insists they remain in Birmingham
34. Horses
35. By shooting a gun at the ceiling
36. Cheltenham
37. John
38. His accountant
39. £3,000
40. A Spanish saddle
41. The Sunshine of Your Smile
42. Percy Piper

EPISODE THREE

1. Two pounds, ten shillings
2. ... the house burns down
3. The IRA
4. Sparkbrook
5. Pub collections
6. Sings a provocative song
7. Proofing water
8. Ada arrives, having run through the streets in a wedding dress
9. The Black Swan
10. He didn't fight in the war at all
11. Grace
12. Whether or not he's armed

13. An operative
14. Money
15. ... bad for business
16. Tickets for the next passage to America
17. Observe and report
18. White statues
19. Heart
20. It belongs to Billy Kimber
21. Gathering in groups of more than three
22. Flanders
23. In a church pew, nursing a bottle of spirits
24. The Garrison pub
25. A flat tyre

26. Three years for sedition
27. He asks if they could still swim across the water like they did when they were young
28. 'This marriage will not stand.'
29. Cradling the head of young Finn, who is asleep beside her on the sofa
30. Freddie and Danny Whizz-Bang
31. A pub
32. Travel
33. I will do my duty, sir
34. 'Trust only kin.'
35. Lady Sarah Duggan of Connemara
36. Prussian
37. Slicing his ear
38. A percentage of the take and betting pitches at his racecourses
39. Tommy
40. She has syphilis
41. Mooneys
42. Samatra
43. DS 9746

EPISODE FOUR

1. A Chinese restaurant
2. … it grows by the day
3. A fish
4. The race has started
5. A small boy
6. Under canvas in a horse-drawn cart
7. She's a prostitute
8. Four
9. There's a booby trap
10. The car
11. A white scarf on a stick
12. Pope
13. He doesn't believe
14. A bullet with Billy Kimber's name on it
15. A tin bath
16. Stanley Chapman
17. A chance for Freddie to leave the city with Ada
18. The cemetery
19. … in a wooden box
20. Protection
21. It has to be at least fifty yards from the beer tent
22. They smell of rotting water and the rats have got to them
23. It's kept at canal junctions
24. Supposedly a Catholic, she doesn't make a sign of the cross at the door
25. 'My appetite for the work has only increased.'
26. … remember what you are
27. A basket of groceries
28. By offering her money to sleep with him for old times' sake
29. Throws it on the floor
30. Rackhams
31. Deliver an invitation to Ada
32. John
33. Buying drinks for her sister and her cousin
34. 10.00am

35. A buttonhole flower for a wedding
36. A mushroom picker
37. A car
38. Esme Martha Lee

39. The mingling of blood
40. The police
41. Kennet
42. Grayson

EPISODE FIVE

1. 1919
2. Eggs and bread
3. ... have principles
4. Tea
5. Black star
6. Street kids
7. ... carny
8. A licence
9. Their father is the victor
10. Pollyanna
11. 'A selfish bastard.'
12. Money from the till
13. Daniel Owen is still alive
14. America
15. Religion
16. Casinos
17. By inviting him to step into the ring for a father-to-son fight
18. Water and cordial
19. A broomstick
20. Commanding Officer
21. Friday
22. Wait for his signal before brandishing a gun
23. Sergeant Moss and his men

24. A map with directions
25. On the sixth chime
26. Burned it
27. Vengeance for the killing of her father
28. Sympathy
29. Daniel Owen's grave
30. His father
31. She resigns her commission
32. An engagement ring
33. ... starvation
34. He fails in his attempt to hang himself
35. Urges him to flee with her
36. The gramophone is broken
37. 'We'll help each other.'
38. Squeezes his shoulder
39. Associate Bookmaker
40. £100
41. Word put out in Ireland that he was not involved
42. The National Union of Railwaymen

EPISODE SIX

1. Brushing his teeth
2. Sleeping
3. In bed
4. Praying for Tommy and his brothers
5. A special, special customer
6. Whore
7. Winston Churchill
8. '… but also just the same.'
9. Three and five
10. She'd been caught with a home-made spirit still for making gin
11. The Prime Minister
12. A New Year's Honour
13. The National Association of Racecourse Bookmakers
14. Worcester
15. Karl
16. Danny Whizz-Bang
17. A pint and a chaser
18. In the back room behind the bar
19. The Bull Ring market
20. A hairpin
21. He wanted to work with horses
22. The next day
23. Nipper at Hay Mills
24. Two Riley vans
25. Three to one
26. Small Heath Rifles
27. Grace Burgess
28. Harry Fenton
29. Freddie Thorne
30. Ada Shelby
31. Danny Whizz-Bang
32. The head
33. To ask him what he said to Tommy
34. Jeremiah Jesus
35. '… may we all die twice.'
36. London
37. Champagne
38. The Solomons
39. Tossing a coin
40. Kingsman
41. Stratford Road
42. Royal

SEASON TWO

EPISODE ONE

1. She wounds him with the pistol concealed in her handbag
2. 1921
3. Prams
4. Freddie Thorne
5. Pestilence
6. Four Bugattis
7. For protection while he expands the business into the capital
8. Polly finds green confetti on the floor of the Garrison
9. A small boy
10. A hessian sack

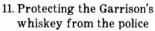

11. Protecting the Garrison's whiskey from the police
12. Ada Thorne
13. She has a son who wears irons on his legs
14. Hanging from a meat hook
15. 12.00am to 4.00am
16. The Irish Desk
17. A silver wolf head
18. 'I know where you live.'
19. Two thousand
20. £150
21. Smoke and trouble
22. Nobody
23. Company Treasurer
24. Six months
25. … at the southern end of the Grand Union
26. Typewriting
27. To find out if the daughter taken from her is alive or dead
28. Blacksmith
29. She knows how they 'push the glass'
30. The body of the man he assassinated
31. Someone throws a bottle of wine at Tommy
32. Mario fires a rifle at the ceiling
33. A life drawing session with a nude model
34. He is behind the IRA operation to blackmail Tommy, and wishes to recruit him for a bigger task
35. Hanging
36. She can type while Tommy covers her eyes
37. Let us break bread together
38. Extract a gold tooth from Tommy's mouth
39. Major Campbell
40. The Black Lion
41. Eighteen
42. Opium and bromide

EPISODE TWO

1. Kneeing him in the groin
2. By stretcher
3. Pass his cigarettes
4. A banker
5. He knows that Tommy carried out a killing for the IRA
6. Horse oil
7. Four days
8. Heathrow
9. Two thousand
10. Rum
11. Hammering a nail up his nose
12. Armed men
13. Mandalay
14. A gold ring through his nose
15. A gun concealed in her purse
16. The key to a London townhouse
17. Warwickshire
18. By hurling a wine bottle at him

19. A pair of scissors
20. It's her birthday
21. Bringing home her two children, whom he plans to track down on her behalf
22. Arthur pulled a gun on them when they said they needed paying
23. Requesting an export licence in return for his work as an agent of the Crown
24. … mongrel
25. Henry
26. Polly's address
27. Six or seven times
28. To take his gun
29. 'The war is done! Shut the door on it.'
30. Tongue and pickle
31. He's on the payroll of the Peaky Blinders
32. Australia
33. Fires a gun into the ceiling
34. To introduce him to cocaine as a pick-me-up
35. Drinking whiskey
36. Grace Burgess
37. Burns it
38. In the hope that Ada can smooth things between Tommy and Polly
39. In bed with a man
40. Michael Gray
41. A murder
42. Sweet Afton
43. Crime

EPISODE THREE

1. A man is garrotted in the background
2. The Daily Mail
3. Organising lodgings
4. So the police meet their quota and leave Shelby Brothers Ltd alone
5. A wooden gun
6. 'They stay kids.'
7. Super
8. Kicking him down Watery Lane
9. The chest
10. He'll blow up the wishing well on the village green
11. Bakers
12. The bakery
13. It's likely to explode
14. Jewish women are off the menu
15. She didn't realise he had a spare key
16. She knows he'll provide squalid living conditions
17. A maid
18. Austin
19. The mother of the boxer he killed in the ring
20. Four
21. The crates are heavy
22. Grace's police identity card
23. Egg and cress
24. Their agreed meeting is not until Sunday
25. His lodgings are in fact a brothel

26. Umbrella maker
27. The murder of the Digbeth Kid in jail
28. Remove her clothes
29. His men need to feel protected
30. Stealing a car
31. The Epsom Derby
32. Michael Gray
33. Squeezed between a boat and a canal lock
34. John's
35. Sandwiches
36. Because they know what they want
37. 2,000 guineas
38. 'Bad things.'
39. 'I'm all right to drive.'
40. The Winning Post
41. A teddy bear
42. Scorpion

EPISODE FOUR

1. Harold Hancox
2. A pay-off
3. Irene O'Donnell is working with the Crown to assassinate the same man
4. He knows that Irene's associate is a spy
5. Arthur pays off the copper
6. Mario the manager
7. Billy Kitchen
8. Cavorting with two women in a bathtub
9. He touches a recent cut on his temple and notes blood on his hands
10. Accounts Clerk
11. Three years
12. Telephone Polly to keep her informed
13. Because she has always wanted to see an authentic gambling den
14. Born riding
15. Billy
16. Cordial
17. A horse that will pay out at Epsom on an each-way bet
18. Grace's Secret
19. Tommy suggests Michael will move to London and lose contact
20. Spitting into their palms and shaking on it
21. A gold watch and chain
22. Poplar
23. Alcohol is prohibited in Nova Scotia, and at a premium on the black market
24. Temptation
25. Olives
26. Selling drugs directly is too risky as the government is cracking down
27. To time how long it takes for the officer to ask what purpose he has here
28. The lodger
29. He kisses Alfie on the cheek three times
30. Camden Road

31. His bookies can return to Epsom
32. An elephant
33. Good to soft
34. She's still coming to terms with widowhood
35. A map
36. The Marquis

37. The barman makes the man aware that Michael is the son of Polly Gray
38. Burned down the pub
39. Grace's American husband
40. Field Marshall
41. Riley
42. Mild

EPISODE FIVE

1. A goat
2. Celebrate Passover
3. 'Shalom.'
4. Moss is the commanding officer on this operation
5. To say 'Amen'
6. Treacle
7. Tommy Shelby
8. He's shot through the head
9. Reclaiming the Eden Club from the Peaky Blinders
10. Slicing his face with a razor
11. Daubing his face in blood from the sacrificed goat
12. Arthur shot Billy before Alfie's men overpowered him
13. Michael's involvement in the pub fracas and the retribution that followed
14. Goldfish
15. By asking if they should light a fire in the guest room
16. Knowing Tommy is unafraid to die, he needs further leverage to ensure he carries out his mission

17. Grace
18. Billy Kitchen's gang, who control the waterway, believe Arthur killed their man
19. Take him away from the family
20. Queen Mary Lee
21. The Black Patch
22. He wants to sleep with her
23. Five
24. The guards told him what she'd done to secure his release
25. Shovelling horse manure
26. Six cans of petrol
27. Her half-blind auntie
28. Tommy knows Chaplin's bodyguard
29. To taunt him by letting him know that he's about to sleep with Grace
30. They're seeking fertility treatment at Harley Street
31. Drawing horses
32. Post a letter bomb through the door of the military figure that Tommy must assassinate

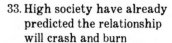

33. High society have already predicted the relationship will crash and burn
34. Tea
35. Testing his locked desk drawers
36. A globe
37. He realised the house is so heavily guarded that any attempt to assassinate the man at his place of residence will guarantee his own death
38. He must ensure the target receives an invitation to the VIP enclosure
39. Winston Churchill
40. … get lost
41. Chaplin is said to have been born in Black Patch, home to the city's gypsy community in the late 1800s
42. Three

EPISODE SIX

1. Major Campbell and Winston Churchill
2. The New York Times
3. Making a pot of tea
4. Insurance
5. 'The good old cause.'
6. Bottle of whiskey and a gun
7. An eating utensil
8. Johnny Dogs
9. Alfie has honoured his part of a deal by withdrawing witness statements against Arthur
10. He's planted a grenade with a wire trip behind a barrel in the bakery
11. 7.00am
12. … an anarchist
13. 100:1
14. Sit in the corner
15. 35%
16. Outside Ada's house
17. Lookout
18. She's emptied the betting shop safe
19. Ulster Volunteer Force
20. A countryside verge
21. Take over Sabini's pitches
22. 20 years
23. The police will be distracted by an incident in the owners' enclosure
24. Nom de Guerre
25. The horse has thrown a shoe
26. Queen Victoria
27. She's pregnant
28. Where the bets are laid
29. To write her price on the sole of her shoe
30. Major Campbell
31. It's cordoned off as the King will shortly be in the vicinity
32. The gun fails to fire
33. Fires it into the air three times
34. Irish

35. A bookmaker's track premises licence
36. Mr Sabini will be considered to be 'the King's assassin'
37. She has influence on the board

38. In a telephone booth
39. 'In the bleak midwinter.'
40. Hamilton Christmas
41. Happy Bristol
42. The Small Heath Rifles

SEASON THREE

EPISODE ONE

1. Winston Churchill
2. 1924
3. Lilac
4. In The Bleak Midwinter
5. Michael
6. Paintings
7. Regimental uniform
8. Charles
9. Arthur's speech
10. Lipstick
11. Kaledin wishes to talk business at a wedding
12. Arson attack at his restaurant
13. Arthur is about to blurt out that Grace's first husband killed himself
14. Sober up
15. Constantine
16. He's drugged the horse with a mixture of morphine and water
17. The Shelby Foundation Charity
18. Finn Shelby
19. aunt
20. The Soviet Embassy
21. The Duke only trusts family

22. Sergeant Moss
23. … to take meat
24. Tokyo
25. Punch
26. Winston Churchill
27. The Foundation Charity
28. No guns in the house
29. The gatehouse
30. Grand Duchess
31. He gave the wrong codename
32. He slept with the wife of one of the colonels who sat for him
33. A red
34. A wharf at Boston Docks
35. Ragtime
36. 'Always within punching distance.'
37. A bare-knuckle boxing fight
38. Charlie Strong
39. Stashing the $10,000 in the walk-in safe
40. Michael Gray
41. A carrot
42. Anti-communist forces

EPISODE TWO

1. Lanchester Motor Company
2. The foreman
3. The keys to bay six
4. 'Give it to your charity.'
5. Tarpaulins
6. Switch on an interior light
7. businessmen
8. Faces his chair away from Hughes
9. He has counted the military items they require
10. The Ritz
11. Violin
12. Two
13. Charlie Strong's yard
14. A bullet in each knee
15. He spits in the mud
16. bastards
17. The book is property of the people
18. Cocaine
19. Linda Shelby
20. Romanov has defaulted on his bills
21. A toe
22. A blue sapphire
23. Romanov's niece
24. The Chinese laundry
25. Taking several pubs controlled by the Changrettas
26. Three handwritten letters
27. The leader of Birmingham City Council has accepted her invitation to the foundation dinner
28. Had it made into a necklace for Grace, which he presents to her
29. Paperwork
30. Sport
31. … kids
32. The Madonna of Moseley
33. A Doberman
34. Hughes claims to have visited his son's nursery at Spark Hall
35. … fine
36. 'And stolen in Birmingham.'
37. Union convenors will be watching
38. It's cursed
39. A waiter
40. A horse
41. Round
42. The Co-operative Crematorium

EPISODE THREE

1. Under the stars
2. To see his son
3. An increase in donations to the Shelby Foundation Charity
4. The Grace Shelby Institute
5. Flowers
6. They've cut his throat and he's dead
7. Cunard

8. She taught the boys at school
9. The Secret Service
10. Michael deals with legitimate business, which is a priority since Grace's death
11. By proposing a toast
12. Johnny Dogs
13. Wales
14. Her photographs and clothes
15. … waking up a girl
16. Webley
17. Go to the house
18. The Queen of Sheba
19. Communist
20. Sack them
21. They know the names of his children
22. Embroidery
23. She's not educated
24. contradictions

25. She returns to her pose
26. Bethany Boswell takes it
27. Find someone who can
28. 'Have you got a light?'
29. Places it in a drawer
30. Wraps her arms around him
31. A new life.
32. Reciting the Lord's Prayer in Italian
33. The blackbird singing
34. Arthur shoots Vicente dead to spare him and Tommy further torment
35. 'We're not that sort of men.'
36. Boston
37. Vigilance
38. Tea
39. 'I have secrets.'
40. Cigarettes
41. Third Class
42. A towel around his waist

EPISODE FOUR

1. A stag
2. Boston
3. Silver Dagger
4. … dies
5. He doesn't trust the maids
6. Tell him she's a Shelby
7. Murderer
8. Lord Kitchener
9. A plot to kill a priest
10. … dogs pissing up the wall
11. She's sleeping with Tommy
12. 'A foolish man.'
13. Acquire property in America

14. Linda
15. Handle money or slips
16. It's a holy day
17. The Bull Ring
18. 'Hallelujah!'
19. Proof that the priest is a Soviet informant
20. Revolution
21. So she will have to stay the night
22. Cocaine
23. Lichfield
24. … you obey the rules
25. She asks if they would like whiskey
26. She's in love with him

27. Her perfume
28. Kill the priest
29. Ada used her scholar's pass at the British Library
30. A secret tunnel to the cellar from the other side of the river
31. Planting a Russian-speaking associate inside the house as a staff member
32. The Executive Committee of the Union of Bookies and Allied Trades

33. She's too soft
34. Arthur confided in Linda
35. The priest who heard Polly's confession
36. Imperious
37. By ambulance
38. Sacks all the former soldiers on his staff
39. To force the British government to break off diplomatic relations
40. 24-8-22
41. Lemonade
42. His father

EPISODE FIVE

1. Head
2. Because Hughes abused Michael as a boy
3. Three months
4. Morphine
5. Boiled
6. Firing pin
7. paradise
8. On the opposite side of the river
9. Reading glasses
10. Seeking an abortion
11. He walks out
12. He clasps Arthur's hand with both his hands
13. A glass ashtray
14. Alfie has two dozen men at his disposal
15. A detail of armed Cossacks
16. To check for Russian tattoos that would mark them out as enemies
17. His cap

18. Head of Property & Acquisitions
19. Smith
20. The room next to Karl's
21. Her portrait is finished
22. The Russian exiles intend to kill the Shelby brothers during the theft
23. In case of a French invasion
24. His wrists are bound
25. His mother was persecuted by the Russian ruling class
26. £70,000
27. Rumpelstiltskin
28. Crimea
29. 'It's good.'
30. Removes his wedding ring
31. He sees a vision of Grace
32. Fuck Them All
33. She has killed a policeman
34. Arthur
35. 7

36. septic
37. A jewellery box
38. knowledge
39. Bring down the organisation
40. Leviticus
41. Rum
42. Khlysty

EPISODE SIX

1. The Grace Shelby Institute for Orphaned Children
2. Fedora
3. safe
4. The Colonies
5. An office
6. Within the next twenty-four hours
7. Heavy clay
8. A model of Tommy's horse
9. A nurse
10. Maypole
11. Inside a car parked outside the office
12. Notes and fragments
13. The Times
14. Lily of the Valley
15. To hand over the Fabergé egg and all the stolen jewels
16. Her waters have broken
17. Tommy never mentioned the existence of the Fabergé egg to him
18. detonators
19. Evens
20. He's left one name off the list to protect him
21. Michael shoots him
22. She looks too sure of herself
23. Prepare to hang him
24. Smith & Wesson
25. Carbon monoxide poisoning
26. They picked the men on board who will perish in the explosion
27. It's too wet
28. A razor
29. Arthur told Tommy he would do it
30. Charlie is safe
31. Weeps
32. A French jeweller
33. Her signature on a contract to legitimise the sale
34. Vienna
35. £3,000
36. contemplation
37. Polly
38. The Chief Constable of Birmingham
39. Linda
40. Tommy
41. Immortal, Invisible
42. Lord Tristan Aldar

SEASON FOUR

EPISODE ONE

1. January
2. Mr Patrick
3. Two
4. Rolling a cigarette
5. Windsor Castle
6. Murder and Sedition
7. He stole it from Wilderness House during the robbery
8. John, Arthur, Michael
9. In The Bleak Midwinter
10. An OBE
11. 23rd December
12. He's wearing glasses
13. Midland Hotel
14. Toy guns
15. The Singer factory
16. John
17. Boston
18. Babies
19. Snorting cocaine
20. A bribe and a drink
21. A drainpipe is hanging loose
22. Merry
23. Harbourne
24. Spaniel
25. He soiled himself
26. Billy
27. The men's toilets
28. Wire-cutting
29. Sweetheart
30. 27
31. A black hand
32. Opening a garage
33. Sicilian
34. A gun
35. Remove his hat
36. Ten
37. time machine
38. Charlie Strong's yard
39. Flushed them away
40. October
41. Goose
42. A meat hook
43. A hay cart
44. Vodka and tonic
45. Maypole 245
46. Her pocket

EPISODE TWO

1. Nothing
2. They're lacking experience
3. Get out
4. 'In the bleak midwinter.'
5. She lunges at Tommy
6. peace
7. On the road
8. 60:40
9. Vendetta
10. A bullet with his name on it
11. 50
12. Unrest in the workplace is brewing
13. Truce

14. The name of the goalkeepers for two local football teams
15. A gypsy caravan
16. Jeremiah
17. A dagger
18. Ada Thorne
19. … football
20. They had already passed through John
21. Five weeks
22. … get it away
23. A night with Aberama's daughter
24. Buy a flower for Tommy's grave
25. Lizzie
26. … a witch
27. Shadow-boxes
28. She intends to stir a communist uprising
29. Not to use a whip on the horse
30. A rope and a bell
31. Heavyweight
32. … temper
33. New York
34. A cap
35. afraid
36. To discuss the import of car parts to France
37. A cattle truck
38. During the trouble on the factory floor
39. Flicks it across the table
40. The Wenlock
41. 29
42. Funacci

EPISODE THREE

1. Farmhands
2. A protestor who smashes a bottle of flaming petrol on the factory floor
3. 10 bob
4. Apples
5. His stepfather has passed away
6. A pistol
7. Isaiah and two Lee boys
8. … lost my own life
9. Japan
10. Strikers have broken into the paint shop
11. … the devil
12. A wedding
13. Arthur has requested that he should pull the trigger
14. A hammer
15. Drowns him in a vat of paint
16. Burns them in a factory furnace
17. Inkberrow
18. Spotted Dick
19. The mother of the boxer slain by Arthur in the ring
20. Ada Thorne
21. It was Arthur who shot Vicente Changretta
22. Polly Gray
23. A one-way ticket to Glasgow
24. Communist Party members
25. Stations three men with police badges outside Devlin's house
26. Bye, Bye, Blackbird

27. Special Constable
28. Consumption
29. Passchendaele
30. Blackpool
31. Burns it in the fire
32. Wild rovers
33. Into the yard at dawn
34. Take the bets

35. 'Nice women don't do that kind of thing.'
36. The canal
37. Digbeth and Saltley
38. 'Be a man.'
39. Julius Caesar
40. Austin
41. Deputy Vice President
42. Four

EPISODE FOUR

ANSWERS ▮ SEASON FOUR

1. 21st
2. Charlie Strong's yard
3. Artillery Square
4. The towpath
5. Hawkers selling pork
6. No firearms
7. A white handkerchief
8. The tea party is in fact a decoy
9. Rolls Michael's wheelchair away from his reach
10. Tar and feather her
11. Bad luck
12. ... we have a deal
13. The gun misfired
14. Rolls-Royce
15. The officer remarks that the cart belongs to gypsies
16. His driver's throat has been slashed
17. Arm
18. ... smoke blowing out of a mortuary chimney
19. They took out not one Italian but two

20. Barge
21. Dangerous
22. ... different
23. She asks Lizzie to pay it in at the bank for her
24. Train strike
25. sadness
26. A telephone booth in the countryside
27. £10,000
28. Lizzie is pregnant
29. A black star
30. Goliath
31. ... in a beer glass
32. Shot
33. A little sweet
34. God
35. Steelworkers
36. Dinner with Jessie
37. Lean on the car horn
38. It incites violence
39. Polly Gray
40. 333
41. Raging Robbers
42. 5th February

EPISODE FIVE

1. A machine gun
2. Washing lines
3. Places their hat over their face
4. vengeance
5. He refuses the money, no longer willing to work for the Peaky Blinders
6. Three shillings for a two shilling horse
7. Advertise for someone to fill her position in the company
8. Vials of cocaine
9. Loses his balance
10. Their garden
11. hedgehog
12. Rabbit
13. The police were after him
14. At his ankle
15. When her head was in the noose
16. To assert that she'll hold him responsible if any harm comes to her son
17. His cousin
18. … ridiculous it is
19. 200
20. Because Tommy is a good friend
21. They must be circumcised
22. 'You plan to kill us all.'
23. She's been strip-searched
24. What drinks they ordered
25. Burn it
26. … avoid detection
27. Tommy is aware that Ada would be meeting him
28. Two
29. They were both in the Warwickshire Yeomanry in France
30. Her strip-search ordeal
31. Birmingham
32. The names of her contacts who are gunning for revolution
33. £2 million
34. 'Why not?'
35. Charlie Strong's yard
36. Everything Jessie knows about socialism
37. A top hat and a coconut
38. Weapons
39. 20%
40. Certainly I will be with thee
41. Markers made of grass, twigs or leaves to show fellow travellers the way
42. A gypsy princess

EPISODE SIX

1. The fight has rules
2. revelation
3. Time
4. Monkey puzzle
5. By the pier
6. Strip-search
7. Tommy offered her a weekly allowance
8. The gender of the baby
9. Spit back

10. Too strong
11. A boxing glove
12. A gunshot
13. Polly
14. Welterweight Champion of Midlands South
15. She drops into a chair
16. Take his eyes
17. Charlie Strong
18. Aberama Gold
19. 'I chose my mum.'
20. SS Monroe
21. To wait until the funeral has finished
22. All the Shelby businesses
23. Alfie has booby-trapped the office door
24. He never visits her
25. ... take away everything that you have
26. On his knees

27. Alphonse Capone
28. Matteo
29. A table leg
30. Polly and Linda
31. 300
32. Peace
33. A holiday
34. Alfie's dog, Cyril
35. ... in bad blood
36. In France from the gas
37. Licks the blood from Alfie's face
38. Releasing him from the Peaky Blinders to join his family in Glasgow
39. Labour MP for Birmingham South
40. Union Jack
41. February 12
42. 2/500

SEASON FIVE

EPISODE ONE

1. 1929
2. The Lickey Hills, Warwickshire
3. The Angels of Retribution
4. Finn
5. Detroit
6. The ticker tape machine
7. Monte Carlo
8. Ten
9. 'And we were most definitely on board.'
10. She wants to meet his family
11. Smashing through the partition wall

12. Ada's townhouse
13. It died
14. He'd overheard Johnny saying in Romany that Tommy had put the horse down
15. Presses the muzzle to his own head
16. Friday
17. The broker advised him that prices would rebound
18. ... a kindness
19. Medicine
20. He has too much to do

21. So that Tommy can stay clean from any criminal enterprise in his role as **MP**
22. Robin Hood
23. Sharp-witted and decorative
24. A magic wand
25. He's had his rent halved
26. Stingo
27. The man was pimping children and bribing a senior judge
28. Clearing the streets
29. Westminster
30. Cash is king
31. The identity of the father
32. Chinese
33. Their constituencies border one another
34. Tips a bottle of wine across the papers on Suckerby's desk
35. Two more military contacts
36. Major Campbell
37. By revealing that's undertaken his own research into the journalist's personal affairs
38. Champagne
39. The lift
40. Tailor Shop
41. Daily Echo
42. Nolan Bank

EPISODE TWO

1. A machine gun
2. … and see the seeds you have sown
3. Lets the wind carry it away
4. Charlie runs towards him from the house
5. Detonates them in a hail of bullets
6. The occupied six counties
7. Making deals with men to take down Tommy and divide up the racetracks
8. Tommy's political activities and position in a socialist party could be useful to her
9. Fireworks
10. Throws her a coat
11. Pours a drink over his face
12. A general
13. Liverpool
14. To hang it from a necklace
15. Levitt had a Commons pass and Tommy's name was in his diary
16. … frivolity
17. She demands to know if he's telling the truth about the incident on the ship at Belfast
18. Tommy has contacts in the hotel who can keep an eye on Michael
19. A finch
20. May Carleton
21. Fascism
22. The Chancellor of the Duchy of Lancaster
23. … bores me

24. People in the north
25. Lay down their weapons
26. Tommy is hurting or betraying himself
27. ... but only in my heart
28. Meeting Gina
29. A spent force
30. Protection at fascist rallies
31. Tommy suggests that there could be consequences for Michael's unborn baby if he's lying

32. Payback for the money he lost in the crash
33. He's dropped with a bullet to the shoulder
34. Breaking his jaw
35. His primary horse-racing tracks
36. Footballer
37. Two years
38. It's Ruby's birthday
39. Johnny Dogs
40. Richard II
41. Snow Hill
42. Trevelyan Education Bill

EPISODE THREE

1. The children in her care have been abused
2. Smashes the lenses
3. He withdraws all funding
4. A bunch of red roses
5. 45
6. Gina has a maternity appointment at hospital
7. Aberama is in love with her
8. His boxing gloves
9. An oily rag
10. Don't smile
11. ... the devil
12. The Gladiator
13. She's seeing another man
14. The murder of the journalist, Mr Levitt
15. Deputy Leader
16. The Quakers
17. No Birmingham solicitor would dare oversee the divorce of a Shelby man
18. She put the phone down

19. She died from Spanish Flu
20. Take her on a longer journey than necessary
21. ... saying some very stupid things
22. His sister
23. The Fury family
24. ... you and I will be done
25. 'My brother and I are the same person.'
26. His focus is on communist activity
27. The King
28. Johnny Dogs
29. A miniature Statue of Liberty
30. Long Island
31. Champagne
32. Holding their daughter's hand
33. Bournville
34. They talk
35. Search for the truth within
36. Petrol

37. Nailing him to a cross
38. January 1st 1930
39. A primed grenade
40. To buy an ice cream
41. Meriden
42. A bullet

EPISODE FOUR

1. 'Happy or sad, Tommy?'
2. Barge
3. Business
4. Charlie simply finds things before they're lost
5. Jimmy's funeral costs
6. Isaiah
7. York and Lincoln City
8. ... all the lovely things that people like
9. The snug at the Garrison
10. Songbirds
11. losers
12. He is being held at gunpoint
13. ... with no hands
14. Lies
15. The ceiling
16. Throw it in the canal
17. She's stepped in horse manure and removed her heels
18. They'll get stopped by the police
19. Coal
20. San Francisco
21. Half the loss incurred in the stock market crash
22. ... put out your fires
23. A dock
24. A girl called Karen who hates him
25. Polly's hand in marriage
26. Lizzie Shelby
27. He believes that as a younger man he may have slept with Lizzie
28. Laudanum
29. Managing Director
30. The cheque must be underwritten by Mosley
31. Opium, cocaine and brandy
32. meat
33. A tendency to trust people
34. She tosses him a coin for the drink he bought her
35. Arthur
36. He tosses a pebble into her lap
37. poor commoner
38. Frederick
39. Polly Gray
40. Three
41. A razor
42. 16th November

EPISODE FIVE

1. A banqueting table
2. Derringer
3. Iodine
4. Opium
5. Aberama wants him to be best man at his wedding to Polly
6. ... the mighty mood

7. He spits on the ground
8. … and marches on!
9. The British Union of Fascists
10. Trust him
11. It's lower class
12. bitterness
13. Control of the racecourses in the north
14. … the King
15. Drink less
16. To join him with the ballerina in his bedroom
17. The docks
18. It would've been a kindness, and she wants him to live with what he's done
19. Kicks the ball back
20. Younger has experienced resistance from his superiors
21. … wrong
22. Sergeant Moss

23. She didn't love him
24. An IRA assassination of a British military officer
25. Ten
26. … come home to me
27. A bottle of whiskey
28. Irish
29. The Titanic Gang
30. A machine gun
31. On the edge of his knife
32. … burn in that furnace with him
33. Peter
34. His pocket watch
35. Sergeant Major
36. In his mouth
37. He hopes his situation might change
38. After midnight on Wednesday
39. Solihull
40. Five
41. HY 2056
42. The Western Isles Bank

EPISODE SIX

1. He has learned that Tommy's alliance with Mosley is a cover to spy on him
2. On a narrowboat
3. Gardeners
4. He intends to break the law
5. He expresses an interest in spending an evening with the Shelby family
6. The man is sleeping with his wife

7. It's become more profitable than fixing the races
8. … the real man flew out
9. Football and women
10. A glass of 'so what?'
11. Tied to a lamp post
12. With Charles at his violin lesson
13. Three
14. A full restructuring of the company
15. Mr Jones
16. Throws it on the fire

17. The Americans don't wish to deal with a street gang
18. A slap around the cheek
19. A revolver and a dustbin lid
20. He'll be sent back to the asylum
21. Bingley Hall
22. In the wings
23. To get the boat loaded with opium to Tommy's Chinese contacts
24. The girls at the telephone exchange
25. ... selling your stories to the highest bidder
26. Alfie wrote him a letter asking after his dog

27. The rally is in Birmingham
28. Her resignation from the company
29. She committed suicide
30. Charlie Strong's yard
31. Salthouse Lane
32. Check his pocket watch
33. Go home
34. Bottles
35. 'Two apple crumble.'
36. Leaving the stage until order is restored
37. Intelligence
38. The fields
39. Work
40. Oblivion
41. 7.30pm
42. Land of Hope And Glory

ANSWERS ▮ SEASON FIVE